RIA ISLAND

Cambridge Bay

Queen
Maude
Gulf

Chantrey
Inlet

Arctic Circle

BAFFIN ISL

NUNAVUT

Garry
Lake

Baker
Lake

SOUTHAMPTON
ISLAND

QUE

eliance
rift

Ennadai Lake

Hudson Bay

tony
apids

Churchill

Reindeer
Lake

York Factory

Southend

Gillam
Ilford

MANITOBA

The
Pas

Norway
House

CHEWAN

katoon

Lake
Winnipeg

Red Lake

ONTARIO

Jam

CANADA

ED STATES

Thunder
Bay

NORTH DAKOTA

Ely

Lake Superior

TRUE NORTH

TRUE NORTH

Exploring the Great Wilderness by Bush Plane

GEORGE   ERICKSON

The Lyons Press

Guilford, Connecticut
An Imprint of The Globe Pequot Press

The Lyons Press is an imprint of the Globe Pequot Press.

Printed in Canada

10 9 8 7 6 5 4 3 2 1

The Library of Congress Cataloging-in-Publication Data is available on file.

This book is dedicated

To the Bernoullis, a family of seventeenth-century
scientists who fled to Switzerland to escape from persecution
by religious zealots. Daniel Bernoulli discovered the
principle that helps lift our wings to the sky.

To Nicolaus Copernicus, Galileo Galilei, Charles Darwin,
and their many contemporaries who, often at great risk,
opened our eyes to grandeur and advanced the
sciences that provide our many comforts.

To Orville and Wilbur Wright, two independent thinkers
who, in 1903, achieved the world's first successful, powered,
piloted heavier-than-air flight. (The local paper didn't
consider the event worth reporting. The United States
Army later called the use of airplanes a "crazy" idea.)

To the bush pilots who bring supplies and
human contact to remote corners of the world,
and to all who seek new horizons.

Notes

This is a book of nonfiction. A few liberties were taken with the sequencing of events, but all of them actually happened.

The natives that we once called "Eskimos" prefer the word "Inuit," the Inuktitut word for "the people."

To convert Canadian costs to American, subtract approximately one-third.

In keeping with our antiquated U.S. system of weights and measures, temperatures are given in Fahrenheit, and volumes are listed in gallons.

Contents

Preface 1

Part One

Chapter 1: Minnesota to Ilford, Manitoba 7
Chapter 2: Ilford to York Factory, Manitoba 23
Chapter 3: York Factory to Churchill, Manitoba 33

Part Two

Chapter 4: Churchill 49
Chapter 5: Churchill to Baker Lake, Nunavut 69

Part Three

Chapter 6: Baker Lake to Chantrey Inlet, Nunavut 83
Chapter 7: Chantrey Inlet 97
Chapter 8: Chantrey Inlet to Garry Lake, Nunavut 109

Part Four

Chapter 9: Garry Lake to Reliance, NWT 123
Chapter 10: Reliance to Fort St. John, British Columbia 145

Part Five

Chapter 11:   Fort St. John to Juneau, Alaska   165

Chapter 12:   Juneau to Whitehorse, Yukon Territory   195

Chapter 13:   Whitehorse to Fort Simpson, NWT   215

Part Six

Chapter 14:   Fort Simpson to Coppermine, Nunavut   239

Chapter 15:   Coppermine to Yellowknife, NWT   259

Chapter 16:   Yellowknife to Stony Rapids, Saskatchewan   277

Chapter 17:   Stony Rapids to Minnesota   289

A Brief Chronology of Powered Flight   301

Bibliography   303

TRUE NORTH

Preface

*T*HE ROOM where I write overlooks the tea-tinted waters of a northern Minnesota lake, a view that I share with a common loon. When I taxi my seaplane to and from our pier, the loon yodels a raucous theme while he performs his water-walking act. Convinced that he has once again decoyed my rumbling yellow bird away from his sanctuary, the loon settles low in the water, then gracefully slips beneath.

The loon and I share an interest in my Cub, but we do so from our own perspectives. Where the loon sees only an annoying interloper, I behold a magic carpet, the realization of a long-held dream. As a boy, I'd dash to the end of our log crib dock whenever I heard the stuttering start of a neighbor's seaplane. Enthralled by its reverberations and slow pirouettes while its engine warmed, I'd fidget in anticipation of power and spray. With one hand gripping our spruce-tree flagpole, I'd hang out over the water, my imagination riding co-pilot as the aircraft bounced from the waves and cleared the trees, then I'd return to reality as it faded from sight.

A lifetime later I write in a small, birch-bordered cabin overlooking the same log crib dock, thrice rebuilt. The wall to my right bears charts of Canada and Alaska, each map webbed with flights from my past, for the dreams that I dreamed at the end of the dock have changed from fiction to fact.

Rows of Kodachromes decorate the wall to my left: a crescent tundra beach where sandhill cranes cavort and cry, a herd of ten thousand caribou caught in midstep as they clatter past, and a Super Cub standing vertically on its prop and float tips at the edge of a northern lake.

The shelves above my desk hold stacks of books, clippings and travel notes. Some of the notes are neatly typed. Others, set down in a bobbing seaplane among the reeds of a mist-laden bay, are a barely legible scrawl. Still more settled into spiral notebooks beneath the canopy of a nylon tent or in the tar-paper austerity of an abandoned Arctic mission—its priest long missing, undoubtedly dead.

When I work with my notes, I often drift back to another time and place—to the turquoise waters of the Coppermine Gorge or to the banks of the Great Whale River, where arctic char played between my floats while I worked on a damaged engine.

My ninety horsepower Piper PA-11 is a transition model between the famous J-3 Cub and the beefier Super Cub, a descendant of the ornithopters envisioned by Leonardo da Vinci, the fifteenth-century scientist who saw birds not as fluff and feathers but as an "instrument working within mathematical law, which instrument it is within the capacity of man to reproduce with all its movements."

Equipped with long-range fuel tanks, the light and dependable Cub is ideal for lengthy tundra tours. On its cowling and on the vertical plates that cap the tips of the wings, its name is written in navy blue script: Tundra Cub.

The name is appropriate. The Cub has traversed the Yukon and measured the tides of Nome. Skimming the margins of Hudson Bay, it has dipped a wing to polar bears and delivered me to the banks of the Thelon River, where fifty yards into the bush I performed a nervous pirouette, surrounded by the shaggy descendants of worlds long past—musk oxen.

Now, with our long Minnesota winter just a memory, it's summer once again. The former Yugoslavia is still in fractured ferment. Interreligious strife, overpopulation and hunger soil a globe beset with theologies of breed and the realities of greed.

Having written my legislators and paid up my dues, I will seek renewal in the sights and sounds and scents of the North, in its people, stories and myths. Flying a course determined by weather and whim, I'll return to the rotting cabin of three travelers who starved to death in the Thelon Sanctuary, and visit the Nahanni River's Headless Valley, where two brothers literally lost their heads in a fruitless search for gold.

Though I've no room to spare, I'll fly with Bernoulli, who supports my wings, and with centuries of his peers. In a fifty-year-old aircraft born of their contemplations, I'll renew my longstanding love affair with the North, escorted briefly by a common loon.

One

MINNESOTA TO
CHURCHILL,
MANITOBA

1

Minnesota to Ilford, Manitoba

I am tormented with an everlasting itch for things remote.

– HERMAN MELVILLE

*I*T'S THE THIRD WEEK OF JULY. Soft summer winds have finally swept aside Lake Vermilion's amber pine-pollen veil. Rising from the depths, schools of whitefish lip watery ringlets where the last of the mayflies flutter down. As Sagittarius prowls the nighttime skies, fireflies twinkle in our evergreens, and it seems like Christmas once again.

Far to the north, the lakes of the Northwest Territories have finally shed their sheaths of ice. On Great Slave Lake, a diesel-driven barge is fighting a cold northeasterly wind as it struggles toward a tiny town called Snowdrift and an even more remote weather station named Reliance. Riding low, the barge is laden with machinery, building supplies, appliances, three-wheelers, groceries and a fifty-five-gallon barrel of aviation gas that bears my name.

In years past, I've been accompanied on my northern flights by a passenger, or occasionally by another aircraft, but this trip will be different, for the unforeseen has removed my companions, and I'm facing a solo flight.

A month ago I was one of four pilots eagerly reviewing maps and fueling sites, but appendicitis, loss of employment and a threatened divorce have sidelined the other three. Though I regret their difficulties and will miss their company, I'm buoyed by my freedom to choose destination and course without consultation, with only myself to please.

Flying alone doesn't worry me. I trust my equipment, my training and common sense. And though solo travel has its hazards, what good are our dreams if we lack the courage to follow?

Now, with its floats riding deep in the water, the Tundra Cub awaits. A mountain of gear has disappeared into its small baggage area, the back seat and compartmented floats. Beneath my seat, I've packed four books: Diane Ackerman's artful *Natural History of the Senses*, Carl Sagan's *Demon-Haunted World* and Barbara Walker's *Woman's Encyclopedia of Myths and Secrets*, which the London *Times* proclaimed the "best educational book of the year." The fourth is an old friend, Vilhjalmur Stefansson's *Friendly Arctic*, the intriguing book that first turned my thoughts to the North when a broken leg provided a brief vacation from high school.

A five-pound packet of sequenced maps lies atop the books. Removing the Winnipeg chart, I lay it over the cameras, bug dope, notebooks and pens in the makeshift aluminum tray that hangs beneath the Cub's instrument panel.

Before leaving, I bend a two-foot length of clothes-hanger wire into a precise right angle and set it upright on the pier beneath the noonday sun, then point the horizontal arm north and file a nick in it to record the length of the shadow cast by the vertical arm. Packed away in one of the float compartments, my wire will emerge a few days from now at the edge of an Arctic sea. There, with the twenty-three-hundred-year-old logic of Eratosthenes, I hope to measure the earth as he once did, with the shadow of the noonday sun.

Pushing away from the pier, I set the Cub's throttle to idle, flip the magnetos to Both, prime its engine with a few shots of fuel, step to the front of the float and give the prop a spin. The magnetos snap crisply. Another spin, another snap. "Now," I say to myself, for the Cub always fires on the third swing. Her engine snorts, then steadies to an even rumble.

As I settle into my seat, the Cub and I embrace. Webbed together with seat belt and shoulder harness, we become man/machine, making lazy circles as the engine warms.

My mind often shifts to the plural "we" whenever the Cub's in motion. Like a sailor romancing his ship, I call her Old Girl or Cubby. When her engine's ready, we pivot into a gentle southwesterly wind, building speed as I shove the throttle forward. She roars and shakes, first nose high like an accelerating motorboat, then level as she climbs onto the hydroplane-like step built into the bottoms of her floats, her knifelike keels slicing the water into sheets of spray.

We surge ahead, gaining speed as the chattering vibrations of our corrugated runway diminish, then cease. Transformed, the man/machine smiles and shivers, loving the vibrations that prickle our frames. Fusing thought with motion, we alter our wings with a touch of aileron, banking north toward a sparsely settled country that the Iroquois called Kanata.

The boreal forest below obscures the Canadian Shield, an ancient remnant of eroded mountains that spreads a granitic ellipse north from the Adirondacks and Lake Superior across two million square miles of Canada. Where the soil is sufficiently deep, tall stands of pine, birch and aspen masquerade as virgin forest, but they're really second growth. All of these hills were shorn like sheep just a hundred years ago.

After a short flight, the Tundra Cub passes the U.S. Customs facility at Crane Lake and descends toward a maple leaf flag on the shore of neighboring Sand Point Lake. There, a roadless Canadian Customs facility serves summertime boats and seaplanes. And although I'm "clean," I'm hoping that the agent won't ask me to unload my carefully packed gear. Fortunately, he remembers me from summers past and, clipboard in hand, sticks to the essentials.

"Where to this time?"

"Well, Churchill first. Then maybe the Arctic coast. If the weather cooperates, I'll head west to Alaska."

"How long will you be in Canada?"

"Two weeks for sure, no more than three."

"Are you carrying firearms?"

"I have a rifle. As you know, it's required that far north."

Nodding agreement, he signs my permit as a bulky de Havilland Beaver seaplane rumbles up to the pier, followed by an eighteen-foot fishing boat with three canoes in tow. The agent wishes me a good trip and turns to the Beaver, which is spilling tourists onto the pier.

As the Cub accelerates, her wings split the air into two layers. The lower layer flows straight back across the wings' flat undersides, while the upper layer, which must cross their longer, curved upper surfaces, becomes stretched like a rubber band. The space between the molecules in the upper layer increases, creating the area of low pressure that helps lift my wings and confirms the work of Daniel Bernoulli, who discovered that raising the speed of any fluid, including air, lowers its pressure.

Level again at a thousand feet, I head north across Rainy Lake, a lengthy portage-free section of the Voyageurs' Highway. For almost two centuries, thirty-foot birchbark canoes bearing up to three tons of supplies plied this watery thoroughfare that connected the Great Lakes to Winnipeg, Saskatoon and a tiny settlement called Edmonton until the canoes were displaced by rail near the time of our Civil War.

The Montreal-based North West Company, which dominated this "southern" fur-trade route, preferred short, stocky voyageurs—compact men who wouldn't usurp valuable cargo space but could still tote two ninety-pound "pieces" across the nine-mile Grand Portage from Lake Superior to the upper reaches of the Pigeon River. Urged on by a bonus, some carried three. Despite claims that it was easier to get into heaven than to portage the Grand, a few managed four. One voyageur, a hugely muscled black man named Pierre Bonga, is said to have portaged *five*—an amazing 450 pounds! And though they made their living on the water, most of the men couldn't swim, a shortcoming that the company actually preferred, believing that nonswimmers would take fewer risks with their valuable birchbark canoes.

Seine Bay appears, and with it a tugboat trailing a fat pendant of pine and aspen logs to International Falls and the mills of Boise Cascade. Over Redgut Bay, the Cub's shadow intercepts a linear, water-darkened log boom reminiscent of a Trident submarine that I once watched exit Pearl Harbor. As the cigar-shaped boom flattens the foam-flecked chop, I'm pleased that this slow-moving "vessel" will yield studs, rafters, plywood or paper, while the Trident held nothing but death.

Looking up, I scan the Rainy's westward flow in search of the Northwest Angle, the thirty-mile thumb that Minnesota pokes into Canada's belly to the west of Lake of the Woods, but it's lost in the afternoon haze. Believing (wrongly) that the Angle contained the source of the Mississippi River, the United States required the extension in the border-setting 1814 Treaty of Ghent.

When the Cub crosses the Trans-Canada Highway, I switch my radio to 121.5 megahertz, the emergency frequency that I usually monitor. Far above, a Boeing 767 strings a slender vapor trail toward Winnipeg. As the aircraft descends into warmer air, the frozen exhalations of its engines thin and disappear.

I wonder, could it be the same Boeing that I'd overheard one fine July evening in '83 as the Cub and I departed from Red Lake? While skipping through the frequencies to reach 121.5, I'd stumbled onto the transmissions of an Air Canada jet that had just lost power in both engines. Gripped by the gravity that tugs at every aircraft's wings, the huge jet had just begun a long, 140-mile glide toward Winnipeg from forty-one thousand feet.

When the captain realized that the 130-ton Boeing and its sixty-nine passengers would never reach Winnipeg, he turned toward a former World War II training base at Gimli, an Icelandic village on Lake Winnipeg's western shore. Lacking hydraulic pressure to lower the flaps or wheels, the crew cranked the gear down, but the nose wheel refused to lock into place.

The stricken 767 swept out of the sky toward the abandoned runway, then cleared the fence at 180 mph. Two of the main gear tires exploded; the front gear collapsed, igniting a fire as the Boeing skidded down the runway on its nose. But with no fuel to explode, what might have been a disaster turned into an outstanding success.

Now, as the Trans-Canada Highway falls behind, I envision the passengers and crew, first anxious, then frightened, then gloriously relieved, having found safety at a little town called Gimli, which in Icelandic means "Paradise."

When visions of Gimli's mouthwatering *ponnokokur* (crepes rolled in sugar) begin to prod my appetite, I remember stowing a sack of cherries behind my seat. Loosening my seat belt, I squirm around and grab the bag while the Cub flies itself. The deliciously sweet, succulent cherries tempt me to eat handfuls, but I'm restrained by vivid memories of the gluttony-induced diarrhea that I once suffered during the height of the plum and cherry season at Grand Junction, Colorado.

I'm the Johnny Cherrypit of Canada, spitting a pit out the open window every ten seconds or so. Imagining that each will take root and survive, I envision perplexed canoeists in the midst of the Ontario wilderness gaping at ruby red cherry trees laden with luscious fruit.

An hour passes, then two. Boredom blows at me like a headwind. Kansans might be enthralled with the emerald forest below, but it's no different from northern Minnesota's, and I see that every day. Finally, when a dot on the horizon becomes the community of Red Lake, I lift the mike and transmit,

"Red Lake radio, this is Piper 4745 Mike."

"Piper Four five Mike, this is Red Lake."

"Red Lake radio, Four five Mike is fifteen south. Landing at Green's."

"Piper Four five Mike, altimeter is 30.02, wind is southwest at ten knots. Report on final."

At Green's seaplane base, the Tundra Cub wedges between a hulking radial-engined Norseman and an equally impressive de Havilland Otter. In the sixties, I stood on this same wharf, chuckling at an ancient Fox Moth seaplane, a World War I–era biplane that housed three passengers directly behind the engine. The pilot sat above and *behind*, a reversal of the usual arrangement. Now, my 1947 Cub could also be called an antique.

As I secure the Cub, a woman arrives with a seagull cradled in her arms, its white breast stained with blood from a fishhook lodged in its mouth. Perhaps weakened or imbued with hidden wisdom, the gull waits calmly while I retrieve my tool kit, then remains surprisingly passive as I snip the hook and slide the shaft from its flesh. I return the gull to its feet, where it takes a few steps, then dashes my weakness theory by leaping into raucous, glaucous flight.

A huge part-Newfoundland dog ambles over. He leans against me, begging to be petted—and I discover that he's loaded with ticks. As I pluck them off, Large waits patiently, then rolls over for a more thorough job. Looking like eight-legged burgundy grapes, the ticks make satisfying plops as I toss them into the lake, shattering flotillas of water beetles that are whirling away the day.

Fuel is expensive in Canada. Twenty-six U.S. gallons comes to $US90—more than twice what I'd pay at home. I offer my Master-Card to "Laura," Green's Airway's auburn-haired clerk, then phone the Department of Transport (DOT) to file a flight plan to Churchill. (In much of Canada, pilots are required to inform a responsible party of their route and destination.) As I turn to leave, "Laura" slips out from behind the counter and follows me through the door.

"I heard you file for Churchill," she says. "I've always wanted to go there. Not for long, though. It's too cold, you know."

"I don't blame you," I reply. "I've been there eight or nine times, and I haven't tired of it yet."

"It's the polar bears that intrigue me," she continues, "and the white whales, too. Everyone who stops here on their way south raves about them." Then, as I'm about to tell her about Churchill's abandoned forty-cannon fortress, she asks, "Are you just on a short holiday?"

"Two or three weeks. After Churchill I'm heading north to Baker Lake, then up to the Arctic coast. If the weather holds, I might end up in Alaska."

She stares at the plane, her eyes searching. "God," she sighs, looking directly at me, "I'd give *anything* to go along."

Surprised, I stammer, "Yeah, well . . ." then wave a hand at what she can plainly see—a passenger seat filled with gear. Besides, there's that thing called marriage, which my wedding ring proclaims.

As I taxi away from the pier amid a storm of fantasies, Large begins to howl. When I turn into the wind, "Laura" is stroking his huge head with one hand and waving with the other. I raise a hand to her, my fingers spread as if to grasp something, then lift the water rudder and pour on the gas.

The enlivened Cub snarls and rises shaking onto the step. Power flows through our frames as the hairs on the back of my neck begin to prickle in anticipation of flight. Temporarily freed from gravity, we climb toward a wider horizon and a broader, more unified view. When wings and rockets and things yet undreamed finally carry us to the edge of space, I wonder, will we ever grasp it all?

The land has changed. Back near the border, lighter greens of birch and aspen dapple dark forests of tall spruce and pine. But ahead, a mottled plain of shorter black spruce, jack pine and bog reaches for the horizon, encroaching on dwindling ghettos of aspen and birch that struggle in thinner soil and a cooler climate.

It's at least four hours to Ilford, so I climb to smooth air at eighty-five hundred feet as the afternoon sun highlights distant Lake Winnipeg, a two-hundred-mile-long remnant of Lake Agassiz, the immense flood that inundated northern Minnesota, much of North Dakota and most of Manitoba some ten thousand years ago. Fed by the waters of a dying ice age, Lake Agassiz honors Louis Agassiz, the brilliant young naturalist who, in the early 1800s, confronted the Swiss Society of Natural Sciences with two seemingly preposterous claims: that the deep Swiss valleys had once been filled by mile-thick mantles of ice, and that the great blocks of mountain granite that dotted the distant plains had been carried there by glaciers and not by Noah's flood. Instead, Agassiz proposed that "God's great plows," the glaciers, had slowly ground across Europe, overwhelming everything in their paths.

Because the Flood theory had provided a convenient compromise for geologists and theologians alike, Agassiz found only ridicule, and despite the evidence, the Genesis flood held sway. Nevertheless, after a long and often bitter campaign, Agassiz finally replaced the Flood with fact and won the posthumous honor of a glacial lake bearing his name.

Not long before he died, Agassiz wrote, "Every great scientific truth goes through three stages. First, people say it conflicts with the Bible. Next they say it has been discovered before. Lastly, they say they have always believed it."

His brilliance in one field, however, was no guarantee of wisdom in another. Applying some of the same arguments that had been used against him, Agassiz vehemently opposed the meticulous work of a methodical genius named Charles Darwin. Unfortunately, he died before learning that Darwin was right, and he had been wrong. In closing his mind to Darwin, Agassiz set a pattern for those who still promote schemes to have Genesis taught as science in the public schools today.

When Deer Lake draws near, I search for a small, amoeba-shaped lake with a granite-shouldered island that still bears grooves carved by Agassiz' rock-studded glaciers. On the island, a tiny cabin nestles in a balsam-rimmed cove, its red roof matted with russet pine needles and emerald green moss. The cabin, now empty, once belonged to a Deer Lake resident named Oscar Lindokken.

Oscar was pushing eighty when my younger son, Lars, and I taxied up to the Deer Lake seaplane base. Dressed in a red-plaid flannel shirt, jeans and rubber boots, lanky Oscar could have been the model for Jonathan Jo, the A. A. Milne character with "a mouth like an O and a wheelbarrow full of surprises."

Besides resembling Jonathan, Oscar turned out to be equally re-sourceful. Grabbing a wing as we taxied in, he helped secure the Cub, chatting all the while.

"Hi, I'm Oscar Lindokken. Nice Cub you've got there. A friend of mine had one just like it. Where you heading?"

"I'm not sure," I answered. "But we'd be happy with a decent place to camp and a few walleyes or trout."

"You can use my cabin," offered Oscar. "It's the only place on the lake. The keys are in the outhouse, and the boat and motor are ready to go. I haven't been there for a month—lots of fish along the north shore." As he marked the cabin on my map, he added, "And don't talk about payin' me. I'll be glad just to have the place looked at."

For two days Lars and I enjoyed Oscar's cabin, his secluded lake and its marvelous fishing, then left his outboard full of fuel and a big note saying thanks.

A year later, I returned to Deer Lake, only to learn that Oscar had died without seeing his island again. Now, as Oscar's sanctuary falls behind, I remember his generosity and how he typified the many Canadians I've met. Friendly, eager to be helpful and generous to a fault, Oscar truly embodied "the spirit of the North."

The southwesterly winds slowly switch to the north, bringing a soli-tary thunderstorm to block my path with gusts that bend the pines below as easily as prairie winds ripple fields of wheat. With a touch of rudder and aileron, I detour around the storm's western (and safest) flank while nature torches trees with shards of lightning, then douses them with torrents.

Hindered by the head wind, the Cub's wavering shadow slowly crosses concentric growths of jack pine, spruce and bog, then lazes across a fresh, forest fire burn softened by a haze of violet fireweed. An osprey with a fish in its talons descends to its nest. Moose tracks meander across the bottoms of shallow ponds, each one dotted with white sweet-scented water lilies, the North American version of the lotus that Buddhists revere, believing that if such a beauty can rise from the mud, there is hope for humans, too.

As the last rays of the setting sun gild the metal roof of the Hudson's Bay Company store, I measure the distance from Beaverhouse Lake to Ilford, my destination du jour. One hundred miles remain; the Cub cruises at ninety-two. Knowing that I'll need every bit of the long northern twilight for a landing well past sundown, I feed in full throttle, then crank in some nose-down trim to offset the climb that would otherwise follow. My airspeed rises to ninety-four.

Thirty miles pass. I add more nose-down trim to begin a long descent, and the downhill-running Cub hits one hundred, thirty mph *slower* than a Pete Sampras serve. By the time I level off above the trees, the western sky has dimmed from poppy red to rose, and we're back to ninety-four.

A string of bog-rimmed lakes parallels my course. As each lake passes and the sky slowly dims, I ask myself if there will be enough light to land on the *next* lake, and the answer is always yes. If in doubt, I'll land, for I'd rather spend a cramped night in the Cub than risk a landing on a surface that I can barely see. Finally, a pinprick of light appears on the horizon, and within minutes, the Cub crosses the nine-hundred-mile-long railroad that connects Winnipeg to Churchill, and Ilford flashes by.

Reducing power, I bank away from the purpling eastern sky, slowing the Cub as we clear the trees that encircle Moosenose Lake. The Cub responds to a gentle pull on the stick, raising her cowling toward the rosy afterglow of the Manitoba sky. She flares out over the water, her engine a quiet rumble, her slipstream receding to a gentle hiss. Hard-wired by hands, arms, body and brain, the Cub and I commune, sensing the subtleties of lift and drag that flow across our wings. Aided by peripheral vision, diminishing sound and softening control feedback, we descend like a bird, releasing speed as we plan the approaching stall. Three feet, two feet, then one. Raising the nose a trifle, we skim across Moosenose Lake, our floats slicing its serenity, then settling toward repose.

Ilford was once the hub of the North, home base to the cat-trains of the Sigfusson Line and Lindahl Transport. Fanning out over frozen bog and bay, the cat-trains hauled explosives to mines and supplies to Oxford House, God's Lake and a dozen or more remote outposts. But now, with the trains replaced by aircraft, and the dwindling town connected only by rail to the rest of the world, Ilford's population has shrunk dramatically. Only a few trappers and tourists remain, drawn by the "soft gold" of the North: fur and fish.

Ilford has three, maybe four, miles of road, all gravel, and since no one has noticed my arrival, I begin the trek to town, passing a sagging icehouse where crates of whitefish once chilled while awaiting transport south. On the opposite side of the road, tall columns of lavender fireweed camouflage ranks of rotting steel-shod sledges that once followed growling D-8 Cats. As if they were the dinosaurs of transport, their bones sag into the roadside heath.

Like a dog, I lift my head to inhale cool spruce-scented air still laced with summer's sweet perfumes—glad to be done with diesel exhaust and the clamor of sirens and horns.

In the sixties, pickups rattled down this road while I held my breath against their dust. At the Gold Trail Hotel, two trappers noisily vied for the floor—one eagerly guiding his audience through a visit to the girls at Split Lake, while the other told of the time that Sigfusson's "swing" dropped through the ice into sixty feet of water. This evening, however, barely an insect hums. In the distance, a dog barks; a three-wheeler whines.

Hoping to find my old acquaintances, Kip and Mickey Thompson, I knock on the door of the Gold Trail Hotel. Next to a sign reading "Licensed Beverage House" another complains "Closed Due to High Taxes." I wait, then knock again. No response. When I ask at a nearby house I'm told, "They're open—just pound harder." I again belabor the weathered door, finally bringing a light and a face to it.

Yes, they will rent me a room and rustle up some food, but the elder Thompsons are gone, replaced by their son, Kirk, as full-chested and straight-backed as his father. Later, when Mickey radios in from their Silsby Lake camp, we reminisce about bulldozing their Lake Waskiowaka airstrip out of the bush, and about the German shepherd pup they sold me many years ago.

The pup was supposed to have been a shepherd/Newfoundland cross, like her siblings that were born the year before. The mother was definitely a shepherd, but the Thompsons weren't so sure about Dad. After calling my wife, who said, "Well, OK—gee, maybe not . . . I wonder if we should . . ." I lured the pup out from beneath the hotel, where she'd been living on fish heads since her mother had been shot, looked her over, paid Kip $50, and carted her off to the plane.

One problem remained: what to tell the U.S. Customs agent. Because I didn't know the regulations for importing dogs and didn't want to detour to Kenora to get shots (and knew it would be stupid to try to hide her) I decided to let the inspector conclude that my new pup was *returning* to the U.S.

On arriving at Customs, I plunked her down in front of the inspector and began to secure the Cub. I answered the usual questions as he gave the Cub a cursory check and then turned to the dog. "What about the puppy?" he asked. "Got any papers?"

"No," I said, with a look of puzzlement, "I don't, but they didn't ask for any on the way out."

"Well," he said, "she looks OK, so you can go."

That night, I took Lady into the shower and removed what appeared to be eight pounds of dirt from a ten-pound dog.

The Thompsons' guess about her Dad turned out to be wrong, for Lady matured into a beautiful German shepherd, the guardian and friend of my wife and sons and my best buddy for eleven short years. When arthritis had almost totally immobilized her, I carried Lady to my veterinarian's office. There, as I cradled her in my arms, an injection stopped her heart.

During the long drive back to our country home, I fought the tears and the ache in my throat. Unable to continue, I pulled to the side of the road. Lowering our station wagon's tailgate, I buried my face in her still-warm fur, and my grief came pouring out.

The Gold Trail Hotel is showing its age: stair treads creak; floors sag and a few of the doors won't close. Thanks to the patchy permafrost below, the hotel tilts slightly toward the railroad tracks as if longing for the life and lights of Thompson, a nickel-mining town not far to the west.

During the night, I'm wakened by an unusual sound. At first I think I've startled myself with my own snoring, but there it is again. It's the call of the Muskeg Express, the train that I once rode to Churchill, ensconced in a sleeper that swayed to and fro while it "sped" along at thirty mph, its velocity restricted by a rail bed undermined by discontinuous permafrost.

I gawk from my second-floor window as the engine plows through daisy-strewn meadows and rafts of fog tinted pink by the predawn sky. Dogs howl; two elderly people get off, another on, delivered by a speeding three-wheeler just as the train departs.

Back in bed, I think again about the Muskeg Express—how my wife and I and four friends once took an airliner to Thompson, then boarded the train in midafternoon. Once we were under way, I sought out our neatly uniformed conductor and asked, "Any chance of riding with the engineer for a while?"

"I think so, sir," he replied. "When we stop at Wabowden, just climb out and walk to the front of the train. I'll tell the engineer that you're coming." Later, as I trudged toward the engine, I conjured up images of the engineer—probably a mature man, grayed at the temples like myself, a serious man with a uniform befitting someone who commands a few hundred tons of rolling freight and dozens of precious passengers.

Instead, I was greeted by a smiling, thirty-something engineer wearing a ripped oil-stained T-shirt, through which a portion of his ample belly protruded. However, as others have noted, clothes do not make the man, and our pleasant visit was surpassed only by the delicious breakfast we were served the following morning while the forest dwindled and miles of tripod telephone poles (the permafrost again) saluted our passage.

A shout from below says "Seven o'clock." By eight, I'm fed and back at Moosenose Lake, checking the oil and gas and pumping out the floats, which are divided into compartments to prevent a single leak from flooding the entire float. Fortunately, the Cub's floats are still quite tight, and I'm soon on my way to York Factory, a centuries-old fur-trading post on the eastern shore of an inland sea that's known as Hudson Bay.

2

Ilford to York Factory, Manitoba

What a pitiful business is the fur trade. . . .
Think how many mushquash and weasel skins the
Hudson's Bay Company piles up annually in their
warehouses leaving the bare, red carcasses on the
banks of the streams through all British America . . .
the place where Great Britain goes amousing.

— HENRY DAVID THOREAU

*A*HEAD LIES GILLAM, the final town on a dead-end road that may someday stop at Churchill. Wedged between the railroad and the Nelson River, Gillam was even smaller than Ilford until Manitoba Hydro dammed (many say "damned") the river and throttled the Nelson's flow.

Those who know bush pilot history might wonder if the town is named for Harold Gillam, the famous Alaskan pilot whose skill and luck earned him the title "Thrill 'em, chill 'em, never kill 'em Gillam," but it's not. Instead, the town takes its name from Zachariah Gillam, the master of the *Nonsuch*, the English ship that returned to England in 1668 with an eye-popping load of New World furs. Buoyed by Gillam's success, British investors quickly moved to form a company that would eventually rival the power of kings and become, for many, almost synonymous with Canada: the Hudson's Bay Company.

The river that flows beneath my wings, however, is nothing like the river that greeted Captain Gillam. Seven dams now hoard its flows, spinning out megawatts of electricity throughout the year to power-hungry homes and businesses along the U.S./Canadian border.

A few hundred miles upstream, water diverted into the Nelson from the Churchill River has eroded the shores of Southern Indian Lake. Manitoba Hydro claimed that the shorelines would stabilize within five years, but twenty years have passed and they still crumble. As the land has eroded, mercury once locked in permafrost and vegetation has found its way into fish, fowl and humans. The Southern Indian natives, with their resorts made worthless and their communities threatened, were forced to leave their homes and move even farther north. Large as it is, the Manitoba Project may eventually be dwarfed by projects on the eastern (Quebec) side of the bay, where an impoundment the size of France will inundate entire ecosystems and alter the weather as well.

The Cub's shadow leaps the Limestone dam as the river explodes from the penstocks into a wide, pasturelike valley. I descend to within fifty feet of the valley floor, weaving between ancient islands that have ridden springtime floods for thousands of years but now lie anchored in seas of grass.

The estuary broadens as it enters Hudson Bay, the inland sea named for Henry Hudson, an obscure British mariner who, after sailing the *Half Moon* up the Hudson River as far as present-day Albany, aimed his new ship, the *Discoverie*, farther north in 1610.

It was already fall by the time Hudson entered the bay. Gambling that the wide expanse of water would lead to the Pacific, he sailed on until it was too late to turn back. Hudson and his men barely survived a horrible winter, and when spring finally arrived, the crew mutinied, setting Hudson, his son and seven loyal sailors adrift in an open boat. The mutineers returned to England, where they somehow avoided death by hanging, but Hudson, his son and the seven sailors were never seen again.

Leaving the Nelson behind, I angle east across thirty miles of quagmire and bog toward the mouth of the nearby Hayes River and a historic post called York Factory, the center of the Hudson's Bay Company fur trade for almost two hundred years. The forest below seems solid and dry, but when I peer down through masses of alder and spruce, reflected sunlight continuously flashes upward from the water-filled sponge below. As a consequence, most of York Factory's few visitors arrive by canoe or by air. (Although the word "Factory" in Hudson's Bay Company place names seems to imply a product, it means that the head man, the factor, lived there.)

York Factory is looking up. Where I once tied to willows, compelled to regularly tend the Cub as the tides slipped up and down the Hayes, a floating dock offers safe mooring, and the airplane tends itself. Wooden stairs now climb the steep clay bank, and as I top the last step, I'm greeted by a slender Indian woman in a white sweatshirt bearing the image of a smiling polar bear beneath the word "Churchill." A baseball cap promoting Trapline guitars shades her dark brown eyes.

Offering her hand, she says, "Hi, I'm Betty Settee."

"Betty," I respond, "you haven't changed a bit since I stopped here maybe four or five years ago."

"Oh!" she exclaims, embarrassed at not having recognized me, "I thought you looked familiar. Are you back for another tour?"

"I sure am."

"OK," she replies, "but before we start, I just put the teapot on, so how about some tea and cakes?"

As I gingerly sip Betty's scalding tea, she reminds me that her husband, Jim, supervises the York Factory site, her job being to escort the occasional tourist when he's occupied.

"You know, Betty," I say, "when I first stopped here in '69, I slept in a little building with three archaeologists who were looking for fur-trade artifacts."

"That building," says Betty, "eventually became my living room." Then, waving a hand at her new quarters, she adds, "but believe me, I like *this* much better. It was finished in '94."

Relaxed and knowledgeable, Betty makes good company, and an hour slips past while we exchange tales. She describes the thirty-to forty-foot flat-bottomed York boats that replaced freighter canoes in the early 1800s. Propelled by as many as eight oarsmen, each carried up to four tons of goods and settlers upriver to Norway House and Winnipeg, then up the Red River to homestead the northern plains. The last boat, she says, was built in 1924.

I contribute that here, in 1930, two high school seniors named Eric Sevareid and Walter Port ended an epic canoe trip that began in Minneapolis—a trip that tested their endurance, their wits and their friendship and provided Sevareid an entrée into journalism by becoming the backbone of his first book, *Canoeing with the Cree.*

As we stroll along the narrow boardwalk above a sprinkling of red-lobed dewberries toward the Factory's stark-white three-story centerpiece, I ask Betty, "Didn't the Hudson's Bay Company arrive in the 1600s?"

"Yesssss," she says, drawing out her answer as she searches for the date. "They built Fort York, as they called it then, in the 1680s. But, you know, the Company, or the Bay, as we call it, actually started out as the Governor and Company of Adventurers of England Tradeing into Hudson's Bay, and it wasn't even a British idea. It was proposed by two *French Canadians* named Radisson and Groseilliers.

"Anyway, with the help of Prince Rupert, they got King Charles II to give the company a monopoly on trade in Hudson Bay and its entire drainage system in 1670. They called it Rupert's Land, and it covered almost half of Canada plus parts of North Dakota and Minnesota."

"Did you know," I ask, "that Radisson is French for 'radish' and Groseilliers means 'gooseberries?' And didn't those two eventually switch over to the French?"

"That's right," she replies. "They started a rival company called the Compagnie du Nord when the Bay wouldn't let them set up inland posts. Expecting to be welcomed, they took off for Quebec with two tons of English furs, but the New France officials seized their ships and fined them a fourth of their cargo for trading without a license. Groseilliers gave up and retired, but Radisson returned to the British, who'd finally realized the value of inland posts and welcomed his return.

"But the sad part is that Radisson, after years of service to the Company, returned to England broke. He begged the Company for work as warehouse keeper; they turned him down. He died at seventy-four and was buried in an unmarked grave."

"So, was it the railroad to Churchill that finally shut York Factory down?"

"I suppose so," she says, "but that was probably just the last straw. By the time the railroad reached Winnipeg in the mid-1800s, the post had already begun to decline. In 1870, the HBC—which some say means Here Before Christ—sold its land claims to Great Britain for $1.5 million. When World War II ended, they shut the Factory down and left it to rot. Now, the Bay is just another retailing chain.

"Most of my people moved inland to Shamattawa or God's Lake, or to the Split Lake reserve near Thompson. A few found work with the railroad or at the nickel mine. With a sweep of her hand, she adds, "Frankly, if it weren't for the government preservation work, all of this would be gone."

The depot—"the Big House"—is all that remains of York Factory's original fifty buildings, but it's still an impressive sight. Letitia Hargraves, the wife of one of the factors, was so impressed by the little community that she imported a Viennese piano and became the talk of the North. Her husband, however, took a more skeptical view, describing York Factory life as "nine months of winter varied by three of rain and mosquitoes."

Shaped like a square doughnut, the depot encloses an equally rectangular inner courtyard. One hundred twelve-pane windows look outward from its walls. On the side that faces the Hayes, a third floor supports a sentry's cupola.

Moving inside, we stroll across planks worn smooth by moccasins, mukluks and bales of fur. "Look up here," says Betty, pointing to a thick wooden wedge atop one of the many eight-by-eight posts that support the second floor. "Because the outer walls of the building rest on the ground, they rise and fall with the annual freezes and thaws more than these sheltered inner posts. To keep the floors level, they put wedges between the inner posts and the beams of the second floor. When the frost lifted the outer walls, they drove the wedges in, then hammered them back in the spring."

Spotting a pile of rusted ax blades, I ask Betty, "How old would these be?"

"A few are from the 1700s, but most are newer."

As I turn the battered blade in my hand, I begin to understand the success of the fur trade—why natives who had toiled with sharpened stones or a chunk of copper would covet a simple ax: a few strokes and a tree is felled—wood for a week in a day.

On the second floor, Betty stops beside a structure that runs ladderlike from floor to ceiling with but one four-by-eight "rung" set five feet above the floor. "This is all that's left of the fur presses," says Betty. The jack screw that the crosspiece held is gone, but carved across the frame of the press in boldface type is an aging record of its source: HARLAND, LONDON. Operated like an overgrown book press, the jack screw compressed ermine, mink, wolverine, fox and beaver pelts into bales for shipment to London, where, in the bustle of Garraway's Coffee House, a nearly spent candle urged bidders on; the last bid entered before the candle guttered out the winner. A variation involved a pin pressed into the side of the candle: the winner was the last to place a bid before the pin fell free.

For the most part, furs were eventually sewn into coats and robes. Beaver hats, however, were already de rigueur by the seventeenth century, thanks to a Charles I decree that proscribed materials other than beaver for the making of hats. (In 1661, the diarist Samuel Pepys recorded that he had purchased a "bever [hat] which cost me 4 pounds, 5 shillings," a sum that exceeded the annual wages of many workers.) Besides being expensive, the hats caused a more insidious problem: the mercury used to manufacture the cheaper, look-alike rabbit-fur hats poisoned the workers, giving birth to the phrase "mad as a hatter."

"This," says Betty, as we leave the fur press behind, "is the stove room."

Thinking she said "throne room" I glance about, bewildered. Along the walls are the largest assortment of stoves I've ever seen. Rusted and bent, they stand at muster, ready to beat back the cold. Fronting the huge firebox of one of the stoves are doors wide enough to accept a two-foot log—sideways.

"These are Carron stoves, imported from England in sections and assembled on the spot," says Betty, moving between two of the largest and placing a hand on each—at shoulder height.

Beyond the stoves, an assortment of anchors, neatly coiled chains and an array of ship's hardware terminates in pyramids of two- to twenty-pound cannonballs. Most are unblemished, but a few have been plucked, scarred and spent of anger from the surrounding fields, their scent of powder gone.

Hefting one of the midsize balls, I say, "These would be great for lawn bowling."

"You're not the first to think of that," she replies. "After the Factory closed, vandals rolled those cannonballs down these halls into antique whiskey-bottle ten pins. They even tore siding from the building for fuel rather than cut brush."

Another stairway leads to the empty workmen's quarters of the third floor. Here, clay pipes once puffed and workers cheered when the first stoves arrived in 1841, bringing moderation to winters so severe that "the mercury in our thermometers froze so hard that it could be fired from a musket barrel without breaking." Despite the hardworking warehouse stoves, condensation on midwinter walls froze nightly into flowerlike blossoms.

Some sought relief from the relentless cold and isolation in liquor: during the week between Christmas and New Year's Day

1861, the average resident consumed two gallons. But liquor cuts two ways, and the fort's journals bear tales of suffering and suicide.

On the river side of the building, a ladder lifts us from the third floor into a confining cupola. Far below, near the banks of the Hayes, a sturdy foot-thick flagpole that was once a ship's mast lies in a carpet of grass. At its side, a cannon nestles in the heath. Gone without a trace is the hundred-yard-long six-foot-wide boardwalk that once connected the depot's front doors to the riverbank.

As my eyes scan the horizon, I imagine myself a sentry, shivering in the cold while far below the passing Swampy Cree sing to ward off the evil spirits that reside in the *Kihci-waskahikan*, "the Great House." My attention, however, is held not by the natives, but by a ship dropping anchor downstream at Five Fathom Hole. I strain to see her colors, wondering is she friend or foe? Does her hull hold rum, or ranks of soldiers intent on destroying the Fort and pirating the bales of "soft gold" that fill the floors below?

As we leave the building, Betty looks carefully in all directions, and I know the reason. Though we're only six hundred miles from Minnesota, we're surrounded by polar bears. In fact, Ontario's Polar Bear Provincial Park lies even farther *south*.

"Wapusk?" I ask, using the Swampy Cree word for "polar bear," and Betty nods her reply. "We had three yesterday. They're protected, you know. A shot will usually frighten them off, but if we have to, we're allowed to shoot to kill."

"Has that happened?"

"Not yet."

We leave the warehouse behind and stroll to the carriageless cannon. Squatting, I grasp its muzzle with both hands and make a ridiculous attempt to lift one end. As I withdraw my hand from its corroded bore, I remember two men named Thompson. The first was an American Loyalist named Benjamin Thompson (later Count Rumford) who returned to England in 1776, where he oversaw the manufacture of artillery pieces.

Struck by the extreme heat produced during the boring of cannon barrels, he immersed a section in water while it was being bored. The water eventually boiled. By careful weighing and measuring, Thompson disproved the idea that heat was a material substance, proved that heat was caused by motion, and the science of thermodynamics was born.

About the same time, an official of the Hudson's Bay Company sent a letter to London's Grey Coat School for orphaned boys, requesting "four boys trained in navigation." Only two were available. One, on learning his fate, ran away. The other was David Thompson, a charity student, age fourteen. Three months later, young Thompson landed at York Factory and began to survey the wilds to the west. (The town of Thompson bears his name.)

During his thirteen years of service, Thompson, like Radisson and Groseilliers, grew increasingly frustrated by HBC restrictions. Fed up, he quit the "mean and selfish" Bay in 1797 and joined its new and efficient rival, the Montreal-based North West Company.

When Thompson changed horses, no one was more pleased than an influential "North Wester" named Alexander Mackenzie, who was also destined to fame. With Mackenzie's support, Thompson surveyed some eighty thousand miles by canoe, foot and horseback, becoming the first to find a largely navigable route across Canada to the Washington coast. In so doing, Thompson won praise as "the greatest practical land geographer the world has ever produced."

By age forty-six, Thompson had aquired regular investments in the North West Company that allowed him to retire, but after moving his Métis (half native, half white) wife and his children east, he became restless and returned to work, surveying the new U.S./Canada border east from Minnesota's Lake of the Woods.

David Thompson tried to make the world a better place, but in the end, it proved his undoing. He loaned his congregation funds to build a church. They defaulted. He canceled their debt. He set his sons up in business. They failed. He paid their creditors.

Near the end of his life, having already pawned his treasured surveying instruments and his clothes, he had to borrow money for food from a friend. Like Radisson, he appealed for relief to the

Hudson's Bay Company, which had in the interim bought out the North West Company, but was rebuffed. Destitute, he was taken in by relatives in Longueuil, Quebec, where he combined his journals and memories into a manuscript called *Travels*. Lacking money to publish his memoirs, David Thompson died at eighty-five, ending a life of service, charity and honor.

Remembering that Betty hails from Churchill, I ask if she knew Gordon Paul, the Shell dealer who had befriended my father and me on our first trip to Churchill.

"He moved away," she says. "To Winnipeg, I think."

"Quite a man," I continue. "He offered my father and me free use of a fishing cabin that he'd purchased on South Knife Lake."

Her look softens.

"I grew up in that shack . . ." she says, her voice trailing off.

As I wipe my sweating forehead, Betty pauses beside a shaded thermometer. In one of the many ironies of the North, here in polar bear country where temperatures can fall to sixty below, it's ninety-three degrees.

When I fire up the Cub, it idles motionless beside the floating dock, its usual forward motion arrested by the current of the Hayes. With a wave to Betty, I add power. The Cub surges onto the step, accelerating as I lift the right wing to free one float from the river's drag. We spring into the air in a climbing turn, seeking the safety of altitude before leaving York Factory behind.

Far below, a small figure waves. At Betty's side stands her guardian against polar bears, her north country dog. A husky? A malamute? Perhaps a wolf/Alsatian cross? Of course not. Her protector is a feisty eight-pound Pomeranian!

3

York Factory to Churchill, Manitoba

*A lake is the landscape's most beautiful and expressive
feature. It is the earth's eye; looking into which the
beholder measures the depth of his own nature.*

— HENRY DAVID THOREAU

B ENEATH A BLUE PORCELAIN SKY, the Tundra
Cub returns to the mouth of the Nelson River,
where hundreds of beluga whales rocket through
cool silty water in pursuit of herringlike fish called capelin.

Opening the Cub's windows to ease the full-bore heat of a mid-
July sun, I lean forward to expose my sweat-soaked back to the
swirling air. My sticky shirt dries, then peels away like shedding
skin. Fluttering, it sends cascades of goose bumps rippling across
my shoulders and down my arms.

In the distance, a rusting, two hundred-yard-long finger of steel
juts out from the Nelson's northern shore. The battered skeleton
of a dredge lies in ruin at one end of the pier, abandoned early in
the twentieth century when it failed to keep pace with the river's

silt-laden floods. At the other end, a handful of swaybacked, flattened buildings lie in ruins—the remains of Port Nelson.

Turning northeast, I descend to two hundred feet and begin to search the rock-studded flats and willow-fringed beaches for polar bears. As expected, the beach is loaded with bears, but whenever the Cub draws close, they mutate into bleached, hump-shouldered boulders. Then, directly ahead, one boulder moves, followed by two at its side—a mother bear and two cubs. The Cub flashes past as she pivots, confronting my big droning bird.

I've found polar bear heaven—single bears, bears in pairs and bears in groups up to five. Some lounge in azure sand-rimmed pools, while others loll on lush swamp grass. One bear, perhaps startled out of sleep by the Cub, jumps up and runs off with surprising speed, reminding me of the futility of trying to outrun a bear.

I suddenly develop a case of nerves. If my engine failed, I'd be forced to land in the shallows that David Thompson deplored two centuries ago: ". . . the sea, when the tide was in appeared deep; [but] by the Ebb retired to such a distance that the sea was not visible and showed an immense surface of Mud with immense boulders of rock from one to five to seven tons weight."

Once down, the Cub would be at risk from wind and wave beside a body of water that rivals the Mediterranean Sea. From its tiny antenna, my ELT (Emergency Location Transmitter) would be shouting to the satellites, "Here I am, here I am," while I counted rifle shells and tried to forget that a polar bear's strength and curiosity are exceeded only by its sense of smell.

I climb a thousand feet, then spot an eastbound freighter far out in the bay, its languid progress revealed by a feeble wake. If it holds course, in five hundred miles it will pass just south of the Belcher Islands. Farther on, it will steam into the bay's most striking feature: a semicircular, three-hundred-mile-wide bite taken out of its eastern shore.

Rugged and rocky, the eastern side of Hudson Bay is as vertical as the western side is flat—perhaps the result of a colossal meteorite strike far out in the bay. In fact, the arcs of the Belchers, the Nastapoka chain of islands and the land surrounding the bite, besides focusing on a common point, enclose an area laced with iron.

If the freighter continues, it will find shelter in the mouth of the Great Whale River, where years ago, I stood beside a different Cub with an engine cylinder in one hand and a connecting rod in the other.

I had flown across the top of Lake Superior to Ontario's Lake Nipigon, then followed the Missinaibi River north to food and fuel at Moosonee. Tired from the long flight, and not realizing that the James Bay tides reached upriver as far as Moosonee, I taxied through glass-smooth water toward the fuel dock and cut the engine, expecting to gently drift to a stop. But when the Cub continued to move briskly toward the pier, I realized that the deceptive, lakelike surface on which I'd landed was *tidal water* sliding rapidly back to James Bay. I was coasting downhill without brakes.

Fortunately, an alert dockhand flopped onto his stomach with arms outstretched to stop one float as I leaped to the front of the other, sat down and extended my legs. Thanks to his quick thinking and our human shock absorbers, the floats escaped damage and I learned yet another lesson about operating in unfamiliar surroundings.

When the fog cleared the following morning, I flew across the marshy terminus of James Bay, then north past the Rupert and La Grande Rivers, whose watersheds have been inundated by Hydro-Québec. Sixty miles south of Great Whale River, while cruising over rolling wooded terrain, I heard the sound of my engine begin to change. I removed my headset, only to have the noise vanish in the engine's roar. But with the headset back on, I could hear it again. Fortunately, I'd had enough hours behind the Continental engine to know its voice, and something was going wrong.

I tried the usual remedies: running on either of its two ignition systems instead of both. No change. Switched fuel tanks. No change. I pulled on the carburetor heat to melt any carburetor ice. No ice. (As an engine pulls air through its carburetor, the air pressure drops à la Bernoulli, accompanied by a drop in temperature. Add further cooling from vaporizing gasoline, and carburetor temperatures can run fifty degrees colder than the air they breathe, instantly freezing humidity to their walls. In times of high humidity, carburetors can slowly choke themselves with ice while inhaling seventy-degree air. Alert pilots notice the gradual drop in power and turn on "carb heat," which feeds the carburetor engine-warmed air from inside the cowling.) Out of ideas, I looked for a beach and landed.

By the time the Cub's floats nudged ashore, the clicking had become hammering. I opened the cowling but found only a trace of oil at the base of the left front cylinder. Suspecting a cracked cylinder, I disconnected its spark plug wires so that they couldn't fire (aircraft engines have *two* spark plugs for each cylinder) and started the engine. No buzzing and no hammering. Probably a cracked cylinder.

I decided that if the cylinder couldn't fire, it might hold together until I reached Great Whale River. If it blew, I'd shut the engine down and land on the nearest lake.

After tying the wires away from the plugs, I started the engine and took off on the remaining three cylinders. Down from its usual ninety horsepower to about sixty-five, the Cub struggled onto the step and began a lengthy takeoff run. I climbed until I had enough altitude to glide to the next lake, then turned north, flying with reduced throttle to ease the strain on the damaged engine.

When Great Whale River finally appeared on the horizon, I relaxed and, like a tourist, began to look around. Suddenly, between glances, half of the town disappeared behind a huge gray cloud, as if a tremendous explosion had blown it apart. Concern for my engine vanished with the town, then returned as the "smoke" dissipated and I spotted a Boeing 737 that had just landed on the village's gravel runway, its reversed jets whipping up an immense dust cloud that had hidden the tiny town.

Unbelievably, the first person I met as I hiked into town turned out to be a diesel mechanic who offered to lend me his tools.

Since aircraft engines, unlike car engines, have cylinders that can be individually replaced, I removed the suspect cylinder, ran a hand around its juglike interior and immediately found a crack extending almost all the way around. Had it completed its circuit, the cylinder head would have blasted through the Cub's cowling, an outstanding event that's guaranteed to attract even the most comatose pilot's attention.

Not knowing if any of the associated parts had been damaged, I ordered a complete assembly flown in from Timmins. Two days and a wad of money later, my "assembly" arrived *unassembled* amid another Boeing-generated explosion of dust. Fortunately, repairing the engine required only a careful reversal of the removal process, and in a few hours, with a smooth-running engine and a test flight completed, I headed north along the rugged Nastapokas toward distant Fort Chimo in search of the George River caribou herd and the tiger trout that prowl the rivers of northern Quebec.

As the freighter fades from sight, I turn inland toward the headwaters of the Owl River, one of the prime polar bear denning areas in all of the world. I'm flying along the tree line, a vague transition zone where forests dwindle and the tundra begins.

The tree line doesn't bisect Canada from west to east, as many assume. Instead, it follows the fifty-degree isotherm southeast from northern Alaska to Churchill, where it leaps Hudson Bay to wander through northern Quebec. Known as the "taiga," or the "Land of the Little Sticks," tree-line country varies from parklike beauty farther inland to the soggy mix of sparse forest, marsh, rock and bog that rims western Hudson Bay.

Because pregnant bears occasionally burrow into the fall tundra, then switch to snow dens as winter arrives, I descend when I reach the Owl, rolling the Cub from side to side as I slow-fly the winding river while searching for polar bear dens.

The Owl, like most rivers that flow through flat country, meanders across the land like ribboned Christmas candy. (The word "meander" derives from Turkey's convoluted Menderes River. The Greeks called it the Maiandras, the Romans the Maeander.) In time, erosion cuts through the narrow stem of land within the loop and builds a sandbar across the old channels to create an oxbow lake, its U shape a reminder of the loops that once confined the necks of laboring oxen.

As I roll out of a hard right turn, a yard-wide opening near the top of the bank catches my eye. I circle the area, searching for lingering bears, then line up with the river and ease back the throttle. As the Cub clears the tips of the stunted spruce, I push her nose down, drop the left wing and kick in right rudder, forward-slipping down between the river banks, then level out as the Cub's floats kiss the face of the Owl.

I secure the Cub to a boulder, slip the Marlin rifle from its case, lever a shell into the chamber, lower the hammer to Safety and climb the gravelly scree.

To avoid surprising any local residents—a badger, a wayward black bear, a skunk or a wandering polar bear—I shout "Hey!" as I climb. Twenty feet from the opening that I spotted, I stop and listen. Only blackbirds rasp a response.

I heave a stone into the den and wait. Climbing higher, I shine my flashlight inside. The shallow den extends inward only three to four feet. Claw marks score its walls. Lying scattered across the floor is an earthy mix of bone scraps, hair and musty leaves. Were the cave bigger, I'd be tempted to crawl inside despite its gamey odors, but with all of it visible, what's the point?

Leaving the den behind, I climb to the top of the bank. I hadn't noticed it from the air, but the grass is thoroughly flattened. Shallow holes dot its surface, as if fox or wolf cubs have been honing their digging skills. The lower branches of the trees have been chewed but not in the way that a deer, caribou or rabbit would strip away bark. Instead, the entire area looks like a wolf cubs' playground.

As I slide back down to the Cub, my stomach complains that Betty's tea and cakes don't make a proper lunch, so I dig out my thermos, the camp stove and a handful of fig bars, then retrieve a can of Dinty Moore beef stew from a float compartment. A few minutes later, the aromas of hot chocolate and beef stew rise above the playground.

The north is rife with insect horror stories, some accurate, some overblown and many of them preventable had their tellers chosen campsites away from running water to avoid blackflies, or in open windswept areas that keep mosquitoes at bay. But for some reason, on this windless day in prime mosquito country, there are very few insects. Those few, perhaps drawn to the heat and fragrance of the bubbling stew, dance in the vapors above the stove. As I watch, one of them plummets into the simmering gravy. Aha, I say to myself, a little extra protein.

With my hunger appeased, I crush the can under my heel and toss it into a bag for later disposal. I refuse to leave trash behind, and I won't travel with those who do. If we can carry full containers in, why shouldn't we haul the empties out?

Taxiing upstream to the end of the long curve on which I landed, I turn downriver and add full power. When the Cub climbs onto the step, I lift one wing to follow the river's arc. The Cub breaks free in seconds and leaves the Owl behind.

To my great surprise, the northwest horizon is hidden in fog. By the time I reach the north-running railroad, the billows have cut off Churchill, so I turn west toward Owl Lake in a race against the fog.

I cross a wide ribbon of sand. Stretching far to the north and south, this inland beach is another remnant of the ice age, a "raised" beach that once rimmed a larger Hudson Bay. While burdened by the mile-thick sheet of ice, the land slowly subsided, only to be flooded by the rising ocean as the ice age finally waned. Relieved of its immense load, the earth began a four-foot-a-century rebound. Now, the ancient beach lies seventy miles from and four hundred feet above Hudson Bay amid a sea of dwarf spruce and jack pine.

Fog is already spilling over the lake's western shore by the time I circle to check for shallows and snags. As I tail the Cub onto the beach, the mists slip in, visibility plummets to a hundred yards and the cool air suddenly quivers with the hum of a million mosquitoes. I retreat to the Cub. Why put up the tent in case the delay is brief?

The mosquitoes, however, have followed me in, and the Cub is filled with their whine. Retrieving a can of insecticide from the tray beneath the instrument panel, I give the cockpit a spray. The result is miraculous: mosquitoes go down like kamikazes, while the foot soldiers stagger and fall. With my life preserver for a headrest, I slump against the side of the cockpit and slide my hat over my eyes. A mist begins to fall as I slip into sleep, lulled by light rain hissing on the fabric of the Tundra Cub.

I awaken with a headful of hammers, then realize why the mosquitoes died so quickly—too much insecticide in such a small space. Squinting through my pain, I open a window to savor the air while hoping that the insects dancing in the shelter of the wing won't notice, but they do. How ironic. Here I am, finally surrounded by females who want me for my body—and they're mosquitoes.

Having driven myself from the plane, I've no choice but to pitch the tent. Fortunately, it's one of those pop-up jobs that's supposed to rise so quickly that one must stand back to avoid being injured. I hurriedly throw in my sleeping bag, rifle and camera, some M&Ms and my foam mattress. Then, after downing two aspirin for my aching head, I slaughter the mosquitoes that have followed me and seek relief in sleep.

It's still light when I awaken. Better yet, a thin glimmer of sunshine warms the western horizon. On my wrist, Mickey Mouse wears his perpetual smile, and proclaims it's 8:00 p.m. I'm famished. After retrieving my telescoping fishing rod from the Cub, I flick it out to full extension, attach a battle-scarred spoon and stroll along the beach, adding my footprints to an assortment of moose, heron and seagull tracks. At a likely-looking spot, I raise the rod, tip back my wrist and send the lure flying. As the red-and-white lure passes the midpoint of its arc, I suddenly realize that the mosquitoes are gone.

I have a theory, a mixture of observation and whimsy, about mosquitoes and other blood-sucking insects. Just as there are seasons for all things, there also seem to be schedules within the seasons. The chunky mosquitoes that clumsily drone about and painlessly probe my flesh appear at different times from the tiny whiners whose annoying sting always precedes an itching welt. To minimize competition, perhaps the ancient insects agreed to divide the territory and parse out the day.

The blackflies, weak fliers that mature in running water, saw the logic in staying near their place of their birth, so tend to plague those who frequent rivers and streams. The more agile mosquitoes, however, divided up the day: culex 1 patrols the dawn, culex 2 prowls at midday, with culex 3 assigned to dusk. Thus, some sort of insect is usually available across the liberally aquatic North. Nevertheless, at times they err, and, like gas stations, become either scarce or omnipresent.

The lure strikes the water. I begin a slow retrieve, then crank quickly for a few seconds. As the flickering spoon approaches, something strikes the lure. The line jerks, slicing a V through the water as I set the hook.

Holding the rod high, I let its arc absorb the frantic struggles from below the surface. With a sudden dash the fish overcomes the reel's clutch, stripping line from its spool. But a few minutes later, a three-pound northern pike lies exhausted on the beach, its gill-plates flaring—gasping for water and drowning in air. Though it has my sympathy, I will eat this fish for supper. And maybe breakfast, too.

I dispatch the pike with a blow to the head. Pressed into the sand, my paddle becomes a plank on which to fillet the pike. Knowing that northern pike, like their pickerel and muskellunge kin, have a *very* slippery coating, I get a good grip before I begin my first cut.

The flesh opens cold, firm and creamy white as my knife makes vertical slits behind the gill plates, then slices down its back from head to tail along each side of the spine. Guiding the blade downward along the outer curve of the ribs, I angle the blade inward toward the visceral cavity. A final slice down the belly separates the two fillets. I lay them skin-down on the paddle, then slide the blade between skin and flesh with a gentle sawing motion. Cleaned, buttered and floured, the fillets are soon sizzling in a battered frying pan atop my Coleman stove.

I once owned an ancient camp stove, a hand-me-down from my father-in-law. Like an antique blowtorch, it had a small reservoir beneath the fuel line that led to the burners. Releasing gas into the reservoir and igniting it vaporized the fuel in the line. For some reason, I always ended up with more gas than the tiny reservoir could hold, the overflow causing an eye-popping geyser of flame. As friends leaped back in alarm, I'd patiently wait for the blaze to subside, then explain that I'd attended the Incendiary School of Cooking with a major in Conflagration.

My new Coleman, however, needs no priming. Better yet, it burns any gasoline, so fueling is simple—just open a quick-drain on one of the Cub's wing tanks.

My menu will be pike fillets, cream of mushroom soup, a hard roll, raw carrots, coffee and a few Oreos. Unfortunately, I forgot the tartar sauce, but I'll take care of that in Churchill.

The northern, which my Canadian friends disdain, calling it a "jackfish," is delicious and could easily pass for a walleye. As I finish the last of my Oreos, I momentarily stop munching to appreciate the silence, then scrub my dishes and brighten my beach with a driftwood fire.

I've always liked the company of a fire, a small fire, an intimate, friendly fire that draws me close. Small fires are user-friendly, and better yet, they toss fewer sparks, a big plus near airplanes, forests and tents.

With the fire crackling and my clean-up done, I carry the northern's remains far down the beach and heave them into the lake. Since I'll be staying the night, I'd rather feed fish, turtles or herons than attract wolverines, skunks or bears.

The wide, almost level beach is rimmed with lichen and moss-encrusted dwarf jack pine, black spruce and birch. Except for the obstruction of an occasional pine that's grown beyond its grasp and toppled into the water, the beach could pass for a tilted sidewalk or a perfectly graded road. In the distance, a loon calls with a voice that's different from the call of my friend back home. It could be an arctic loon.

By the time I return to camp, a thin strip of sunset has transformed the jack pine horizon into the silhouetted teeth of a logger's two-man saw and the fire lies in embers. As I slide across the cool nylon exterior of my sleeping bag amid loon calls, forest fragrance and the fire's glow, I recall the opening sentence of Diane Ackerman's *Natural History of the Senses*: "How sense-luscious the world is." No one will ever say it better.

Morning brings the scent of sunlit tenting, the sight of clearing skies—and thoughts of a sweet roll rescued from the Gold Trail Hotel.

When the Cub rises from Owl Lake, the fog's still thick to the north, so I head west to the Little Churchill River. Thirty minutes later, I'm standing at the front of a float, flipping a jig ahead of the slowly drifting Cub. I let it settle for a second, then add a few twitches. Ziiinggg—it's time to start cranking.

It's a big walleye, quickly followed by several more, but I'd rather have a smaller fish, a two-pounder just for lunch. Finally, after releasing three of its large kin, I catch my next meal just as the current carries the Cub to a sunlit island with a sloping, granite shelf that will serve the Cub quite well.

I rope the Cub to a toppled pine, then return to my still-thrashing pike. As I drag him ashore, my eye catches a lens-shaped fragment of stone—a chip of my bedrock beach. I'm no expert on rocks, but I'm sure that my sharp-edged chip of the Canadian Shield is at least two billion years old. If so, it's just a youngster, for much of the Shield is older still. And as I finger my slender piece of our continent's backbone, which we now can date with ease, I remember that such precision wasn't always possible.

In the fourth century, St. Augustine, the venerated Church father who ordered non-Catholics to "convert or die," proclaimed creation to have occurred in 5500 B.C. About thirteen hundred years after Augustine, a seventeenth-century Irish bishop named James Ussher again took up the task. But with nothing more than the biblical "begats" to work with, the archbishop did even worse than Augustine, declaring with laughable precision that time began on "the beginning of the night that preceded the twenty-third day of October [my birthday, how nice!] in the year . . . 4004 B.C."

When humans were finally free to employ the tools of science without the hinderance of religious dogma, it soon became obvious that the earth was incredibly old. In pursuit of its age, some scientists estimated the time needed for erosion to bring the oceans to their then present salinity, while others worked with the probable cooling rate of an originally molten earth.

By the end of the nineteenth century, Lord Kelvin, who was the first to allow for the heat generated by gravitational contraction, had extended the age of the earth to fifty million years. Still, something was missing. That something turned up in the work of Antoine Henri Becquerel, who first described radioactivity in 1896, and in the laboratory of Marie Curie, who isolated radium a few years later, which, being 100,000 times more radioactive than uranium, eventually took her life. Her notebooks are still to "hot" to handle.

Upon learning that radium produced enough heat to melt an equivalent weight of ice every hour as it slowly "decayed" into lighter elements, scientists had to acknowledge that even Lord Kelvin's results had fallen far short of the mark. A few years later, when it was discovered that all of the unstable elements decay at predictable, uniform rates, scientists realized that the clock they'd sought had been hiding in the rocks themselves, and the door to the age of the earth sprang open.

Imagine, for the moment, that we have been given a pail filled with red marbles that we must count at noon every day. On the first day, all 512 marbles are red. The following noon, however, we're surprised to find that 256 (half) have turned blue, leaving 256 still red. On day three there are only 128 red marbles, the rest having turned blue. Day four yields 64 reds and day five only 32, as half of the remaining red marbles turn blue every day. Scientists, observing this transformation, would say that red marbles have a half-life of one day.

Now imagine that we've been given a pail with a *mixture* of red and blue marbles, then asked how long ago the pail was filled with red marbles. Knowing that the half-life of red marbles is one day, a quick count of each color would provide the answer. Half red—one day old; one-fourth red—two days old; an eighth red—three days old and so on. With such a clock, geologists have determined the age of the earth.

Geologists, however, work with elements that have immensely long half-lives. The half-life of carbon 14, for example, which all living matter contains, is 5,570 years. Near the far end of the scale is uranium 238, with a half-life of four billion years.

Equipped with half-life dating methods, scientists quickly verified what a few had long suspected, that the rocks of the Shield are among the oldest of all, ranging back some four billion years. In comparison, the half-billion-year-old rocks of the continental fringes are mere children. At the midatlantic ridge (or at any erupting volcano), new "land" is pouring forth.

I kill the walleye with a blow to the head, then decide to try my sharp-edged stone as a fish-cleaning knife—Modern Man Employs Stone Age Tool. Thirty seconds later, having gained new respect for my predecessors, I quit before I injure myself.

When the Cub heads north under clearing sunlit skies, I look down on the Little Churchill with fondness. It's a delightful river, a clear river, home to walleyes, grayling and char. Punctuated with mild rapids along its placid course, the Little Churchill is a recreational canoeist's dream. Its namesake, however, the emaciated Churchill River into which it flows, is a terrible disappointment. Rising far to the west in Saskatchewan, its voluminous flows once challenged voyageurs and canoeists with reaches of froth and foam. But now, with most of its water diverted to the Nelson, the Churchill's withered remains expose a wide and rocky bed. Once a vigorous giant, the Churchill has become a feeble centenarian whose shriveled body no longer fits its bones.

Two

CHURCHILL TO BAKER LAKE, NUNAVUT

4

Churchill

*Churchill brims with history—
most of it dismal.*

[**S** CURVY CAUSED] "great pains in the loins, as if a thousand knives had been thrust there. . . . The body was discolored as when someone has a black eye, and all the limbs were powerless; all the teeth were loose, so that it was impossible to eat. . . . We seven miserable persons who were still lying there alive, looked mournfully at each other, hoping every day that the snow would thaw and the ice drift away," wrote Capt. Jens Munk.

The year was 1620. Three survived. Sixty-one died.

When Churchill's five-million-bushel grain elevator punctures the Cape Merry horizon, I select 122.2 mhz on my portable cigarette-carton-size transceiver, summon my most professional tone and casually announce, "Churchill radio, this is Piper 4745 Mike."

"Piper 4745, ahhh Mike, this is Churchill radio."

"Churchill radio, Four five Mike is twenty south, en route to the fort and the Ithaca. I'll need fuel at Landing Lake.

"Four five Mike, Altimeter is 29.86. Wind is south ten knots. Traffic is an inbound Convair twenty minutes north. Monitor this frequency and report on final."

To let the radio operator know that I've understood his transmission, I respond with "Four five Mike, Convair inbound, report final." Such brevity is only custom at remote fields like this, but at major airports that have a constant stream of transmissions, it's absolutely essential.

The Churchill River flares into western Hudson Bay as I swoop low to photograph a wharfside freighter, the first of some thirty ships that will call during a short July-to-November shipping season that's restricted by Hudson Strait ice. Riding low in the water, she's already burdened with prairie-province wheat.

Across the river, on the rock-strewn tundra of Eskimo Point, a centuries-old fiasco known as Fort Prince of Wales rises above the heath like a granitic flat-topped wart. After forty years a-building and eleven years of British use, the fort fell to the French, surrendered by a short-handed garrison in 1782.

As I cross the fortress, I lower a wing to scan the courtyard. Inside the battlements, tourists trailing a rifle-toting guide lift their heads to follow the Cub. Ghostlike, the Cub's shadow flits over the tundra, dances across the river's whitecaps and darts through the demarcation line between the beige silt-laden river and blue-watered Hudson Bay, where pods of torpedolike belugas roll among the swells.

Though we call them "whales," belugas are, in fact, large porpoises that run to sixteen feet and weigh about half a ton. The young wear suits of battleship gray; on maturing, they'll don the adults' white.

In 1961, the freighter *Ithaca* lost her steering and anchors in a colossal Hudson Bay storm. Driven aground a dozen miles from town, she squats among the boulders, dry-docked forever. There, despite her gale-canted funnel and a hull holed by cutting torches and wind-driven ice, her cranes still beg for a cargo as if she's ready to put out to sea.

As I orbit the ship, the afternoon sun cuts through the *Ithaca*'s wheelhouse, spreading golden light across a binnacle that's held its final course. I'm tempted to rent a car, bring a grappling hook and a rope ladder and climb aboard. I envision myself standing at the helm of the landlocked ship, grasping wheel handles worn smooth by a seaman's grip. If I lived here I'd have done it long ago, but I put it out of my mind. I haven't the time and it's too risky to try by myself.

The seaplane docks at Landing Lake are even shabbier than I'd remembered—a disintegrating assemblage of planks that threaten aircraft floats in any wind. The only decent dock is reserved for fueling, so I head that way, leaving tie-down decisions for later.

Someone calls when I remove my headset, and I swivel in search of the source. He calls again; I laugh at myself. It's an arctic loon.

Thirty minutes later, a Northwinds Shell truck rumbles into sight, backs up to the Cub, and out jumps Al. Thin as a strut and wearing a smile that begins at his ears, he yells, "Hi, there! Where'd you come from?"

"York Factory," I reply.

As I hoist the hose to the top of the wing, Al warns me, "Get a good grip on that hose. This pump is fast."

Although I take his warning seriously, the recoil almost rips the nozzle from my hands as the first of the Cub's two eighteen-gallon tanks fills in seconds, jetting a geyser of blue-tinted fuel into my face and eyes. I'm the victim of equipment designed for brutes with several hundred-gallon-tanks and sidewalk wings that you kneel on while the pump rams in the fuel. As I wipe hundred-octane gas from my burning eyes, Al apologizes, adding, "Hey, I'll take off a couple of gallons from the bill for spillage." At $3.84 a gallon, it's appreciated.

With the Cub secure, we jolt off toward town.

"You lived here long, Al?"

"Three years," he says, rolling his eyes. "Three lonnnnng years."

"So you're not planning to stay?

"No way," he replies. "My girlfriend's trying to find work for me in Winnipeg, but job or not, I'm leaving come winter." While Al laments his separation from his Winnipeg sweetie, I ponder a town of a thousand with an airport suited to a city a hundred times its size. Built and operated by the U.S. Air Force during World War II, the base reverted to Canada in 1945.

My driver is the antithesis of W. E. (Ernie) Senior, the enthusiastic publisher of *The Taiga Times*, Churchill's mimeographed "newspaper" during the sixties. Ernie, the quintessential booster, not only had great plans for Churchill, but he was also one of the few who cared about Churchill's minority ethnic groups, writing often on their behalf.

Ernie predicted (correctly) that tourism would someday provide a major boost to Churchill's economy, railed against Manitoba Hydro's diversion of the Churchill River and lobbied for an all-weather road from Churchill to Winnipeg. Forty years later, Ernie's road is still a dream.

As we follow the three-legged utility poles into town, I ask Al to take a turn past Churchill's unique Eskimo Museum, which has been curated since its 1941 inception by Brother John Volant, a walking encyclopedia of Inuit culture. There, I've spent hours under Brother John's wing while he patiently answered my questions in his breathy, cigar-scented, Brittany baritone. Captivated by his charm and the knowledge he'd accumulated during decades in the Arctic, my father and I once invited him to join us for supper. To our surprise he replied, "I'll have to ask the bishop for permission," and hurried off. That evening, we dined on T-bone steaks at the Hudson Hotel while Brother John served up tales of an Inuit culture that he knew as well as his own.

Perhaps only the natives stay in Churchill. When I ask if Brother Volant still runs the museum, I learn that he left for Winnipeg in 1991. Art Cripps, the dark-haired free spirit who shepherded tourists around town in the sixties is with Manitoba Hydro in Gillam. Gordon Paul, the friendly Shell dealer who purchased the shack in which Betty Settee was raised, has moved south to Winnipeg. The only Caucasian resident I've known who stayed to the end was Angus MacIver, the rawboned septuagenarian Scot who ferried tourists across to the fort in his freighter canoe and chronicled his adventurous life in a book titled *Churchill on Hudson Bay*.

Despite its frontierlike character, Churchill has gradually changed. In the seventies, the Hudson Hotel burned to the ground, leaving embers and rumors of arson. Later, the Churchill Hotel vanished in flames and similar speculation, leaving an opening for the Tundra Inn, the Arctic Inn and the Polar Hotel. But the most obvious improvement is a sprawling building called the Town Centre. Built in the seventies on the rock ridge that separates the town from Hudson Bay, the centre, with its wide expanses of glass overlooking the bay, is Churchill's administrative, recreational and health service hub. On its several floors, the centre houses a hospital, the school, a gymnasium, curling rink, bowling alley, movie theater, hockey arena, swimming pool and cafeteria.

The centre's halls abound with native images. Boldly colored, imaginative hangings of Inuit art line the corridor to the cafeteria, where an ingenious artist has sculpted a ten-foot tall polar bear statue/children's slide out of a huge block of spiked-together planks.

Architecturally, Churchill runs from Quonset hut to California modern, including an interesting tourist trap/trading post, an excellent restaurant, a supermarket/variety store, a bakery, a Parks Canada theater, a two-story wooden teepee and a co-op that sells Inuit carvings and native crafts—all of them dwarfed by the grain elevator that provides a big chunk of Churchill's seasonal economy.

Churchill's polyglot population of whites, Indians and Inuit rises each year with the mid-July to November tourist and shipping season. Then, when the summer sun has finally removed the ice (and prohibitive insurance rates) from the Hudson Strait, freighters steam into port, their crews adding bits of Polish, Danish or German to a Main Street accustomed to English, Inuktitut, Chipewyan and Cree.

Al drops me off at Steve Bosnjak's Churchill Motel. Steve, a hard-working Croatian immigrant and middle-aged bachelor, hires his tourist-season waitresses from southern Manitoba. He treats them well, calls them his daughters and they call him Dad.

The Muskeg Express has just pulled in, and Steve is too busy to talk, so I stow my gear and hike toward the river, eager to see how the Métis have fared. In the sixties, the Métis were still living in a grubby area beside the river called "the Flats." Unwanted by both natives and whites, and virtually ignored by the government, they survived in makeshift tarpaper hovels. There, they somehow managed a precarious hand-to-mouth existence in country that hosts five million mosquitoes to the acre and is known as the "home of the windchill."

As I walk, I'm surrounded by the sounds of industry: a tug working the harbor, trucks gearing down for the turn to the elevator, the idling diesel engine of the Muskeg Express. But in a single moment the din is displaced by the sensuous scent of the sea. Breathing deeply, I inhale not Ilford's delicate mix of wild rose and evergreen but the fecund tide of the estuary, rich with the fragrance of life.

A sun-warmed smile spreads across my face as I realize that the daisy-strewn fields that surround me were once the shantytown Flats. Aided by the support of an awakened government, the hovels of the Flats were finally razed and new housing provided. Today, rag-clothed Métis children no longer stand before their flimsy shacks to stare numbly into the cameras of well-dressed tourists from another world.

Churchill's social problems accumulated during decades of governmental mismanagement and indifference. Three hundred years ago, a fairly stable population of some ten thousand Chipewyans occupied the land to the west of Churchill. Then Europeans arrived, bringing alcohol, syphilis and smallpox. By the twentieth century, as few as a thousand remained. Of that thousand, about a third slowly gravitated to Hudson's Bay Company posts within a few days' paddle of Churchill.

When the railroad reached Churchill in 1929, the HBC moved their post one hundred miles northwest to Duck Lake to avoid competition from newly arrived free traders. According to *The Taiga Times*, "Except for the HBC manager, the servants and a few old men and women, no one lived at the Duck Lake Post for the entire year.

Trapping began in the fall and lasted until spring." Summer, with the band reunited, was more like a holiday. The event of the year, however, was Treaty Day, the natives' *ka-soniyaskak*, the "time of money," when the Indian agent arrived amid a great show of pomp, accompanied by a Mountie and sometimes a doctor and nurse. At the appropriate time the head of every family received his treaty money, after which he rushed to the Bay to buy whatever he could afford, except for alcohol, which was forbidden.

When the forties and fifties brought a slump in the market for long-haired fur, the Bay closed many of its inland posts, Duck Lake included. As *The Taiga Times* reported, "Faced with the Company's departure, the Indian Affairs branch decided to move the Chipewyan band to Churchill, where it would be closer to administration, schools and employment. A quick economic survey was conducted . . . concluding [some say falsely] that the Indians at Duck Lake are starving and Chipewyans are wantonly decimating the caribou herds."

In 1957, when the time came to move, the federal Indian Affairs department offered to transport the entire band by plane if they would abandon their dogs and sleds—their means of livelihood. The majority chose to move by aircraft, only to discover that space was extremely limited. As a result, many housekeeping goods, outboard motors and other essentials had to be left behind.

The Chipewyans were housed at a site called Camp 10, an area that one reporter charitably described as "extremely unattractive." Those who had driven their dog teams from Duck Lake camped across the Churchill River in small patches of brush while trying to eke out a living by fishing and trapping.

The Chipewyans quickly came to hate life at Churchill. Unable to speak English, and by nature shy and bush-like in attire and mannerism, they were ill equipped to compete for jobs and social status. Lacking education and organization, the Chipewyans bottomed out.

Years of unemployment and inactivity led to alcohol abuse. Unscrupulous whites profited by purchasing toboggans, traps and caribou meat from the Chipewyans for one-dollar bottles of wine. In

1960, when the sale of liquor to Indians became legal, the use of alcohol at Camp 10 soared: one Royal Canadian Mounted Policeman noted that 95 percent of work at Churchill involved Camp 10.

Time, intelligence and a change in governmental attitudes eventually brought improvements to the Chipewyans and to the Métis as well. The Camp 10 ghetto was abandoned in favor of a new settlement called Dene ("the people") village, and as the natives learned English, the job market slowly improved, and the process of integration began.

Like most frontier communities, Churchill had its share of entrepreneurs, but few have matched Johnny Bilenduke, the optimist who started a hog farm, feeding his hogs garbage from the air base. The polar bears, on discovering pork chop heaven, often had to be driven away six times a day. Finally, as Bilenduke lamented, "One day they learned how to climb my chain link fence, and that was the end of my hog farming days."

Canada is home to two-thirds of the world's twenty-five thousand polar bears, and Churchill rightly calls itself "the polar bear capital of the world." Visit Churchill in June, and most of the bears will still be out on the ice, hunting seals. But when the ice leaves the bay in July, the bears return to the coast to top off their season with jet black crow berries, blueberries and tidbits from the Churchill dump, where tourists photograph them from the safety of Tundra Buggies, a bit of four-wheel-drive entrepreneurism that has turned out very well.

In the late seventies, Len Smith decided to cash in on the tourist trade. Realizing that cabs and rental cars were unsuitable (a car window won't stop a determined bear) Len decided to build a safe off-road vehicle that could carry a couple of dozen passengers. Working from plans in his head and parts from a bucket loader and a few other vehicles, he topped his four-wheel-drive creation with a huge box, added floatation tires, put in a wood-burning stove and a bathroom and began carrying tourists. Today, up to thirty-six passengers can watch bears from a larger vehicle's open observation deck or from windows set well above their eight-foot reach. As his business grew, Tundra Buggy Tours added a fifty-foot bunkhouse-on-wheels that sleeps sixteen, plus a diner with a full kitchen and tables for twenty-eight.

Because polar bears tend to congregate in the Churchill area before freeze-up, they're plentiful from late August to November, but during the mild mid-July and August days that encourage trips across the river to the fort, a Tundra Buggy ride might yield only gulls, geese and ptarmigan—or, if you're lucky, a caribou or arctic fox. Then, pilots have the advantage, for the scattered bears are easily seen from the air.

Known to the Inuit as Tornarssuk, to the scientist as *Ursus maritimus*, and to much of the world as Nanook, the Ice Bears' circumpolar range makes them citizens of Canada, Greenland, Norway, Finland, Russia and the United States. Hunting the margins of the circumpolar pack, Nanook slides silently across the ice to stalk a sleeping seal, dives into the ocean for mussels and kelp and dines omnivorously through the summer on whatever the land provides. And although we call them "polar" bears, denning females have been found on James Bay, the southern tongue of Hudson Bay, just four hundred miles from Lake Superior. Pregnant bears remain ashore when the bay begins to freeze, digging into snowdrifts downwind from hummocks and ridges. Cubs, usually two, but occasionally one or three, are born in late December or early January. Weighing little more than a pound at birth, the cubs cannot hear for three weeks, and another week will pass before they can see. By the sixth, they're walking, and when mother breaks out of the den in late March or early April, the cubs are ready to roll.

Were it not for firearms, polar bears wouldn't need protection, as adult males can weigh 1,500 pounds, depending on the season and their success with the seals. (The largest polar bear on record weighed 2,210 pounds and stands in the Anchorage, Alaska, airport.) In 1956, the U.S.S.R. banned polar bear hunting, setting an example that eventually led to international limits on polar bear kills and to the creation of sanctuaries like Ontario's Polar Bear Provincial Park.

Unfortunately, Nanook's curiosity and fine sense of smell often lead to trouble with humans. Churchill-area cabin owners board up their shacks with plywood and lay spike-studded planks on their steps, but the bears routinely rip off the plywood and plunder the cabins. Even so, despite their power and occasional ferocity, Churchill area polar bears can be surprisingly amiable, sometimes even declining to dine on chained sled dogs in favor of playing with them, as evidenced by remarkable public television videos that have featured polar bears playfully wrestling, cavorting and hugging anxious-looking, chained sled dogs before flopping down beside them, exhausted from their play.

Still, the bears are not to be taken lightly. At Churchill, bears mauled people in '66 and '67, killed a child in '68, a man in '83 and a woman in '98. During the 1980s, an average of two bears a year were shot at Churchill alone.

On one occasion, a ground crewman guiding an airliner to a parking place became increasingly irritated when the pilot ignored his signals and kept flashing his taxi lights. Disgusted, the crewman turned to walk away and discovered a polar bear rearing up behind him. As the crewman ran to the plane, the pilot revved the engines and drove the bear away.

Most bear encounters result in retreats and, occasionally, a good laugh. When one bear ambled into the Legion Hall and headed straight for a group of dart throwers, the club steward, an old English army major, shouted, "You're not a member. Get out of here!" The bear left.

Perhaps because they're bear-free for much of the year, Churchill residents vigorously defend their bears. "Look at California," one resident said. "They once had 150,000 grizzlies. It's their state symbol. But they shot the last one in 1922."

After picking up a rental car from Polar U-Drive, I head toward the airport to search for *Miss Piggy*, a wrecked c-46 named for her once-rotund fuselage. After a few false starts down gravel roads that wander off to the Bay, I finally locate the wreck.

One account claims that the twin-engine transport lost an engine while far out over the bay. Heavily loaded, *Miss Piggy* slowly descended until it was within thirty feet of the rotting summertime ice. There, it flew in "ground effect," aided by a cushion of air trapped between the ice and the aircraft's wings. Barely flying, the c-46 labored on toward Churchill, but when it encountered the gentle mile-long uphill slope to the airport, *Miss Piggy* couldn't climb. Shearing off a scattering of black spruce, *Miss Piggy* smashed across truck-size boulders, her aluminum skin screeching as she slid to a stop. The crew survived because the pilot brought the aircraft in under control, saving lives with good airmanship and a sturdy hull.

Pushing the unlikely possibility of a bear encounter from my mind, I grab my camera and, leaving the car door open, climb from a boulder onto the port wing, then stride across the buckled aluminum sidewalk toward a fuselage bearing a red lightning stripe and the name LAMBAIR in bold black print.

I peer into the dimly lit, empty cargo compartment. Broken windows scatter slivers of light into the tunnel of the fuselage. Making my way forward, I discover that the instruments have been stripped from the panel, leaving behind an expanse of empty eye sockets from which wire nerves dangle. The windshield is shattered inward, broken not by the crash but by the rocks of vandals.

As I leave the fuselage, I stop for a moment beside a streamlined engine cowling faired into the top of the wing. At its front, a magnificent, eighteen-cylinder engine once poured out more than a thousand horsepower. But engines, like their builders, eventually tire and die, sometimes with little warning. The engine and its mate from the starboard wing have been removed, disassembled and inspected. Damaged parts became scrap. Still, I wouldn't be surprised if somewhere, a few of *Miss Piggy*'s cylinders have found new life on another crankcase and are still hauling freight and passengers for those who trust their aircraft and the engines that make them fly.

Spotting a dead six-foot-tall spruce near the end of the wing, I break it across my knee and smooth its stub with my pocket knife.

How many summers built this inch-thick trunk? I remove my glasses to combine my myopia with the magnifying power of my wide angle lens and begin counting. Three counts later, I know that my inch-thick spruce, if it died recently, took root during the term of President McKinley and struggled on for a hundred years.

The road to town passes little islands of stunted spruce trees wearing snow-blasted "bare midriffs" over drift-protected skirts of greenery. Above their barren waists, a few short branches struggle against the prevailing wind, while on their southeast sides, healthy branches stream away like windblown scarves. Like synchronized ballerinas frozen in midpirouette, their arms point away from the northwest wind.

As I motor past ponds littered with ducks, geese and shorebirds, I suddenly come upon two lounging roadside bears. I pull to a stop, and while they ignore me snap photos from fifteen feet. Perhaps they've heard about Ursus Alcatraz, the jail that provides an alternative to expensive helicopter rides out of town for trapped delinquent bears. But like its namesake in San Francisco Bay, this Alcatraz is also empty; no caged Nanooks pace to and fro while awaiting the reprieve of solid Hudson Bay ice.

The sun's still high, though it's 9:00 p.m.—definitely time for supper. At the Trader's Table, my placemat depicts two seated polar bears bending over steaming mugs of coffee while the amber glow of candlelight warms their pearlescent fur. By the time I've downed the last of my porterhouse steak, my evening plans are made: a bottle of Molson ale, a little television and a bed at the Churchill Motel. Life is hard on the northern frontier.

"Fred" tells me that he runs a river-taxi service "on the side," which means that he takes tourists across to the fort, but lacks a commercial license and insurance. But because Fred's attitude is "you're the boss," and he has a shotgun with firecracker shells to ward off inquisitive bears (and the price is right) I pass up Sea North's long and beamy, thirty-two passenger six-hundred-horsepower, aluminum launch and downsize to Fred's fourteen-foot Alumacraft and his twenty-horse Mercury. Besides, Sea North's vessel draws much more water than Fred's and must time its trips to the tides. Fred, however, can come and go at will, and he'll stop at Sloop's Cove, a concession that Sea North cannot make.

Fred's an old-timer, having lived at Churchill for thirty-six years. His short, bony, fiftyish frame shows surprising strength as he hoists the Merc onto the transom and, with one hand and a knee, shoves the Alumacraft into the river.

Fred turns upstream, and within a minute I spot jets of mist rising above the swells. "Belugas!" I shout, but Fred's already seen them. Seeing their exhalations is easy enough, but getting close quickly becomes a chore, for while we cruise back and forth on the surface, the whales make use of the depths.

When Fred cuts the motor as we enter Sloop's Cove, the brief silence is suddenly broken by a loud puuffffff directly behind us, and as we turn, another puuffffff. Four of the thousands of belugas that visit the Churchill River have followed us into the cove—three adults and one juvenile. Slipping through the water like alabaster columns, they pass within fifteen feet, their exhalations sounding like speech teachers demonstrating plosives to a diction class.

As we climb the weathered granite, Fred describes the beluga hunts that ended in '67: "Someone got the bright idea to can the blubber, sell the hides and market beluga meat for mink food. If I remember right, the going rate for a beluga was about $1.25 per foot. They'd motor up to the whales and shoot or spear them and tow them off to the plant. In case you're wondering, no one knows how many wounded belugas escaped, later to die in the bay.

"The factory was just a rough-board building on the edge of the tidal flats. They'd winch the whales into the plant and strip off the blubber. Outside, dozens of severed beluga heads were strewn about, each head oozing tiny streams of blood past green algae-coated boulders. The shallows had turned a faded pink.

"But the demand for muktuk never materialized, and the cannery failed. Later, the government found high levels of mercury in the meat."

Thirty yards from the shoreline, a deeply rusted mooring ring is pinned to the rock. Why so far from shore? Because post-ice-age rebound has raised the ring a good nine feet, adding yards of sloping shoreline during the 250 years since its anchoring-pin was driven home.

Fred slows when he reaches the top of the rise, taking care to avoid the inscriptions at his feet. Scattered across the light gray outcropping are more than a dozen names and dates, and one grim illustration.

One inscription, adorned at top and bottom with decorative scrolls, reads

Richard J Johnson

1773

A larger, more elaborate engraving remembers the last commander of Fort Prince of Wales:

S L Hearne

July ye 1 1767

The illustration, however, depicts a hanging. Chiseled into the stone by amateurish hands are the words "John Kelley—From the Isle of Wight" and "1765." According to Fred, Mr. Kelley stole a Christmas goose and in so doing cooked his own.

By the time we arrive at the fort, the rising tide has done us a great favor, inundating thirty yards of slippery algae-coated boulders. I persuade Fred to help me search for an Inuit grave that once lay close to the fort, but we come up empty-handed. Constrained by rock and permafrost, the Inuit simply covered their dead with stones, and though the mound was prominent thirty years ago, it's nowhere in sight today—perhaps carried off by the thoughtless who search for souvenirs.

The fortress squats under glowering stratus clouds like a dark Macbethan castle, its sixteen-foot-high limestone walls rising above the V-shaped stone ravelin that shielded its timber doors from frontal assault.

As we enter the fort, Flora Beardy, a stocky Parks Canada guide emerges with her flock of tourists. One vacationer keeps insisting that the lovely lavender fireweed surrounding the fort are lupines, while Flora, her moon face wreathed in smiles, tries to correct her. It's an uphill fight.

Fort Prince of Wales forms a square, a hundred yards on a side, with bastions like arrowheads protruding from each corner. The fort, which was begun in 1731, took forty years to complete. Built by the HBC to protect its fur trade, the fort with its forty cannons, still plays at guarding the only deep-water port on Hudson Bay. (Although the HBC claimed to oppose using liquor for pay, it awarded stonemason Thomas Smith an extra ten *gallons* of brandy a year for the risks he took while blasting out rock for the fortress's walls.)

When Samuel Hearne arrived in 1766, he found the fort commanded by an unscrupulous tyrant named Moses Norton, whom Hearne, a deist and an admirer of Voltaire, quickly grew to despise, describing Norton as "one of the most debauched wretches under the sun." (Norton, who was a notorious philanderer, and who had a handful of native "wives," two of whom he is said to have poisoned, required his men to listen to him preach about ethics and moral living.)

On hearing rumors of a river rich with copper far to the north and west, Norton sent Hearne to search it out but supplied him so poorly that the poor man almost starved. Worse yet, the guide Norton provided robbed and abandoned Hearne when they were hundreds of miles from the fort.

Hearne tried again the following year, again with bad "luck" when another of Norton's guides not only got lost but freely shared vital provisions with every native they met. Abandoned again, Hearne turned back, starving and alone. And then, in one of the great good luck stories of history, Hearne stumbled onto a Chipewyan chief named Matonabbee, who led him back to the fort.

Twelve days later, Hearne set out again, this time accompanied by Matonabbee and his eight wives, who, being traditional native women, did most of the work. Matonabbee proved far superior to Norton's guides, for he not only knew the terrain but he could also manage people. On his third attempt, Hearne finally reached the arctic coast near Coppermine. His journey, however, was marred by the massacre of an Inuit encampment that neither he nor Matonabbee could prevent at a place called Bloody Fall.

Nevertheless, Hearne's respect for Matonabbee held: "He had so much natural good sense and liberality of sentiment that he would not ridicule any particular sect on account of their religious opinion. He held them all in equal esteem, but was determined that as he came into this world, so would he go out of it—without professing any religion at all. Not withstanding, I have met few Christians who possess as many good qualities, or fewer bad ones." Hearne praised Matonabbee's "scrupulous adherence to truth . . . his benevolence and universal humanity to all . . . he was always the master of himself."

Toward the end of their return trek, they had nothing but tobacco and snow water. Hearne's toenails fell from his injured feet, leaving "the print of my feet in blood." No mine was discovered: only a few scraps of copper were found. But with his three attempts and five thousand miles of travel, Hearne finally proved that the long-sought inland waterway from Hudson Bay to the Orient simply didn't exist.

Shortly after his return, Norton ordered Hearne to establish an inland trading post far to the west on the Saskatchewan River. When Cumberland House was finally completed, a second stroke of luck fell to Samuel Hearne: Moses Norton died.

Promoted to commander, Hearne took charge of the fort and married one of Norton's Métis daughters, an attractive sixteen-year-old named Mary. Hearne, happily married and content to stay put, would later describe the following years as the best of his life. Unfortunately, they didn't last very long.

In 1782, the French privateer Comte Jean-François La Perouse, sailed up to the fort with three men-of-war at a very propitious time for the French. With only thirty-nine men in a fort that required at least three hundred to man its forty cannons, Hearne was compelled to surrender.

La Perouse torched the interior buildings and drove iron spikes into the cannon's ignition holes, transforming the great stone fort into a great stone folly. He then set off to attack York Factory. Hearne and his men were allowed to return to England, but the fort was never staffed again.

When Matonabbee learned that Hearne had become a prisoner of the French, he assumed that Hearne would be murdered. Believing also that the French would refuse to trade with him, he committed suicide. Without Matonabbee to assist them, his wives and children starved to death the following winter, along with Mary, Hearne's young wife. At about the same time, a smallpox epidemic swept up from the south, and half of the Chipewyan population perished.

The Hudson's Bay Company shipped Hearne back to Churchill in 1783 with orders to build a new post upriver from the damaged fort. Eager for a reunion with his wife and Matonabbee, Hearne arrived in midsummer, only to learn of their deaths. He resigned his command in 1787 and soon fell ill. He died at forty-seven. Chief Matonabbee, Hearne's friend and savior, is honored by a bronze plaque near the path that leads to the fort, but only the Sloop's Cove inscription keeps thoughts of Hearne alive.

Fred enters the fort and heads for a wooden ladder to climb to the top of the walls. By the time I mount the ladder, he's crossed to the windward side and is scanning Button Bay.

In the courtyard below, a few stone walls remain—remnants of buildings in which men shivered through seemingly endless winters, using heated cannonballs to warm frigid nights. Wine and beer, even when stored inside, froze solid. As a remedy, the men dug an eight-foot-deep pit and buried the spirits in horse manure. It worked.

I'm sighting along a cannon barrel toward Sea North's departing boat, when Fred softly calls my name. Pointing over the fortress wall, he silently mouths the word, "bear." I arrive just in time to see a polar bear disappear behind the six-foot-high V-shaped stone ravelin that protected the fortress's wooden doors from frontal assualt.

"Want to follow him?" asks Fred.

"OK," I answer, with a glance at his shotgun.

The bear is fifty yards away by the time we reach the ravelin, ambling toward the river at an angle that will take him through our scent. He stops, lifts his head and turns. Spotting us, he rises on his hind legs for a better look, then drops to all fours and casually strolls away. He might be annoyed, but he certainly isn't afraid.

The bear eases into the river and heads straight for Churchill.

"Jeez," says Fred, "we don't want him on Main Street, eh? Let's head him off with the boat."

By the time we idle alongside, he's a third of the way across, slipping through the water with easy grace, his pearly coat greened by algae growing within his hollow guard hairs. I marvel at his grace, how smoothly his big paddle-feet move him along, how *big* he is, though I guess his weight at no more than eight hundred pounds. Staying a few yards to one side, we slowly turn him back to the fort.

He suddenly dives, coursing through aquamarine water for twenty to thirty feet, then surfaces, as if expecting that we'd be gone. Having failed to elude us, he shakes his head in a halo of spray and heads back to Eskimo Point.

A shaft of sunlight enlivens the western sky as we drag Fred's boat ashore. Assuming that it's a harbinger of clearing skies, I ask Fred to wait outside the motel while I phone the airport. "Yes," they say, "the satellite shows that it's clearing from the west."

I file a flight note, grab my gear and ask Fred for a ride to the seaplane base, where I thank him for his help and pump a few pints of water from the floats. As I step from the end of the float to the slippery pier, my feet suddenly fly out from beneath me and I tumble into the lake. I prepare myself for a quick leap back to shore, but my feet find only soft, yielding muck. I climb out sputtering, remove my clothes and wring them out, then spot blood seeping from a scratch on my leg.

My clothes will dry in the heated Cub, so I struggle into them while smashing mosquitoes on my abundantly exposed skin. As I stow the rest of my gear, I notice the debris churned up by my plunge—great gobs of goose and loon excrement.

Tetanus! It's been *years* since my last tetanus shot, and I dare not leave without one. Fred, who has been smiling at my antics, agrees to run me back to the Town Centre, where a nurse provides my shot. When I offer to pay, I'm told to forget it. I'm a foreigner, and the paper work's too daunting.

The ever-obliging Steve Bosnjak lets me back into my room for a shower and a change of clothes, then drives me back to the Cub. Ninety minutes after my back flip, the Tundra Cub leaves Churchill's ramshackle docks behind. I contact Churchill Radio and report my next destination, Ennadai Lake.

The fort passes beneath my wings while I scan the tundra for Fred's polar bear, but it's nowhere in sight. In the transparent waters of Button Bay, hundreds of free-swimming belugas roll and dive. And as my camera preserves the moment, I regret that we capture these intelligent, social animals whose wanderings span hundreds of miles and imprison them in the bathtubs of our zoos.

"Churchill radio, Four five Mike is 20 miles northwest."

"Four five Mike, I have you leaving the zone at five five-[4:55]. Good day."

5

Churchill to Baker Lake, Nunavut

*I am glad I shall never be young without wild country
to be young in. What avail are forty freedoms
without a blank spot on the map?*

— ALDO LEOPOLD

*L*OOSENING MY SEAT BELT, I squirm around to retrieve a thermos of coffee from the back seat. It's already sugared and creamed, and it sets my mouth watering by the time I find its companion, a delicious Danish from the Churchill bakery. As I savor my in-flight meal, Caribou Lake slips beneath my wings, bringing memories of a trapper described in *Canada* (Life World Library).

"In the winter of 1947, a trapper named Shaback, lying in a makeshift shack . . . made this entry in his diary: '43rd day without food.' The previous September, finding little game and fearing starvation, he had begun to walk down the Caribou River toward civilization. Weakened by hunger, he had holed up in an empty shack. Awkwardly, Shaback carved three words on a piece of wood, went out into the thirty-degree-below-zero cold, nailed the piece of wood on the door of his shack and went inside again.

"Over a year later, a half-breed trapper found the shack and noticed the piece of wood nailed to the door. On it, Shaback had written: 'DEAD MAN HERE.'"

Shaback's story wouldn't have been unusual a century or two ago, but it happened in modern times. Because of Shaback and others like him, I carry extra food, fishing gear, a hatchet and rifle and of course my ELT. And because my dogleg route from Churchill to Baker Lake could easily empty my tanks, I'm carrying ten extra gallons of fuel in two collapsible jugs on the back seat, plus another five in the floats.

The Tundra Cub is a simple aircraft. Move the stick or push a rudder pedal and cables convey each input to ailerons, elevators and rudder. Designed to take off and land around forty mph, the Cub can almost promise that emergency landings will be injury free.

Like the Wright Flyer that skimmed the dunes of Kill Devil Hill, the Cub's fabric skin enfolds a framework of wood and steel. Given proper care, her dacron sheath will stay supple for more than thirty years.

The Cub's chrome-molybdenum tubing is a rust-resistant alloy of iron, the metal of meteorites, our only source of iron until we learned how to process ore. Her cowling, propeller and the spars of her wings are made of aluminum, a metal once so precious that the Washington monument originally wore an aluminum cap, and kings once preferred it to silverware. Her propeller, like that of the Flyer, is simplicity itself: two rotating airfoils with winglike cross sections that pull the Cub along. The Wrights' hand-carved prototype had a remarkable efficiency of 66 percent, but modern aluminum props like the Cub's have raised it to 88.

The Cub's spark plugs are fired by two magneto-driven ignition systems derived from the work of Michael Faraday, the English genius who discovered the relationship between electricity and magnetism in the early nineteenth century. Using his insights, the Cub's magnetos create pulses of electricity by whirling wires within a magnetic field. Were it not for people like Faraday, we'd still be riding horse-drawn buggies and dirty steam-driven trains; we'd be lighting coal oil lanterns and sweating through long summer nights.

With no hydraulics to leak, no starter, generator or battery to fail, the Cub's a Spartan but practical machine. Engine, propeller, airframe and a few instruments—that's all.

Because the Cub is thoroughly checked and relicensed every year, I don't worry about emergencies. Nevertheless, I always know which lake, river, meadow or bog (in that order) I can reach if my engine fails—a precaution that all instructors teach by suddenly closing the throttle and asking, "Where are you going to land?"

Alert students immediately slow to the speed at which the aircraft glides the farthest, then set up an approach to the area they've chosen. When the plane has descended to one or two hundred feet above the ground, the instructor restores power and comments on the student's choice and approach.

The sun returns, bathing the Cub in golden light as the tundra unrolls a carpet of ocher and green around lakes rimmed with orange lichens and butterscotch sand. Deepening, their waters shift from clear to aquamarine, and then to black as the Cub drones through indolent air above the deep, cold waters of Nueltin Lake that join Manitoba to Nunavut.

Well north of the tree line, Nueltin Lake was, for centuries, home to the band of inland Inuit that the Canadian writer Farley Mowat immortalized in *People of the Deer*. The "deer," of course, were caribou. Unlike their coastal counterparts, these Inuit had no ocean traditions, calling themselves the "People of the Willow Thicket." Compelled to move to Churchill in the fifties like the Chipewyans, they, too, found language barriers, intolerance, unemployment, segregated housing, liquor and, eventually, welfare checks.

The Cub angles into a land where winter lasts eight months and the main attractions are fish, game and minerals—and a paucity of people. In April 1999 the eastern half of the Northwest Territories

(20 percent of all Canada) became Nunavut, a new territory under aboriginal control, with a government like that of the Territories.

Looking into smoke-muted light that speaks of distant fires and splashes lakes and ponds with molten copper, I search the horizon for an antenna-studded island that housed the Ennadai Lake weather station, long since abandoned. The island is part of an esker, a long, wandering ridge of sand and gravel deposited by a glacial river. Trailing across the landscape for up to a hundred miles, eskers provide raised highways for migrating caribou and well-drained sites for denning badgers, foxes and wolves. Still, even when I'm sure that I have the island in sight, I can't see the antennas. Then, just as the Cub crosses the island's center, I spot buildings on its western shore, but the antennas are down, their twisted skeletons sprawled across the sandy hillocks like the vertebral columns of giant snakes.

I set up a long glide that will carry me to a landing near the station. To my surprise, two canoes loll at the edge of the beach, their sterns still awash, as if reluctant to leave the water. Far up the sandy slope, two tents flutter in the wind shadow of the bunkhouse. How nice, I think—a little company.

A tear in my chart precludes my reading the altitude of Ennadai Lake, so I arbitrarily set the Cub's altimeter to one thousand feet. Tomorrow morning, if the reading is significantly higher, I will know that a low pressure area is heading my way, and "lows" often bring dirty weather. If the altimeter reads much less than one thousand feet, a "high" is approaching and with it fair skies.

My altimeter is a gift from Evangelista Toricelli, Galileo's successor at the Florentine Academy, and from Blaise Pascal, his seventeenth-century contemporary—two scientists who concluded that we live at the bottom of an ocean of air (which is why it's so difficult to maintain a vacuum) and invented the barometer.

On observing that mercury always rose to the same height in different lengths of evacuated tubes that had their open, lower ends immersed in mercury, Toricelli reasoned that the weight of air could support only a limited column. The height of that column, the barometric pressure, is equivalent to the weight of the ocean of air over-head, an ocean that rises and falls like its watery counterpart, although not with such tidelike regularity.

Pascal, who had concluded that the weight of the air should change with altitude, took Toricelli's work one step further and devised a barometer that could measure mountains. My altimeter, which is a nothing more than a mechanical version of Pascal's baro-meter, converts air pressure into height above sea level. By setting it to the altitude on the chart (if it's recorded) or to an arbitrary alti-tude that I'll remember the next morning, I've a good idea what sort of weather's approaching, usually from the west.

Surprised that no one has arrived from the tents, I secure the Cub, then transfer the extra fuel to the wings and dig out the mak-ings of supper. Perhaps the paddlers are snoring in their sleeping bags, exhausted by their exertions. Perhaps they're semipurists, canoeists who fly to and from the barrens, but then claim that pass-ing aircraft sully their wilderness experience. As I haul my gear toward the tents, I consider a more likely possibility: they're proba-bly hiking the dunes where I wouldn't have seen them during my approach.

I pause a few yards from the tents, disgusted to see that every window in the nearby buildings has been shattered. Turning to the tents, I utter a quiet hello. No response. Another hello, a bit louder. Still no response.

Not wanting to waken them if they're sleeping, or to intrude if I'm being avoided, I trudge along one of the toppled antennas until I reach its concrete base, then face into a warm, humid breeze that keeps the mosquitoes at bay. I mustard my bread, add a few slices of ham, pour a cup of coffee and recall the very different Ennadai Lake that I found back in '68.

When my father and I taxied up to the pier, the crew streamed out of the buildings, helped secure the plane, rolled out a barrel of

Chuipka Airways fuel and worked the wobble pump to fill our tanks with gas.

They insisted we stay for coffee, which the cook transformed into a mouthwatering feast of fresh bread, sweet potatoes, a caribou roast and peach pie. Bribed with food by an isolated crew that was eager for company, we lingered in exchange for tales of Ennadai life: of feeding caribou by hand, of arctic foxes warming themselves against the chimney of the snow-covered cookhouse and of bulldozing a mile-long runway on eight-foot-thick ice for a Hercules transport with a fourteen-thousand-gallon fuel tank in its belly.

The following summer I stopped again at Ennadai Lake, where I found the same crew except for the cook, who, after so many years in the north, had succumbed to cabin fever. When his mood darkened during the short days of winter and he began to threaten violence, the government flew him out.

Two ravens begin to orbit my picnic site. Like their dapper cousins, the Canada jays, their intelligence and legendary sense of smell has won the respect of Indians and Inuit alike. Opening my pack, I remove two pieces of bread and toss them in different directions to ensure that my gift will be shared. When I'm a hundred feet away I stop and turn. The ravens are dining.

Back at the tents, I try another hello, but it, too, goes unanswered. They still can't be hiking, so I'm either being ignored or they're dead to the world and best left undisturbed.

Thinking that the vandalized cookhouse might provide an acceptable shelter, I step inside, but it's a shambles of glass, dirt and debris. Worse yet, it teems with mosquitoes. The shattered windows of the machine shop imply that it, too, will be useless, but I decide to look it over. Inside, shafts of light from the setting sun illuminate a scattering of empty barrels, a workbench and a few coils of wire. As I look about, I suddenly listen in disbelief—there are no mosquitoes. Despite its vacant windows and a wide-open door, not a single insect whines. I walk to the entrance, certain that they'll be drawn to me. A few venture in, but then turn back, repelled, perhaps, by the odor of diesel fuel rising from the oil-stained floor.

When I step outside to retrieve my gear, I'm captivated by an immense bronze sun angling toward the horizon in a scene that rivals the binary sunsets of Tatooine, Luke Skywalker's home. Though mosquitoes dance around me, I'm transfixed.

To the east, a gibbous moon slips yellow light through a toppled antenna. A minute later, its lower half turns toothy behind the meshwork of steel—a moon with orthodontics. And as the moon abandons its earthbound braces, I recall a tropical beach near Lighthouse Cay on the Barrier Reef of Belize.

Poo, our Mayan guide, had heard that my son, Chris, and I had planned to sleep outside. "Not sleep with moon on face," he warned us. When I asked him why, he replied, "Moon makes wrinkles." Poo may be right, but in the land of the Inuit, the moon brings a hunter luck and makes a woman fertile. And since I don't plan to hunt and I can't get pregnant, I'll sleep inside tonight.

I spread a sheet of plastic over the oil-stained concrete and stretch out on my sleeping bag. Eyes closed, I put everything from my mind while I absorb the sounds of evening. If I awaken to similar sounds, I'll quickly go back to sleep, but if I sense a change of wind or wave, I'll immediately check on the Cub. With the recording session over, I drift into the whispering reservoir of night while eau de diesel holds the skeeters at bay.

Just after three o'clock, the sound of a rising wind tugs me awake. When I reach the shore, the Cub is still secure, but the canoes are gone. I whirl in my tracks to confirm that the tents are still in place, then realize what has happened. The empty canoes, with their sterns awash, have been worked loose by waves slanting along the shore. Looking downwind, I spot one canoe bumping along the beach a hundred yards to the north. Beyond it, the predawn light reveals the second, rocking against a tiny spit of sand.

Ignoring the first canoe, I run for the second. If I can catch it, the first won't be a problem, but sprinting across the sloping sand is like running through a tilted bog—lots of effort but slow progress. I finally reach the distant canoe and grab its bow just as it's about to head off across forty miles of water. Panting, I anchor the canoe with my body while the wind cools me down. Then, with my breath regained, I tow it back to its companion and drag them both ashore.

Realizing that the wind will soon raise waves that could jeopardize a safe takeoff, I pack my gear and crank up the Cub. While the engine warms, I check the altimeter, which reads 1,180 feet. A "low" is definitely approaching. Since air flows counterclockwise around and into a low, my southerly winds indicate that the low must lie to the west. Tomorrow will probably bring the phantom canoeists clouds, drizzle and fog. But by then, I'll be far away, flying north out of Baker Lake.

The Tundra Cub breaks loose from the beach, her engine roaring, her wings lifting as she pivots into the wind. With the waves already spanning eight feet and the troughs deepening by the minute, I'm pushing the limits of safety.

Pulling back on the stick, I hold the Cub's nose higher than normal to avoid sucking spray into her carburetor. Even so, as we slam across the first two crests, she gasps on Ennadai spray. The third crest jolts her floats, sending her staggering into the air. The fourth is just a kiss—and we climb away. At two hundred feet I roll left, reverse course and streak past the station at 120 mph. While Ennadai brews a head of foam, the campers sleep on, their tent walls flapping in the wind.

The Cub hurries through the predawn light while I wonder what the campers will make of their wayward canoes. Will they decide that a midnight prankster prowls the shores of Ennadai Lake, or, if they heard the Cub, will they correctly reason that the pilot rescued their canoes? The longer I weigh the possibilities, the more irritated I become. Finally, convinced (unreasonably) that I was heard and ignored and that they will think that I deliberately messed with their canoes, I heave a sigh and push them from my mind.

The Cub's sole navigation instrument is a wet compass—"wet" meaning that its turbulence-induced oscillations are dampened by sealing it in high-grade kerosene. Like all compasses, my pole-seeking instrument is a descendant of the magnetite lodestones that were discovered near the town of Magnesia, Greece, around 550 B.C. Eventually, someone noticed that a needle rubbed against a lodestone would become "magnetized" and when floated, would align itself north and south.

First used by Europeans in the twelfth century, and common by the thirteenth, compasses escaped serious study until they attracted the attention of William Gilbert, the president of the London College of Surgeons, who realized that "the earth's globe is itself a great magnet," and published *De Magnete* in 1600. Gilbert, who denied the earth-centered astronomy of Luther, Calvin and the Vatican, was fortunate to live in a tolerant society—for its time. He was knighted and appointed the queen's physician, while across the Channel, the Inquisition was trying (and later executed) the philosopher and scientist Giordano Bruno for espousing similar views.

Staying low to watch for caribou, I toast the gentle warmth of the rising sun with a thermos of coffee and the last of my Danish rolls while steadying the stick with my knees. Where are the caribou, the wolves and the musk oxen? Have they returned to the hole in the earth from which Inuit legends say they came, pulled out bodily by the first woman?

Like vampires shrinking from the light of dawn, the horizons slowly recede. The sky brightens, and the monochrome tundra releases a mosaic of caramel, russet and green as the lakes slowly shift from gray to aquamarine. Then, faced with three hundred miles of glacier-scarred plain and with only my snoring engine for company, I begin to calculate how much air/fuel mixture the Cub's engine consumes each minute. After all, are the Cub and I not air breathers? Are we not internal-combustion heat-producing beings that fuel ourselves with hydrocarbons? Michael Faraday, the one whose work fires the Cub's spark plugs, would agree: "In every one of us there is a living process of combustion going on very similar to that of the candle...."

Since the Cub's two-hundred-cubic-inch engine "inhales" one hundred cubic inches of air a revolution (two of its four cylinders exhale as the other two inhale), it follows that at a cruise setting of 2300 rpm it consumes 230,000 cubic inches—about 130 cubic feet—a minute. That's seven refrigerators of air/fuel mix every minute, just to get the 20 percent that supports combustion. Today, we call that portion "oxygen," although Joseph Priestley, the Englishman who discovered it, called it "dephlogisticated air."

Priestley, a nonconformist if ever there was one, had the misfortune of being bright, contentious, personally unappealing and a Unitarian—believing in the unity of God instead of the Trinity—a very unpopular combination that inspired a religious mob to ransack his Birmingham, England, laboratory and set his home ablaze in 1791. Lucky Priestley! By escaping to America, where he renewed his acquaintance with Franklin and Jefferson, he fared better than Antoine Lavoisier, the French scientist and father of modern chemistry who gave us the word "oxygen." Charged with being sympathetic to the monarchy during the French Revolution, Lavoisier was brought before a Reign of Terror judge who is said to have sniffed, "The Republic has no need of scientists" and sent him to the guillotine.

My chart has abandoned English names in favor of native names like Angikuni, Tulemalu, Kaminuriak and Tebesjuak Lakes. But as the foam-streaked waters of Yathkyed Lake fall far behind, the Cub approaches Ferguson Lake, a small body of water that I landed upon long ago in order to stretch my legs.

As I secured the Cub, the drone of an outboard motor reached me, and a few minutes later, a boat carrying four men bumped ashore. When I expressed surprise at finding anyone, they countered, "We thought you were the charter pilot come to fly us out. He's two days overdue." All four were geologists, and all had foreign accents—not a Canadian in the lot. Hailing from Germany, Denmark, the Netherlands and India, they'd been employed by a French consortium to search for minerals of commercial value.

When an invitation to tea led to lunch, I updated them on the world they'd left behind. That done, we exchanged thoughts on everything from religion to politics. On the former, they professed indifference; on the latter, they politely advised the U.S. to "get out of Vietnam."

Hungry and ready for a stretch, I decide to land at Pitz Lake, a circular body of water with gently sloping shores that generate none of the turbulence that swirls downwind from steeper slopes. When the Cub's a foot above the whitecaps, I ease off the power, slide to a stop and carefully secure the Cub to a boulder, the only object to tie to on the treeless, barren shore. Should the Cub work loose, it's a twenty-mile hike to where she'd drift ashore.

I whip a Daredevil far out over the lake, only to have my retrieve interrupted by a raucous cry, followed by a short duet. Dropping the rod, I peer over the gravelly ridge that separates beach from tundra. In the distance, two sandhill cranes cavort, perhaps performing a prenuptial dance or nesting display, despite it being late in July.

Creeping along the beach to within fifty yards of the gyrating cranes, I raise my head above the ridge. My hunger disappears, carried off by the dancing cranes on a stage of arctic cotton.

When I return to the Cub, it's six o'clock—breakfast time. But to my amazement, my casting draws a blank. I can't believe it. How can this be? Fishless for the first time in all of my travels, I fall back on my favorite quickie meal, a can of Dinty Moore stew before returning to the skies above the former Keewatin Territory. As large as Manitoba, the Keewatin, now part of Nunavut, has a population density of fewer than one person a square mile. Exclude the eleven hundred residents of Baker Lake, and the density drops to one for every *thousand* square miles.

Baker Lake still bears a few small rafts of ice, some of it delivered by the Thelon River, the main artery of the Thelon Wildlife Sanctuary. Rising far to south and west, the Thelon's tranquil flow offers hundreds of miles of safe river travel for canoeists who seek wild country and wild animals but not wild water. Like a sheltering oasis, the shallow Thelon valley hoards the warmth of the subarctic sun, encouraging growth within a long, fingerlike microclimate that probes a land of stone, brush, lichen and moss.

The Cub skips across the last hundred yards of Baker Lake, pushes through a jingle of candled ice and drifts to a stop at a unique beach where a seaplane that's displayed in the Smithsonian Air and Space Museum once eased ashore in 1931. Headed west to the Orient, the sleek six-hundred-horsepower Lockheed Sirius with a two thousand-mile range epitomized the technology that had developed during the twenty-eight years since the Wrights flew their Flyer to fame. The Sirius, however, was piloted by two who were well accustomed to acclaim: one was a shy Minnesotan named Charles. The other, his radio operator, journalist and wife, was Anne Morrow Lindbergh.

Three

BAKER LAKE TO GARRY LAKE, NUNAVUT

6

Baker Lake to Chantrey Inlet, Nunavut

Toward evening we came upon a grey, glassy lake, bounded by bleak shores a little higher than the marshes. On the shore, the only points of accent in the monotonous landscape, stood three or four white houses. This was Baker Lake.

— ANNE MORROW LINDBERGH,
North to the Orient, 1931

THE LINDBERGHS NEVER RETURNED to Baker Lake to see what a transformation a few decades would bring. No longer just "three or four white houses," Baker Lake boasts an airline, a rambling one-story hotel and restaurant, a craft store, a school, a government center and a herd of three-wheelers that never seem to stop. Newspapers arrive on scheduled flights instead of the yearly Churchill barge, and satellite communications have replaced the often unintelligible warblings of shortwave radio.

As I step ashore, two seaplanes bearing Minnesota registration stickers pull away from the beach. One has a canoe lashed to its floats, a practice that began with the Wrights, who strapped a canoe beneath their aircraft for a flight over New York harbor just in case their engine failed.

In the resoundingly busy Northern store I phone for a barrel of gas. I already know the drill: pay for all fifty-five gallons whether I can use them or not. A half hour later the truck arrives, drops off the barrel and adds $216 to my Visa account—about $US3 a gallon.

"Wow!" I exclaim as I sign the slip, "I used to think that your gas was expensive at $.95 a gallon, but look at it now."

"Yeah," he agrees. "It's plenty high. Just be glad you won't need it at Chantrey. It's even worse there—if you can get it."

Surrounded by a gaggle of bubbling children, I answer a stream of questions: "It's a Piper; it can fly six hundred miles on the wing tanks alone; I'm from Minnesota; I'm going to Chantrey Inlet and then Alaska; I was a dentist; yes, I'm traveling alone; I'm married, but my wife doesn't like flying; I have two sons; no, they don't fly either; it cruises at ninety mph; I carry a rifle, but only for an emergency."

A young entrepreneur stops to ask if I'll be needing all the gas. When I show him the vinyl bag in the floats, he wanders off. And as my hand pump slowly empties the barrel, I recall other years on this same beach, including a near disaster that happened in '81.

On arriving at Baker Lake in a rented Cessna 172 that required hundred-octane fuel, I called the gas truck, leaving a friend to fuel the plane while I headed to the Wildlife office to check on the caribou migration. By the time I returned, the fueling was done, and out of habit, I drained a bit from each wing tank to check for water. But instead of finding pale blue hundred-octane gas, the fuel I saw was clear, and the smell was definitely wrong.

Walking around to the far side of the barrel, I was stunned to read, "Jet-A," a kerosene fuel intended for jet engines. If I hadn't noticed the error, we'd have had just enough gasoline in the fuel lines to fly a mile or two. When the Jet-A reached the engine, we'd have been low over rocky terrain with a faltering engine or, more likely, a total failure.

After reassuring my non-pilot friend that the mistake was not his, I called the Shell office and told them to bring the fuel that I'd ordered. Ninety minutes later we had drained the tanks and fuel lines, flushed them twice, refueled with hundred-octane and were on our way after circling Baker Lake to be sure that the engine would perform as it should.

A few years later, when my longtime flying companion, Wesley Miller, and I arrived in identical Cubs, we were confronted by the pilot of a nearby Beaver who chewed us out for "running around up here in those little things."

"Just how long do you think you'd last in this water?" he grumbled, jabbing a finger at Baker Lake, which still held a few shards of ice. I was tempted to answer that Baker Lake in July was no worse than Minnesota in April, but I restrained myself. Later, we learned that our gruff adviser had wrecked his seaplane during an ill-advised takeoff in high waves. His training as a frogman saved his life, but his passengers drowned.

Returning from Chantrey Inlet another year, Wes and I hiked up to the Rainy Lake Airways camp for a hot meal, only to learn that "Pooch" Liesenfield, the company's senior pilot who had left Chantrey ahead of us, had yet to arrive.

Since the inlet's no more than two hours away, we were concerned, though not very seriously because the low ceilings that had posed no problem for our land-on-any-puddle Cubs could have forced a precautionary landing for Pooch's twin-engined Goose. Furthermore, the lack of radio contact meant nothing, for the Goose's line-of-sight signals would be blocked by the hills to the north and west of Baker Lake. The most reassuring factor, however, was that Pooch had been flying the bush since '36 and had yet to meet his match.

That evening, the Rainy Lake camp resembled a hospital waiting room. Deliberate small talk drifted back and forth above the steady hiss of gas lanterns, interrupted only by an occasional caller inquiring after the Goose. When daylight waned, we turned in, slept

poorly and rose at five to pass another day of low ceilings, speculation and stilted conversation.

A second night came and went, bringing a wind shift and a slight
increase in ceilings and visibility. By the time we'd finished breakfast, Wes and I had decided that the weather had improved enough
to let us look for the Goose. Just as we were about to leave, the cook
came running down, yelling that Pooch had radioed in. Even as he
hollered, our ears picked up the distant, synchronous drone of the
Goose's radial engines. Growing louder and louder, the sound grew
to a skin-prickling roar as he buzzed the town and circled to land.
Returning to camp, we found faces stretched with smiles of relief,
and more than a few surreptitiously blinking back tears. As we had
expected, low ceilings had prevented Pooch from using our direct
route, and to stay within reach of the larger lakes, he'd veered to the
west, where he landed to wait for the weather to change.

With fueling complete, I return to the store to ring up Father
Joseph Choque, who exemplifies another major change—one of
friendly co-existence between rival missionaries, and not just at
Baker Lake, but in the arctic missionary field as a whole.

When I began reading about Alaska and the Canadian North, I
was surprised at the frequent and often scathing criticism heaped
upon northern missionaries. In *The Cruise of the Cachalot* (1899)
First Mate Frank T. Bullen wrote, "No one who has travelled with
his eyes open would assert that all missionaries are wise, prudent or
even godly men; while . . . much is made of hardships, which in a
large proportion of cases do not exist, the men who are supposed to
be enduring them are immensely better off and more comfortable
than they ever would have been at home."

Other authors observed that although whalers and trappers
inadvertently destroyed the Inuit culture, those who arrived in the
name of God had just that end in mind. Realizing that their success
depended on their ability to eliminate the influence of Inuit medicine men, missionaries challenged shamans to prove their claims, a
tactic that ignored the obvious: the challenging religion should provide similar proofs.

In the ensuing contest, missionaries used their ability to predict the annual return of the sun (which science, not religion, had provided) to embarrass shamans. Worse yet, according to missionary diaries, shamans who refused to convert were often severely beaten, receiving a promise of further abuse if they failed to yield to "reason."

James Houston, the Canadian artist, author and entrepreneur who lived with the Inuit from 1948 to 1962, wrote in *Confessions of an Igloo Dweller* that even in those days, missionaries still "demonstrated little kindness or charity toward each other . . ." Speaking of the native beliefs, Houston wrote, "Imagine a religion with no related priesthood, no written word, no head of church, no collection plates, no church! Shamanism can and does co-exist with Christianity in Inuit thinking. Why should it not? What kind of weak religion would shamanism be if after 16,000 years of its known existence it could be knocked down dead by a handful of new, squabbling missionaries who wandered in to the vastness of the arctic world less than a century ago."

In *An Arctic Man*, Ernie Lyall, HBC employee, entrepreneur, and founder of Spence Bay, told of Anglican/Catholic hatreds and the fruit they bore: "When I was in Pond Inlet, if there was one missionary visiting us and he'd see the other coming, he'd go out the back door before the other would come in the front door. Sometimes the people went haywire due to religion. . . . They'd get thinking about this [going to hell] so much they'd just get clear unbalanced. . . . Shamans and shamanism were looked down upon by the missionaries, both Protestant and Catholic, as a bad thing; but the way I look at it myself is that this was the Eskimos' religion then, and I think it should have been respected . . . Christianity was pushed too hard."

According to Lyall, the priest at Pond Inlet rang the church bell at six in the morning, at noon and again at six in the evening. The natives complained, saying, "There used to be seals in the morning out on the ice, and they liked to walk out to get them, but every time the seals heard these church bells they'd all go down their holes and disappear." Many missionaries even forbade Sunday hunting, a cruel and senseless prohibition, given the natives' survival needs.

Unfortunately, for every decent missionary, there were others who would, in the contest for souls, stoop to planting crosses on the graves of natives who'd refused to convert, then tell relatives that the deceased had experienced a last-minute conversion.

If Anglican churchmen reached a camp first, they'd baptize the "willing," and then warn them of evil men in black robes who dressed like women and would claim them for the devil. Catholic priests, in turn, worsened the natives' turmoil by threatening damnation upon those who refused to embrace the "one true faith."

Driven by contempt for native beliefs and their willingness to gain converts by unscrupulous methods, interfaith bickering between missionaries became so commonplace that during their brief stop at Baker Lake, even the Lindberghs noticed the friction, writing that the clergy were "not on speaking terms."

During this same period, Inuit children were suffering priestly abuse at church-run schools. Decades later, when lawsuits brought the offenses in nearby Chesterfield Inlet and other church-run schools to light, the Church that claims to be *the* source of ethics and morality hid behind the statute of limitations.

Unfortunately, the Chesterfield experience was not just an isolated incident in Catholic and Anglican schools. Most missionaries believed it was much more important for the Inuit to get into heaven than to be cured of tuberculosis or properly educated. As a result, by 1960, after half a century of mission-controlled government-supported "education," under 5 percent of Canadian Inuit could read, speak or write English. One in eight had a history of tuberculosis; infant mortality was one in five and Inuit life expectancy fell short of thirty years.

Father Choque, whom I hope to thank for providing information about an abandoned mission at Garry Lake, is out of town, so I search out Henry Ford, a half-Inuit half-Caucasian entrepreneur who's lived in the Arctic for most of his life. Bright and remarkably agile for a man in his seventies, Henry is filling orders for native carvings at his store, Oopiktoyuk Arts, when I arrive.

When Henry mentions that he was about to check his nets, I offer to lend a hand. As we trudge back to the lake, a smiling Inuk makes a show of shielding his eyes. Henry and I glance at each other, then break into laughter. We're lighting up the cloud covered beach—Henry in his red-plaid hat and bright yellow slicker, and me in a gold Stearns windbreaker/inflatable life preserver and loud pink cap.

We climb into Henry's boat, paddle out to the near end of the net and begin untangling a mixed catch of yellow-flecked lake trout, red-spotted arctic char and silvery whitefish from its hundred-foot web. Most of the fish are stiff with rigor, but the recently ensnared thump noisily against the aluminum hull. Twenty minutes later, I photograph Henry beside eighty pounds of Baker Lake bounty, while imagining telling my friends of the time I pulled in twenty fish in just ten minutes. Faced with looks of disbelief, I'll add, "Of course, there was this net."

Over lunch at the Iglu hotel, I decide to hike past the Baker Lake cemetery to fish a small lake where one of my former passengers, Jim Kimball, an outdoor columnist for *The Minneapolis Star Tribune*, once fished for grayling. A half hour later, I puff to a stop amid a scattering of rock-covered graves and a mixture of wooden and iron rebar crosses. One rebar cross has fallen over, so I shove it into the ground, only to be stopped when the tip is six inches deep. I give it a twist and pull it out. The end bears a crystalline mix of earth and ice, a scraping from the great permafrost lens that spreads across the Arctic to a depth of four thousand feet.

One impressive marker rises above the tilting crosses—a memorial to Father Joseph Buliard, the priest who disappeared while serving at a primitive mission at distant Garry Lake. Chiseled into the granite headstone in English and Inuktituk are words of tribute to a man whom many considered a model of selflessness. But Buliard's remains lie elsewhere, for his body was never found. And as I stand before his memorial with my pants flapping in the wind, I wonder if I'll find a hint of his fate when I reach the Garry Lake mission, the last place to see him alive.

At Kimball's Lake I select one of my homemade lures, a removable flip top from an old pop can with a small treble hook attached to the tab, and clip the finger-ring end to my line. Within a few casts, I have a strike, then a solid take, and I soon slip my hand beneath the Arctic version of a sailfish, a fourteen-inch grayling. I lift it from the water, gently remove the hook and set the fish free. As the grayling's flaglike dorsal fin slips below the surface, I imagine it proclaiming that it had been hauled into another world by a gold-clad giant, from whom it escaped by playing dead.

I'd hoped to leave for Chantrey today, but by the time I return to town, it's late and I'm reluctant to battle a strong northwest wind that predicts a long, rough ride. Besides, the Iglu hotel has room to spare, so I grab my gear, check in and luxuriate in the shower's fluid warmth for several luscious minutes while ignoring my energy-sensitive conscience as it entreats, *That's enough!*

Steaming bowls of beef-and-broccoli stew are already circulating around the tables by the time I enter the dining room, and I'm well into my second helping when four Minnesotans walk in—the same four who had left when I arrived. Surprised to see them, I wave them to my table.

"Weather bad toward Churchill?" I ask as they sag into their chairs.

"You got it," the oldest replies, his voice a mixture of irritation and relief. "We hit some light rain, which wasn't too bad, but when we ran into patches of fog we decided to come back—and it's a good thing we turned around when we did. That cold front that came through after we left really slowed us down. Between the head wind and the drag of the canoe, I only had twenty minutes of fuel left when we landed."

They're tired and disgusted, but the stew and a few bottles of Labatt ale slowly work their charms, and we finish the evening over a cribbage board amid wild exaggerations and transparent lies—theirs, of course, not mine.

The youngest, a chunky black-haired lad claims to have caught such a huge trout that the photo weighed five pounds. Another reports a char so large that it took three huskies to bark at it, while a third swears that the local fuel truck driver radioed in to report that he'd finished fueling the Beaver that had just arrived. When the office replied, "What Beaver?" he discovered that he'd just pumped 120 gallons of avgas into one of Baker Lake's smaller mosquitoes.

Rainy Lake's Twin Beech shatters my sleep as it heads for Chantrey Inlet. It's 7:30 A.M. I toss down a breakfast of scrambled eggs, bacon and pancakes, then head for the DOT office, where I file a flight note and call my wife to ask how she's doing. I also check the weather, though it's just an empty gesture. I'll go anyway, ready to land if I must.

The Cessnas are already rumbling on the shoreline by the time I crank up the Cub. When they taxi out, I pull in about two hundred feet behind the last to leave the beach. With myself, my gear and thirty-six gallons of fuel in the wings plus thirty-five more in the cabin and floats, the Cub is heavy, the tails of her floats riding low in the water. Although I'm confident the Cub can climb onto the step quickly enough to avoid overheating her engine, I want that high-heat period to be as short as possible.

The lead Cessna adds power, its nose rising as it plows for fifty yards, then climbs up onto the step. The second follows suit, its 230-horsepower engine blasting a wind tunnel of air back at the Cub as I add full throttle. The Cub jumps onto the step as if helium filled, temporarily buoyed by the man-made blast that lifts her wings. Quivering in the Cessnas' prop wash, she races across their wakes, gaining speed as they pull ahead. As the Cessnas peel off toward Churchill, the Cub breaks free in a climbing turn to the north and levels off at one thousand feet.

Small flat-bottomed clouds like dollops of whipped cream enliven the morning sky. I alter my course to fly over one, then another. Leaping from billow to billow, the Cub's hurrying shadow is surrounded by a lovely rainbow—a colorful "glory" that encircles the Cub's fleeting image.

All sunlit aircraft bear hidden glories. Casting their delicate hues on ground and clouds alike, glories paint muted hoops of spectral light on the soft white flesh of clouds. And as my glory vaults from cloud to cloud, I find myself wishing that I could share the sight with an English genius who was born in 1642, the year that Galileo died.

As a young man, Isaac Newton alarmed the countryside with a candle-lit kite—a model 1660 UFO. Six years later, during the twelve-month period known in English history as the "annus mirabilis," the Year of Miracles, Newton worked out the laws of gravitation, invented calculus and the mirror telescope, formulated the Laws of Motion, wrote the Principia Mathematica and, while studying optics, employed prisms to investigate sunlight's rainbow spectrum of colors.

Enabled by Newton's work with prisms and light, later scientists developed spectroscopy, the unifying method of science that detects the distinctive fingerprints that elements emit when heated to incandescence. With the aid of spectroscopy, we've parsed the earth and probed the makeup of distant stars.

When the thickening clouds conspire to hide the earth, I descend toward the rolling rock-studded hills below. The overcast becomes solid; a mist begins to fall. By the time I'm down to four hundred feet, I spot the Twin Beech heeled up on the Back River's western shore—waiting out the weather. I begin a long glide that crosses the Arctic Circle, the southern limit of a land where the midsummer sun prefers not to set and, six months later, just as often fails to rise.

Though our senses would make us members of the Flat Earth Society, we know that the earth is round. Most of us also realize that the axis around which the earth revolves is tilted about twenty-three degrees from its orbital plane, which is why Northern Hemisphere days are longer when we tilt toward the sun and shorter when we tilt away.

Fortunately (for those in the Northern Hemisphere), the earth is a bit farther from the sun during the northern summer, which slightly reduces radiation to the already hot land masses "above" the equator. Six months later, we're a tad closer, which eases our northern winters.

Goose-down snow begins to fall as I tail the Cub ashore. Phalaropes twirl in the river-edge ponds as sandpipers tiptoe the beach, their heads bobbing as if to avoid the falling dime-size flakes.

Back inside the Cub, I reach for Barbara Walker's *Woman's Encyclopedia of Myths and Secrets*. An hour later, when I'm knee-deep in a bloody Crusade that murdered half of France for the crime of being judged insufficiently Catholic, I'm jolted alert by a pulsing roar as the Beech returns to the sky.

I taxi back to midstream while summoning Capt. George Back's 1835 description of Whirlpool Rapids, which I'm rapidly approaching: "The rapid looked as even and smooth as oil.... There was not, it is true, a single break in the smoothness of the surface, but with such wild swiftness were we borne along, that it required our extremest efforts, the very tug of life, to keep the boat clear of the gigantic waves below."

One hundred fifty years later, adventurer Robert Perkins, the author of *Into the Great Solitude*, paddled the Back during a low-water year and found the rapids tame. But this year the Back's running fast and high, promising a reprise of the rapids that impressed our Captain Back, the first to fully explore and chart the river.

Just for fun, I point the nose of the idling Cub downstream toward the approaching spray, letting the no-longer-subtle slope of the river draw the Cub toward the haystacks ahead. The river's hurrying surface bears not a ripple, its hidden speed revealed only when I glance toward shore. I wait. When my brain finally says, This is stupid, I feed the Cub's ninety horses well before I'd planned, rise from the oil-slick waters and leave Whirlpool Rapids behind.

Franklin Lake, the long expanse of dark, reef-studded water below, tapers off to the north and disappears into history. It's named for Sir John Franklin, the British captain whom the Canadian author Margaret Atwood had in mind when she wrote, "For Americans, of course, the name *Franklin* means Benjamin, or else a stove. But for Canadians it means a disaster."

The Franklin calamity began when Sir John, who had barely survived two earlier expeditions to the Arctic coast, loaded his presciently named ships, the *Erebus* (the dwelling place of the dead) and the *Terror*, with elegant silverware, stacks of *Punch* magazine, a mahogany desk and enough salt pork, beef, beer, potatoes and cabbage for a five-year voyage and set off to search for the Northwest Passage—the fabled water route to the Orient that explorers had been seeking for all of two hundred years.

On a spring morning in 1845, the Franklin expedition set off from the ominously named port of Gravesend and was never seen again. Following a century-and-a-half-long search that consumed five British ships and scores of lives, searchers finally located three graves far to the north of Franklin Lake, where they began to piece together the Franklin tragedy.

After his ships were entrapped by ice and wrecked during the first winter, Franklin and his crew of 128 men waited for rescue for two long years. When none came, they headed south in a desperate bid for safety before winter trapped them again. Abandoning once-precious items, they struggled on, burying their dead where they dropped, victims of famine, scurvy and probably lead poisoning—their canned goods had leaded seams. A few managed to reach Chantrey Inlet and the lake that bears Franklin's name. And then, for some strange reason, they turned back! Not a one survived.

My compass, waylaid by magnetic lines of force that have begun to dip downward, is becoming erratic. Seven hundred miles to the north, our footloose magnetic pole wanders about elliptically some fifty miles a day, perhaps in response to electrical currents generated by the earth's iron-rich core. Were the Cub to cross the magnetic pole and fly the additional eight hundred miles to the north geographic pole, its compass would become increasingly deceptive, wobbling about for a while before swearing we're heading south, though every minute would carry us farther north—toward the home of Santa Claus.

Halfway up Franklin Lake, a fifteen-foot-tall rooster tail highlights the end of the Back River, the beginning of Chantrey Inlet and the site of the Rainy Lake camp. The Twin Beech is already unloading as I taxi through the whirlpools below the Back's final plunge, pulled first one way by the vortices, then another. When the largest spins me away from shore, I let the Cub complete its merry-go-round, then power out of its grip and idle ashore near the Rainy Lake camp.

As I retrieve a rope from a forward float compartment, I glance down through water like liquid glass. A ten-pound trout hovers beneath the float, idling in the current. Mesmerized by its powerful silhouette, I watch as it slowly swims away, only to be replaced by another, and another, and another.

7

Chantrey Inlet

Is it more beautiful than the country of the musk ox in the summer,
where sometimes the mist blows over the lakes, and sometimes
the water is blue and the loons cry very often?

— SALTATHA'S INQUIRY TO A MISSIONARY'S
PORTRAYAL OF HEAVEN

ERHAPS THE INUIT'S modest nature dissuaded them from naming places for people, as we so often do. Instead, they used descriptive words, naming the river that buoys my floats the Great Fish River. Here, the river validates its Inuit name. And as sleek-sided trout pass beneath my floats, I can hardly believe that on these same shores I once swore that I'd never return to Chantrey Inlet.

Three days of rain, snow showers and head winds had plagued me all the way from Churchill. I arrived so weary that even the Back's bountiful fishing couldn't overcome the finger-numbing cold of the Inlet's wind-driven sleet. That late-July night, as I lay wrapped in every scrap of clothing that I'd packed, I decided I'd had enough. When dawn arrived in a shroud of gray, I finally understood why explorers had called this country "the land God gave to Cain" and fled at the first opportunity.

By the following spring, my memories of discomfort had been replaced with visions of huge trout and an Inuit camp that I'd failed to visit. When July finally came, Wes and I headed north again, accompanied by weather that could well have been brewed on a different planet, arriving during a heat wave that peeled off our shirts and baked the shoreline from which we fished.

Slinging six-inch red-and-white spoons into the whirlpools, we hooked a trout or char on cast after cast. Most were much too large for a two-man meal, so we shuttled fish in and out of a rock-rimmed wier, replacing the largest with the smallest as we searched for our supper. Finally, too arm-weary to fish any longer, we settled for a five-pounder.

Across a hundred yards of thundering water, an Inuk stood, "trying his luck" with a spear. Luck, however, obviously played no role, for almost every thrust retrieved a struggling fish. We borrowed a boat from the Rainy Lake crew, then crossed to the Inuit camp, where a team of beautifully furred sled dogs howled us into camp.

A woman seated beside her canvas tent smiled and nodded permission when I held up my camera. She spoke no English, but her meaning was plain when she slipped her chubby child from beneath her parka and cradled him for a photograph.

When Wes pointed to a row of stone columns on a ridge beyond the tents, I remembered reading of Inuit constructions called "inukshuks" whose purpose varied by locale: an armless inukshuk was the counterpart of the lob-pine of the voyageurs—a beacon to head for—whereas an inukshuk with "arms" outstretched might indicate a valley or a body of water with outlets at either end.

This row, however, had served as a "drift-fence" to detour migrating caribou, whose notoriously poor vision apparently interpreted the posts as men or wolves. Pursued by women, the caribou would refuse to pass between the inukshuks, running parallel to them instead toward a place of ambush: a cliff or a body of water where they could be speared from kayaks. Now, although rifles have downgraded inukshuks from useful tools to relics, their crude silhouettes still speak of a time when everything, including life itself, depended on the hunt.

Turning to the clan's weathered patriarch, I pointed to the stone columns. "Inukshuk?" I asked. He beamed with surprise and nodded a reply as I hid my frustration at having only a few nouns in common. Unable to speak Inuktituk, I stood there mute while, with one callused hand, he gripped a four-pound chunk of green soapstone from which a seal was slowly emerging, liberated by the knife clutched in the three remaining fingers of his other hand.

How did this man lose the use of one opalescent, sightless eye? Were his missing fingers lost by accident or removed by the Arctic cold? What, I wondered, does a man who listens to the world on a transistor radio, but has lived the life of his seal-and-caribou-stalking ancestors, remember of that hazardous life?

Had he, like his father, ladled fresh water into the mouth of a dead seal to appease its spirit and slake the thirst it had acquired during a lifetime in saltwater? Did he believe that the seal would tell other seals that here was a considerate hunter—a man worth dying for? Or with his gift of fresh water, did he hope to escape the wrath of Sedna, the sea goddess who brings bad luck to those who treat animal spirits with contempt?

Had he stalked polar bears after silently apologizing to them, explaining his need to feed his family, and rewarded their spirits with a precious knife or an ulu—tools that bears must surely covet? Did he shelter their pelts and show them great respect for four days if a male's and five days if a female's? Following a season of poor hunting, did he change his name to escape the evil spirits that had plagued him?

Although most of the early missionaries and explorers called them "ignorant savages," the Chantrey Inuit somehow survived the ages without wood—not even driftwood—a truly remarkable feat. Here, wood is highly prized. As Gontran de Poncins wrote in the 1941 northern classic *Kabloona*, "The poverty of the natives . . . is so wretched that the least bit of string, the least stick of wood is a treasure in their existence." In a land that offered only hides and flesh, shrubs and stone, fish and bone, the Inuit somehow survived, while those who called them savages died until their successors adopted the Inuit way of life.

When attempts were made to explain World War I to the Inuit, the "savages" were aghast, saying that "white men . . . were strangely unnatural and inhuman." Their language, which has dozens of words for the different types of snow, had none for war, which they decided to call "mass killings."

A gentle, modest people, the Inuit had no concept of illegitimacy and considered paternal lineage unimportant, as all children were related to the larger family. In a harsh land where life was truly treasured, they were tolerant parents who smiled at the misbehavior of children, replying to critics that it would be wrong to punish children who obviously "don't yet have all their brains."

If told that he was a good hunter, the traditional Inuk would claim that he had no skill, only luck. Likewise, a woman would deny being attractive and argue that X, or even Y, was much better-looking. Skill and innovation, however, not luck and modesty, ensured the survival of the Inuit: freezing animal hides onto precious sled runners to reduce wear and crafting seal-oil lamps from bone.

Unfortunately, one sensible Inuit practice brought them condemnation: their custom of wife sharing. Labeled sinful by all missionaries and some explorers, wife sharing was a logical response to the necessities of the harsh arctic environment. If a pregnant Inuk could not accompany her husband on a hunt, an agreeable woman exchanged duties with her, providing another set of eyes to search for game, another pair of hands to manage dogs and build a snow house and someone to cook and mend clothing. The mutual benefits of sexual variety were incidental to the exchange and only occasionally the primary reason.

Thus, it's not surprising that traditional Inuit had few of the sexual hang-ups that are found in "civilized" societies. Their practical approach to sex, their communal concept of a larger family and their willingness to share resources enhanced the odds of survival and produced less stressful lives.

Fifty yards from the patriarch, the young spearman stood beside a growing heap of arctic char and trout. One hand gripped a *kiki-vak*, a three-pronged, trident-like spear with a central shaft and two outer tines armed with inch-long barbs. Since two hands would be needed to spread the outer prongs, Wes asked the young Inuk how he removed the fish from the center tine. With a smile, he said, "Just watch."

Wading a yard into the river, he stood in the shallows, his spear raised as his eyes searched the sunlit ripples. Suddenly he made a quick thrust—and retrieved a struggling trout. Bending over, he spread the outer tines with his hands, bit the trout behind the head and pulled it free of the center shaft. He then thumbed an eye from its socket and popped it into his mouth. When he offered me its mate, I'm sorry to say I declined.

A small child ran down to the river, holding high over his head the primary symbol of change for the Arctic, if not the world—a bundle of twigs tied into the shape of an airplane. Though his grandmother might tell him that geese fly off to the Old Woman Who Never Dies every fall and return with the promise of spring, this child-of-the-airplane will also learn the facts of migrating birds. Airplane held aloft, he flopped onto a nearby caribou hide and flew his bundle high, his body cushioned in caribou hair, his mind far off in the sky.

Now, as I stare down into the cold waters of the Back, I miss my old friend, Wes, my traveling companion for many years, an easygoing, peace-loving *gentle*man who saddled himself with a shrew of a wife whom he steadfastly refused to divorce. Wes finally escaped into death many years ago, done in by twenty years of unrelenting bitchery and a kinder, briefer cancer.

Paul, one of the Rainy Lake guides, arrives and interrupts my thoughts. As we stroll to the camp through thousands of tiny flowers that are busily cramming a summer of life and reproduction into a few brief months, he holds up a hand and points toward a nearby boulder. I look carefully but see nothing. Looking again, I finally spot an immobile, beautifully camouflaged ptarmigan against a backdrop of dwarf willows.

"Want to hear Farley Mowat's ptarmigan poem?" I ask.

"Sure," he says.

"The ptarmigan—a kind of grouse
Lives in the Arctic with his spouse.
The ptarmigan is smart and perky,
And tastes much better than a pturkey."

Laughing, Paul asks if I've ever heard of an Alaskan town named Chicken. " 'Fraid not," I reply.

"Well, they really wanted to name it ptarmigan," he says, "but no one knew how to spell it, so they named it Chicken instead. It's between Dawson City and Tok."

Over lunch, Paul tells me that the campsite across the river hasn't been used for years. And the patriarch with the missing fingers and the opaque eye? Gone, like my old friend, Wes.

As I return to the Cub, I search the noon sky for a clearing trend, but the solid overcast makes it plain that I'll wait for another day. Grumbling, I put up my tent, a job that I'll dislike until someone invents a Viagra pill for tents—or one that springs to life at the touch of a remote. However, once my tent's up, I love its shelter and woodsy smells. With my foam pad, sleeping bag and pillow in place, I decide that a short rest will prepare me for an afternoon of tussling with trout, so I pull a stocking cap over my eyes and let the white sound of the Back's rooster tail sweep my cares away.

When I awaken, my watch reads 2:20—a little late, but not too bad. On looking again, I see that my bleary eyes have reversed Mickey's hands. It's 4:10! I've slept almost four hours! At supper, the cookhouse resounds with the chatter of tired fishermen. One fellow with a group of fishermen from Chicago ribs me, "You sure came a long way just to sleep."

"Yeah, well," I respond with a modest smile, "if I were going to be content with the minnows that I hear you guys have been catching, I wouldn't need much rest either. But I plan to do some big-time fishing this very evening. Matter of fact, here's the lure that I plan to use."

Lifting the lid of a battered cigar box, I hold up a stainless-steel teaspoon with a treble hook in its lip. Laughter erupts.

"Lemme see that thing," one burly fisherman says. As the spoon passes from hand to hand, one fisherman says that he'd love to set out spoons like that for uninvited company. Another rises to his feet, a Molson ale in one hand and the spoon held high in the other. "I christen thee the mother-in-law spoon," he announces while eyeing its gleaming barbs. "May she sup from you but once."

When I ask Paul about renting a boat for the evening, Phil, one of the Chicago fisherman invites me to join him, explaining that as the fifth in a party of five, he has room in his boat.

Later, as we motor into the Inlet, I realize that Phil, in addition to being a worrier, is way out of his element. Persuaded by his buddies to join them for what he thought would be an idyllic weekend in the woods, he almost turned back at Churchill and again at Baker Lake. Now he's just going through the motions, counting days until he can return to Chicago's Lake Shore Drive. Gripping the boat's gunwales whenever we cross a whirlpool, he's the picture of a man who'd prefer to get his wilderness experience by way of a good book and a comfortable recliner while a fire smiles from across the hearth.

Unfortunately, Phil's luck at fishing is as bad as his attitude. Thirty minutes pass, and he has caught one char to my four trout and two char. Having at first declined to try my productive "spoon," he finally relents when I offer it once again.

Phil casts beyond one of the whirlpools and begins a slow retrieve. Suddenly, he lets out a yell. Clutching his rod with both hands, he whips it into a U. "Phil," I say, as his line slices Chantrey foam, "you've got one helluva fish down there."

Five minutes pass, and we still haven't seen his fish. "It has to be a trout, a big trout," I tell Phil, keeping my voice low, then wondering why. More minutes pass. The nylon line that streamed from the reel after each retrieve now points straight down, quivering. "You've got him, Phil!" I exclaim. "He's worn out."

"What d'ya mean, *he's* worn out?" squeaks Phil, rolling his eyes as a grin spreads across his face. Phil cranks in twenty, then thirty feet of braided nylon. The fish takes off again, but his run is short. One more lunge and he's spent, lying alongside the boat. I slip a hand behind his gills and quickly heave him aboard. "Keeper?" I ask Phil.

"*Keeper?*" he says. "I'll say its a keeper! That trout's got a date with a taxidermist," Then, turning to the guide he asks, "Where's the scale?"

Phil's trout bottoms the scale at twenty-five pounds, its weight limited only by Phil's conscience and imagination. "What do you think?" he asks. "Thirty, maybe thirty-five pounds?"

"Probably," I reply, then add, with a wink to the guide, "that's the biggest trout I've ever seen."

After Phil returns my spoon with thanks commensurate to a loan of the Hope diamond, I return to battling trout. "This one," I boast to Phil, "is going to make yours look like an appetizer." Suddenly my line goes slack. When I reel it in, my spoon is gone. "Phil," I say, "You're a lucky man. That fish was so big we would have had to tow it back to camp. This way, you still have something to brag about."

As we troll through the Arctic twilight, I tell Phil that I'm hoping for sunshine tomorrow so I can repeat Eratosthenes' measurement of the earth. I start to explain, but we're interrupted so often by fish strikes that I give up. Finally satiated with fishing, I decide that this one's my last. I bring him to the side of the boat, my arms sore, my wrists shot. I'm worn out, but he's not. With a sudden swirl he slips the hook and disappears, leaving the rod drooping in my tired hands.

During the ride back to camp, Phil burbles, "Sure hope they have plenty of ice for the cooler? Do you have a photo of that spoon?" Then, looking over the side at his stringered trout, he exclaims, "My Gaaawwwd, that's a big fish!"

The guide and I haul the boat ashore as Phil races on ahead yelling, "Hey, hey, guys! Come and see what *I* caught!"

When a one o'clock nature call reveals a stunningly clear sky, my eyes seek Ursa Major, then leap to the polar star, which every mile of my northerly flight has lofted higher overhead. Although we Westerners call Ursa Major the Big Dipper, Homer saw the Bear That Never Bathes, passing on what every sailor knew: that in Mediterranean latitudes, the constellation never touched the sea. In France, our Big Dipper is called *le casserole*; in England, it's the plow; in China, the celestial bureaucrat.

Morning comes wreathed in fog. At breakfast, the cook tent resounds with conversation, much of it focused on talk of measuring the earth, which Phil has announced.

"How do you plan to do that?" asks one of Phil's friends.

"It's really just simple geometry," I reply, "which, by the way, means 'to measure the earth.' About two centuries B.C., a Greek named Eratosthenes became the first Westerner to calculate the size of the earth.

"His predecessor, Epicurus, had already theorized that matter consists of tiny, invisible particles like atoms. Besides rejecting gods as rulers of the world, he also proposed that many other worlds held life forms, all made from the same particles as ourselves. At about the same time, Aristarchus, who had proved that the sun was far larger than the earth, even proposed what we now know—that the smaller earth must orbit the larger sun."

Accompanied by the rattling of dishes as the tables are cleared, I continue. "Eratosthenes knew that on the longest day of the year the noontime sun shone directly down a deep well in the Egyptian city of Syene. Knowing also that the sun cast a shadow of approximately seven degrees at the same time in Alexandria, which lay some 500 miles to the north, he asked this question: If traveling 500 miles across a round earth produces a 7.5 degree change, how far would we travel with a change of 360 degrees? Since forty-eight 7.5 degree arcs equal 360 degrees, forty-eight 500-mile arcs yields a circumference of about 24,000 miles—a surprisingly accurate figure for its time."

When Phil asks, "Would ya run through that again?" I flip a dinner plate over onto the paper tablecloth and trace a circle—the earth. I follow with a straight line piercing the circle to terminate at its center—the beam of sunlight that shone down the well at Syene. Then I draw another radian from the circle's center outward, piercing it about an inch from Syene, and label the junction Alexandria.

"Think of this radian at Alexandria as another well and notice that the curve of the circle tilts it away from the radian at Syene, just as it would tilt a flagpole away from the sun, making it cast a shadow of about seven degrees. Because Eratosthenes had paid someone to pace off the distance between Syene and Alexandria, he knew that the 7.5 degree change represented 500 miles. If 7.5 degrees spans 500 miles, then 360 degrees must cover about 24,000 miles."

I pause, pleased to see nods of insight replacing furrowed brows.

"Before I left Minnesota, which is almost straight south of the inlet, I recorded the length of the shadow cast by the noonday sun on a right-angle wire. Even though I left home four days ago, and we're well north of the equator, the sun is high at this time of year, so Eratosthenes' method should work fairly well, especially since our known, 1,300-mile distance from where I started is probably more accurate than his paced-off span from Syene to Alexandria.

"So," I say, hoisting my mug of coffee, "here's to the science of the Greeks that almost died during the Dark Ages." Then, aware that I've been carrying on, I add, "End of speech."

To help pass the morning, I hike the poppy-strewn tundra with one of the Rainy Lake guides. Beneath our feet lies the same Canadian Shield that supports northern Minnesota, but the land here seems young and raw, and with good reason, for the ice age withdrew from the Arctic long after it left the States.

Rick, a student from the University of Toronto, has a double major in agriculture and astronomy—an odd mix that he obviously savors. Gathering up a bit of the thin, sandy soil, he lets it trickle from hand to hand. "Test this and you'll discover that it hosts only a thousandth as many bacteria as southern loams, which is one reason that plant productivity here is just a few percent of the yield you'd expect to find in the States.

He points to an orange two-inch lichen clinging to the south side of a granite slab. "You probably know that lichen are a blend of a fungus and an algae, but what most people don't realize is that they grow so slowly that photographs taken at fifty-year intervals reveal hardly any growth at all.

"Think of it," he says. "A lichen no wider than my hand might have begun life in the days of your friend Eratosthenes."

By the time we return to camp, the sun has begun to burn holes in the overcast. I retrieve my clothes-hanger wire, some duct tape and a file from the Cub, and get ready to measure the angle of the sun whenever it shows its face.

To my surprise, the experiment has gripped the camp. A dining room table has been carried outside, where it awaits adjustment with my pocket level and rock wedges. That done, I tape my L-shaped wire to its top with the horizontal arm pointing north and its vertical arm upright. There are cloud breaks everywhere, but none cross the camp. Finally, at twelve-fifteen, a huge opening admits a flood of sunlight, and I notch the wire at the end of the shadow cast by the vertical arm. Removing the tape, I lay the wire on a piece of paper, mark a dot at the tip of the wire, then a dot at the mark made in Minnesota and another at the new mark. With a folded paper for a straight edge, I connect the tip-of-the-wire dot with the Minnesota dot and also with the Chantrey dot to form an acute angle. As I take my protractor from my pocket, I'm struck by the silence of the men pressed against the table.

When I read off 18, maybe 19 degrees, Rick whips out his pocket calculator, then realizes he won't need it and talks his way through the math. "Let's see, 18 degrees goes into 360 degrees 20 times, and if a twentieth of the earth's circumference is 1,300 miles, then it's got to be 26,000 miles around. Nineteen degrees would make it about 5 percent less, say just under 25,000 miles—not bad, *not bad!*"

I suddenly realize that my aeronautical charts should verify the 18–19 degree difference. The camp turns out to be a shade north of

67 degrees, and my cabin just under 49, a difference of 19 degrees. Raising the chart, I announce that the precision of modern technology is hereby confirmed with a protractor, a level, a coat hanger and the common sense of Eratosthenes. Someone shouts, "I'll drink to that!" and we're off to the cookhouse for a pre-lunch beer.

As I dig into a heap of baked char, Phil pulls up a chair.

"Where did you get that earth-measuring idea?" he asks.

"Well," I say, "what got me going was an intriguing book and Public TV series called *The Ring of Truth* by Philip and Phylis Morrison. In a tribute to Eratosthenes, the Morrisons recorded the angular height of Arcturus on the side of a south-facing rental truck in northern Nebraska, then measured it again the next night when they were some 450 miles farther south. Using those figures, they calculated the earth's circumference at 26,500 miles. Knowing that I'd be traveling north for more than 1,000 miles, I thought I'd give it a try."

I settle up for my meals, find Rick and ask a favor. "If anyone comes looking for me, would you tell them that I left at noon today, and that I was heading up the Back to Garry Lake, then south to the Thelon River, then west to Reliance on Great Slave Lake, and then on to Yellowknife?" Before I can finish the sentence, Rick has his memo pad out and is taking notes.

A handshake and a wave later, the Cub again waltzes through Chantrey's whirlpools. It's the last of July, the month that the Inuit call Padlersersivik: "when there is no night." While the engine warms, I think back to my first departure from Chantrey Inlet—how I filled a float compartment with snow to cool two homeward-bound trout, then dribbled a few drops of oil onto the Cub's rudder and elevator hinges to prevent takeoff spray from locking them up in the subfreezing Chantrey air.

When the Cub's oil temperature gauge says go, I look around, knowing I'll never again see the inukshuks or hear thundering falls of the Great Fish River. But I'll remember the lure-thieving trout and the one-eyed frost-bitten elder—and a playful boy with a primitive plane on the shores of Chantrey Inlet.

8

Chantrey Inlet to Garry Lake, Nunavut

*One midnight. In a time when most engines were round
and reciprocating. Four of them are hunched on
our wings, snoring through the night. I turn
to look over my shoulder at the navigator.
"Where are we?"
The navigator shrugs his shoulders.
"It beats me. So I suppose we're lost."*
– ERNEST K. GANN, "Flying Circus"

WHEN PEOPLE ASK if I've ever been lost, I explain that with the extra fuel that I carry, the Cub can fly a thousand miles. "I can't get lost," I say, as I pull out my pocket map and drop a finger into the center of the Territories' "Zone of Inaccessibility."

"Head north and you run into the Arctic Ocean; fly east and there's Hudson Bay; to the west you'll hit the Slave or Mackenzie

River; head south and you'll find corn." Still, despite my bravado, the truth is that I've been briefly lost right here while accompanied by my friend Wesley Miller.

We were heading south from Chantrey Inlet in our Cubs, flying the same Back River that's slipping past below. Wes, in the lead plane, had cut overland to avoid following a westward bulge in the river. Forgetting that the Meadowbank River joined the Back in that area, Wes took the Meadowbank for the Back when it slowly came into view. Since I wasn't paying attention, I followed Wes along the slowly curving Meadowbank. Fifteen minutes later, out of habit, I checked my map.

"Wes," I radioed, "things don't look right."

After a long silence, Wes replied, "I guess not."

With our compasses unreliable and the sun obscured, we had lost two important tools. But then I remembered a dependable rule of thumb: if, over a short period, the weather hasn't changed, the wind probably hasn't either.

Since a northwest wind had been blowing when we left, and the weather hadn't changed, it should still have been northwest. Looking down at the wind-streaked lakes below, I could see that we were heading with the wind—forty-five degrees from the course we would have been flying if we were over the Back. Turning the map to line it up with the Meadowbank instead of the Back immediately snapped everything into place, and after we'd spent twenty minutes on a westerly course, the Back returned to view.

I scan the Cub's rudimentary but practical instrument panel. Housing nothing more than a tachometer, altimeter, airspeed indicator, oil pressure and temperature gauge, it is charitably described as a "basic" panel.

The Cub has no navigation radio, no Loran, no gyro horizon or gyro compass. I navigate by "pilotage," using a compass (when it works), common sense and a map, employing the same basic flight skills that led Lindbergh to Paris. Were I to plop one of my friends whose aircraft brim with electronic gadgets into my primitive Cub, he'd surely pop a stroke.

No fuel gauges disturb the panel's simplicity, their function being performed by two vertical glass tubes just above my head on each side of the cockpit. Connected to the wing tanks and set at the same level, the tubes house a small ball that floats at the same height as the fuel in the tanks. Although they're *almost* foolproof, the balls have been known to stick to the side of the tubes as the fuel is consumed, leading brain-dead pilots to fly on and on when a recalcitrant ball rides high. I like the Cub's austerity, but if I were to change one thing, I'd add a Global Positioning System, for even those who get lost in three-tree parks can cruise the globe with GPS. Just as sextants seek the light of stars, GPSs rely on satellite signals. Given a sextant and decent conditions, a trained navigator can locate his position within a mile or so, but a good GPS can fix my position with an accuracy of several yards.

Adding a touch of power, I follow the rising terrain while wishing that Wes, my caribou spotter, was here. Overdue for a new set of bifocals, Wes could barely read a map, but for spotting game he was superb. Where my eyes saw distant willow clumps, he discovered musk oxen; where I found nothing but a patch of brown vegetation or the shadow of a cloud, Wes would find a caribou herd. He was rarely wrong.

The Back suddenly changes character. Slick, fast and almost unbending near Franklin Lake, the inland Back rushes past granite lobes and ridges of glacial till, stringing turquoise ponds on a whitewater thread that descends from a pork-chop-shaped island at the far end of Garry Lake.

On the island's south-facing rib, a wide crescent-shaped beach gleams in the afternoon sun. Set deep in the Inuit's Nunassiaq ("beautiful land"), the island bears a tar-paper shack that years ago I wouldn't have noticed were it not for a tiny dot on my map and the word "mission."

Wes and I had been heading east from Coppermine on our way to Baker Lake. When I spotted the dot, I radioed Wes. "The map says there's a mission on an island ahead. It's close to our route and I'm getting hungry, so what say we stop for lunch?"

If either of us had expectations of finding a mission like those of the American southwest, they quickly disappeared. When I first spotted the tiny black shack, I took it for just another die-shaped glacial erratic, a remnant of the last ice age. This die, however, was precisely shaped and just a little too large.

As we taxied up to the island's Caribbean-like beach, the shack disappeared behind a ten-foot bluff. We set off toward the mission, only to be distracted by the chirp of a sik-sik, an arctic ground squirrel that is one of nature's few true hibernators. Like the dormouse (from the French *dormir*, meaning "to sleep") the sik-sik is poorly equipped to handle winter's extremes. So to conserve energy, sik-siks lower their body temperature below fifty degrees for months on end. Our chirping sik-sik, by slowing its metabolism, adds summers of life with long winter sleeps.

The twelve-by-fifteen-foot, tar-paper mission was equipped with a small entry and an attached storage space on its western side. Two small white crosses—painted sticks nailed together—decorated the roof. Like a black boulder carried to a barren island from the sheer walls of a distant fiord, the mission begged to be photographed under the deep blue Arctic sky.

We passed through the entry and peered inside. We hadn't expected comfort, but even so, we were surprised at the poverty that met our eyes. Against the east wall was a plywood bed. Above it, several shelves offered dozens of bottles, each containing a different remedy. All were labeled in French. As I tried to decipher their meaning, I remembered the tale of a sailor who had served aboard the *Passat*, a four-masted steel barque built in 1911. Because the owners of the *Passat* lacked funds for a doctor, they provided, instead, a small chest filled with bottled remedies numbered 1 through 7— number 1 for chills, 2 for fevers, 3 for ailments of the bowel, and so on. One day, finding the number 7 bottle empty, the first mate mixed a dose from numbers 3 and 4. The results were not reported.

On one windowsill, a red-and-gold icon of a saint glowed in sunlight softened by the dust-dimmed window, while across the barren room, the window's twin admitted muted shafts of light.

A small table stood beneath an open stovepipe through which decades of dust had descended, coating every surface a dull and even gray. On the table lay a scattering of French Bibles, English Bibles, religious comic books in English and Inuktitut and a few letters written in French.

Repelled by the dust and disorder, we took a few pictures and returned to the beach, accompanied by the chirp of the sik-sik, which we lured from its den with bread.

On arriving at Baker Lake, we learned that the mission had been hammered together in 1949. There (according to letters from Father Charles Choque of Baker Lake, Bishop John Robideaux of Churchill and reports in "Eskimo") Father Joseph Buliard, the man whose memorial dominates the Baker Lake cemetery, sought to convert the Inuit until he disappeared around Christmas 1956.

Joseph Paul Jean Marie Buliard began life in the little village of Le Barboux in southern France. In time, the boy with the large name grew into a small, big-eared, bespectacled man, a Mr. Peepers who might easily have been gobbled up by the world had he not turned to the Church. Following his indoctrination, Father Buliard became a congregant of the Oblates of Mary Immaculate (OMI), and in 1939 set sail from Le Havre, France, at the age of twenty-five. His destination: Churchill.

Churchill surprised him, being smaller and colder than he'd expected: "We are in the middle of summer and we have had . . . eight days below [freezing] . . ." That fall, Buliard and two other missionaries shipped out for an abandoned trading post at Repulse, a Hudson Bay inlet six hundred miles north of Churchill. There, they planned to proselytize whoever came their way.

Six weeks after freeze-up, Father Buliard fell through thin ice but managed to climb free and stagger back to the post. His arms and feet began to swell. When his companions thought they detected the scent of gangrene, they radioed for a rescue flight. Three weeks later, a single-engine Junker finally arrived to fly him out. Thus,

Buliard spent his first winter in the Churchill hospital, where, as his fingernails finally grew back, he became even more determined to return to the north.

FatherBuliard spent most of the next nine years in the rocky country to the north of Baker Lake. Often rejected, though occasionally accepted, he sought conversions during an era that saw some priests portraying their rivals as "wolves ravaging the one and only Fold of Christ."

His once-frozen hands proved a constant trial. Despite his best efforts, he often needed Inuit help because, unlike many missionaries, he shared the grim prospects of those he sought to convert while faulting himself for what he called his "meager success." Repeatedly reduced to ill health, Buliard would have to be ordered out for recuperation.

In August 1949, with Buliard restored and the materials on site at Garry Lake, the tar-paper Mission of Our Lady of the Rosary finally materialized on an island known to the Inuit as Siuradjuar—the big pile of sand. From there, he attempted to convert the natives and reconvert Protestants in the area. Traveling alone or with an Inuit family for months at a time, he'd eventually return to his island, where in the winter "the walls became coated with frost, which it [the coal stove] could never entirely melt."

A strict observer of poverty, Buliard gave up his occasional treat of malted milk when he learned its Baker Lake price, saying that it was inappropriate for a minister to the poor to drink such an expensive beverage. He was offered a battery radio with which he could receive the Canadian Broadcasting Company that he missed so much, but he declined, unwilling to include a radio receiver on his list of needs. Unlike his superiors then and now, Buliard would have rejected a crystal palace or a grand cathedral. Neither would he have understood churches that shelter child-abusing clergy, or men like Swaggart, Bakker, Robertson and Falwell, or zealots like David Koresh.

Father Buliard often suffered from hunger, cold and exhaustion, but he rarely complained, the one exception involving the state of his hands, which ". . . make me powerless. I can't get them warm.

And at night, under the furs, when my circulation comes back, the pain and torment drive sleep away."

It comes as no surprise that his years in the Arctic almost certainly ended the way they began—with a plunge through the ice. He even predicted it: "Sooner or later, I'll finish by going through the ice, the rivers up here are so tricky in so many spots. . . ."

Some natives said that he went out in a storm to check his nets and never returned. Others said he drove his dogsled across thin ice that collapsed. Rumors circulated that he'd been murdered, a real possibility, given the Inuit's reluctance to reject their treasured beliefs and Buliard's insistence that they stop exchanging wives. The mission died with Father Buliard. A few months later, nineteen Garry Lake Inuit starved to death.

When I finally learned Buliard's story, I became determined to inspect the "big pile of sand" more closely. Decades had passed since his death, but I wanted to search for clues to his disappearance. From the distant clamor of city life, I yearned to sample the solitude that Buliard had accepted while he longed for the sight of a human face.

The island, like much of the Arctic, is a checkerboard of tundra polygons—hexagonlike "platters" of tundra just a few yards across. I secure the Cub to a half-buried gas barrel and begin to haul my gear to the mission.

A disheveled freighter canoe lies inverted near the entry, its canvas rotting, its stern hacked away for firewood. A wrecked snow-mobile sags nearby. The entry itself is much as Robert Perkins found it in 1987, containing "rubber gloves, used cans of motor oil, snowmobile parts, rusty traps, spools of nylon fishing line, nets." Inside, however, the contents are gone, perhaps carried off by souvenir hunters.

When I step outside, I discover an arctic hare just ten feet away from the steps. It stares at me as I stare back. I am not fox, or wolf, or snowy owl. As long as I stand still the hare remains motionless, the inbred reaction of animals that need to remain invisible in open country—don't move.

Remembering a *National Geographic* film of arctic hares bounding across the tundra on their hind legs, I let out a sudden yell. The startled hare leaps into flight. Sure enough, he's one of their finest. After a conventional bound, the hare rises to his hind legs and quickly disappears.

The cry of a gull tilts my head. Circling through the deep blue tundra sky, the ivory gull follows me as I begin my search. I inspect the western shoreline first but find only sand and solitude. Back at the mission, I mentally divide the surrounding tundra into ten-foot squares and begin to probe each square on my hands and knees. Halfway round the mission, I find several buttons beneath a clump of ground-hugging bearberry. Close by, I discover a packet of rusty needles and a few beads—the tip of a rosary protruding from years of windblown sand.

Near the north side of the building, my fingers find what the vegetation hides from sight—a sprinkling of leather tags about the size of 50-cent pieces. Unfortunately, the printing on all but one is unreadable.

In *An Arctic Man*, Ernie Lyall wrote that from 1941 to 1969, "Eskimos were given numbers because they generally had only one name and a lot of Eskimos had the same ones, and sometimes they even changed their name to something different. All this was very confusing. . . . So the government decided to give them numbers, which I think was a very good thing. Each settlement had its own number. . . . But later on, they started a program that they called 'Project Surname' and everybody was given a second name. . . . I guess whoever suggested getting rid of the numbers said why should Eskimos be known by numbers—it's only people in jails who have numbers."

I carry the disk to the sunlit side of the mission, where I see that one side carries a symbol of the crown rimmed by the words Eskimo Identification Canada. The other confirms Mr. Lyall, reading E.2-507 in its center. Along its lower rim is a handwritten name—Kowak-ferik—and the date 23-4-57.

Returning to the north side of the mission, I extend my sweep on hands and knees, carefully working my fingers through the ground cover like someone searching for a contact lens. An hour passes fruitlessly, then another with poor results. I'm laughing at myself, at my sore knees and tired back. If this were a job, I'd be demanding a rest period and better pay. Besides, the wind has begun to nibble, leaving goose bumps in its wake.

A sense of loneliness suddenly grips me, and as I return to the shelter of the mission, doubts about staying enter my mind. Cold and hungry, I toss a quarter pound of bacon on the Coleman, then stir in a can of Boston-baked beans as the bacon snaps and curls. Slathered on Baker Lake bread, my feast soon revives me, and I set off to explore the eastern half of the island.

When I reach the northern shore, I turn east along its rubble bank, the flesh of an esker laid bare by erosion. I consider looking for fossils, but on this pile that was scraped from the igneous Shield, it would be a waste of time. In the Arctic islands farther north, how-ever, fossils are easily found. There, acres of petrified tropical forests prove that the earth is incredibly old, given the inconceivably slow drift of the continents.

A female caribou comes clopping round the point. The wind is wrong, so she cannot smell me, but at fifty feet she sees me well enough. I stand motionless, savoring her surprise while she swings her rudimentary antlers from side to side as she tries to catch my scent. With a sudden snort, she whirls about, trots into the lake and heads for the opposite shore.

A shiver spawned by the rising wind ripples across my back. A band of dark clouds is approaching, the harbinger of a rapidly advancing cold front. I quicken my pace, determined to reach the island's eastern end before I turn back. Just as I round the corner, it begins to pour. Parjanya, the one who brings monsoon rains to India, has gone a-traveling and soaks me in seconds.

As forty mile per hour gusts buffet me and the wind moans over-head, I break into a run. I'm tempted to head straight to the mission, but I race along the beach. I'm concerned for the Cub, and I'll certainly need dry clothes.

By the time I reach the Cub, it's thirty-six degrees. I'm soaked and shaking with cold—and plastered with wind-whipped sleet. As I near the mission, I'm seized by a shiver-driven urge to urinate. Hampered by trembling hands and bladder muscles that are losing their grip, I almost make a mess of it. Part of my brain whispers, Hypothermia, but the remainder says, Don't be silly—you can't get that cold in five minutes. But I am.

I fumble out of my wet clothes, grab a T-shirt, dry my sandpaper flesh and struggle into wool socks, a sweatshirt and pants. But when I jam myself into my sleeping bag, I can barely manage the zipper. I insanely contemplate retrieving a stocking cap from the Cub, but knowing that the bag's insulation will trap whatever heat I produce, I pull it over my head and begin doing sit-ups. Cold as I am, I laugh at myself as I flop around like a giant inchworm while trying to think warm thoughts.

As the heat of my efforts accumulates, I think of the time that I'd just turned twelve and was allowed to spend a midwinter night at our cabin while my parents went to town. Not realizing that our ancient wood burner leaked vast amounts of air, and reluctant to leave my bed to stoke the fire in the middle of a thirty-below night, I packed it full of wood, filling each crevice with ever smaller sticks. Then, as instructed, I filled the water pail with snow and set it on top of the stove.

Around two o'clock, I awoke, miserably hot and sweating. I rushed into the living room, where I found a red-hot wood burner, its ten-foot-long horizontal pipes aglow to within a yard of the wall as the last drops of water leaped and sizzled on the bottom of the pail.

I quickly propped open the cabin door. As steam billowed into the frigid night, I removed a burner lid and slowly dribbled water onto the inferno while taking care not to spill, which might crack the burner. Fifteen minutes later, the glowing stovepipes finally turned black, as did the stove, and I returned to bed, relieved that I hadn't burned down the cabin—and determined to keep my adventure to myself.

The following morning I noticed something I'd missed during my fright. Every one of our many candles had collapsed. Candles hung limply from wall sconces and lay flattened on windowsills. From the rim of our dining table centerpiece, more than a dozen fanned out like white daisy petals. Knowing that I couldn't explain away the flaccid candles, I confessed to my parents, who were understanding.

Years later, I came across a deformed candle that my mother had tucked away. I restored it to its holder, from which it flops across the windowsill like a dead snake. Visitors glance at it, wondering dare they ask? When they finally do, I smile and begin, "One winter evening, when I'd just turned twelve . . ."

The shaking finally slows, my fingers tingle and the shivering stops. Like the cold-blooded lizards that Australian aborigines believe brought life to earth, then lost their tails and stood erect as they warmed, I am once again a man.

Outside, the Arctic wind moans. Sleep descends amid visions of Buliard dropping through the ice, and of Laura from Red Lake, who had wanted to come along. I decide I will send her a card from Yellowknife saying, "You wouldn't like it."

Morning. Rested and rational again, I can't imagine sending such a message. Why should I prejudice her with a single unpleasant incident out of a hundred delightful events?

Over a makeshift breakfast of coffee, fig newtons and a handful of carrots, I'm embarrassed to admit that I've had enough of Siuradjuar's stark beauty, of the solitude that once seemed so attractive and of the mystery of a man who asked for so little and suffered so much.

In a way, it doesn't matter how Father Buliard died, for he held true to his beliefs and to those who shaped his mind. Nevertheless, with the exception of medical missionaries and those who provide a tangible benefit, I think that Robert Perkins had it right: "I've never been in favor of the missionary spirit. It is a bitter fruit that has destroyed many cultures."

Four

GARRY LAKE TO
FORT ST. JOHN,
BRITISH COLUMBIA

9

Garry Lake to Reliance, Northwest Territories

When men lack a sense of awe, there will be disaster.
— LAO-TZU

THE CUB'S PRIMITIVE HEATER roasts my feet but warms little else as it struggles against the cold, overcome by the cockpit's many air leaks that demand a turned-up collar, a pair of gloves and a stocking cap that's stretched over my headset. As Garry Lake fades from sight, the Tundra Cub slips across the northern boundary of the "Serengeti of the North," the Thelon Wildlife Sanctuary, which my chart delineates with a line of geese. And though every pond and river is V'ed with the wakes of molting geese, the twenty-one-thousand-square-mile sanctuary was set aside not just for waterfowl but for the protection of all wildlife within its borders. Now, while the sun warms my spirit, I scan the tundra for wildlife as the Cub hurries south toward one of North America's largest gatherings of caribou, the Beverly Lake herd.

The Beverly herd, like most of the other great herds, fell to a fourth of its former size during the twentieth century, reduced by mindless opportunists with repeating rifles and possibly by nuclear fallout absorbed by lichen that the caribou fed on. Fortunately, the North American herds are recovering, with recent estimates totalling a million animals.

Because we were loath to accept our responsibility for the caribou's decline, we sought a scapegoat—and found the wolf. Although we knew that wolves took few healthy caribou, we spread poison across the Territories and the provinces during the fifties, killing more than ten thousand wolves and countless other unfortunate animals lured by the scent of the bait. Even far-off Minnesota authorities became carried away, proposing to destroy two hundred wolves a year until the "wolf menace has been eliminated." Fortunately, when people like Farley Mowat, the author of *Never Cry Wolf*, rose to the wolves' defense, reason finally prevailed, and we "discovered" what the natives had always known: that wolves culled the weak, the ill and the injured.

In open country, large animals like musk oxen and caribou have nowhere to hide. Worse yet, the musk oxen's practice of encircling their young and threatening predators with their massive horns proved suicidal against trigger-happy hunters who often slaughtered with abandon. Alarmed at the obvious decline of the musk ox herds, John Hornby, a peripatetic ne'er-do-well who flitted across the Territories in the early 1900s, took it upon himself to become the chief promoter of the Thelon Wildlife Sanctuary and may well have saved the musk oxen from extinction. Had he been as concerned for his own welfare, he'd have lived to see the herds return, but his boundless enthusiasm disdained caution, and in 1927, the year that the sanctuary was created, he and two companions paid the ultimate price in the haven he'd sought to create.

As the Tundra Cub crests the Musk Ox Hills, I ease back the throttle to begin a long descent to the valley of the Thelon River.

Lakes, ponds, rivers and marsh fill every basin for as far as the eye can see—a seemingly incredible sight for an arid region that receives under ten inches of moisture a year.

I pick up the Thelon at Beverly Lake. Flowing east, the water will pass through Beverly, Aberdeen, Schultz and Baker Lakes before coursing the final two hundred miles to Hudson Bay. This year the lakes are ice-free, but in "bad" ice years large lakes like these can thaw very late, and occasionally not at all, creating an unpleasant surprise for canoeists who suddenly find their idyllic river voyage to Baker Lake suddenly slowed by a hundred miles of rotting lake ice.

Although it's early in the season, I'm hoping to come upon the fall caribou migration that so often follows the Thelon's shores— a migration like the one described by geologist and author J. W. Tyrrell in 1893: "Moving masses of caribou [covered] the valleys and hillsides for miles. . . . To estimate their numbers would be impossible. They could only be reckoned in acres or square miles."

Holding to a westerly course, I leave the rocky tundra behind as the Thelon meanders back and forth below. The scattering of trees slowly thickens as the Cub flies deeper into the evergreen oasis, soaring over spruce and willows that once again stand erect instead of hunching low to the ground.

Ursus Islands grow large through the Cub's invisibly spinning prop. Floating like green rafts on an azure river-sky melange, the islands are home to the Barren Ground grizzlies that have always evaded me, concealed by brush dense enough to hide a convention of bears. And though I search the dense alder canopy, the islands again fall behind once again without a single bear in sight.

No caribou, no bears and no musk oxen. If my luck doesn't change, I'll have to content myself with Musk Ox Hill, a sixty-foot-high blister that's rising on the horizon. Known to the Inuit as a *pingo*, meaning "conical hill," Musk Ox Hill is a cousin of the frost heaves that buckle our northern American roads. Pingos, like the sandy eskers deposited by glacial rivers and the gravelly moraines that trace a glacier's margins, are remnants of the Great Cold.

Exclusive to the Arctic, they form when runoff feeds a subsurface core of deep permafrost and freezes, expanding upward to burst through the overburden of silt and clay.

By the time the Tundra Cub passes the tiny cabin at Lookout Point I'm weary of searching for game, so I push the Cub's nose down until I'm twenty feet above the river, pour on the fuel and roll from side to side as I bank through the Thelon's turns. As the shoreline flashes past, waves of goose bumps wash up and down my spine. I am Walter Mitty, come to the rescue in my Spitfire, or perhaps in a Wart Hog—the ugly, low-level fighter bomber of the Gulf War. Darting up the Thelon at all of Mach .13, I hold my heading when the river turns, pull up abruptly to clear the trees, then shove the nose down again as the river rounds the bend.

With my ears monitoring the engine's roar, my eyes constantly measuring the height and distance of the oncoming trees and my muscles evaluating feedback from the Cub, I weave back and forth within the confines of the river's spruce-topped banks. I'm a surfer in the Banzai pipeline—the roaring surf my engine, the speeding surfboard my wings. Whipping up and down the breaker's face, I arc through three G turns, living on the edge while excusing myself with Robert Burns:

> If there be life after death, he lies in bliss;
> If not, he made the most of this.

Aiming again at a wall of trees, I pull up hard to leap another point of land. When I shove the nose down, I'm suddenly looking into an explosion of running musk oxen—huge mounds of fur startled into flight by the intruding Cub.

I pull back on the stick, bank left and gain two hundred feet. Scattered, but regrouping below, are more than twenty musk oxen bulls and cows and at least one calf. I throttle back to two thousand rpm, raise the window and circle for photos.

The musk oxen slowly drift back toward the point, pushing through shoulder-high brush as I slip the Cub to an unseen landing on the peninsula's opposite shore. I'm sure that I won't be able to get close to the herd, so I snap an 80–200 mm lens onto my camera, scramble up the riverbank and begin to push through the thickets.

Something to my left moves. I'm stunned to see a humped-shouldered, seven-hundred-pound bull musk ox staring at me. Less than thirty feet away and looking like an evolutionary throwback with an ominous brow and huge curved horns, he snorts and paws the ground. As his wooly-mammoth-like coat wavers in the wind, I center his bulk in the Nikon's viewfinder while reassuring myself of the musk ox's defensive nature and the claim that they rarely charge.

Musk oxen, like the Inuit, crossed the Bering land bridge from Asia thousands of years ago. But their name is misleading. Although the males emit a pungent, sweetish smell during the fall rut, they have no musk glands.

Known to the Inuit as Oomingmaq, meaning "the animal with skin like a beard," musk oxen are marvels of Arctic adaptation. Aided by short ears, stocky legs and an extremely efficient double coat of fur, the musk ox maintains a body temperature of 101 degrees in temperatures of 50 below and windchills that can exceed minus 90. A dense, wooly underfur called *qiviut* lies tucked within its two-foot-long guard hairs. As fine as vicuna or cashmere, qiviut is said to insulate eight times better than wool. Not surprisingly, qiviut products won't be found at the five and dime. Stocking caps start at $90, and scarves can top $200.

A twig snaps behind me. When I turn, I discover that I'm surrounded by musk oxen, having somehow walked into their midst in the head-high brush. Pivoting from side to side, I snap photos while trying to keep my cool. When I finally run out of film, I face an unexpected problem—how do I leave?

Fortunately, the musk oxen cooperate by drifting away—except for the big bull, who continues to stare at me with his dark brown eyes. As I slowly back away, I gather a handful of freshly shed qiviut from the brush, roll it into a ball and cup it in my hand. I'm astounded at how rapidly my palm overheats, as if I'd pulled on a fleece-lined mitten on a hot midsummer day.

Back at the Cub, I check the oil. She's used a quart since Baker Lake and about twenty-five gallons of fuel. Lifting the three five-gallon plastic bags of hundred-octane fuel from the back seat, I set them on the flat-topped floats, where they look like bulging bags of blueberry Kool Aid awaiting a Boy Scout picnic.

After rolling up my sleeves in anticipation of my usual spillage, I hoist the first bag overhead and pour the fuel into a filter-equipped funnel. In the midst of emptying the second container into the wing tank, a mosquito alights on my arm, followed by several of her friends who tank up while I steady the bag. For a moment I see them sympathetically—just fellow creatures trying to make ends meet. Oh sure, my inner voice interrupts, their ends—your meat. I sweep them into oblivion. When I reach for the last bag of fuel, I discover that it has slumped over the edge of the float and is slowly drifting downstream, which explains the quiet slurp that I heard and ignored while feeding mosquitoes. Not to worry. Gas is so much lighter than water that even steel drums full of fuel will float. Pulling off my boots, I wade into the river and retrieve the wayward bag.

I continue west when the river begins a long loop to the north. The odds of finding caribou will be better if I follow the river, but the overland route will save fuel, so I head for a ruined cabin and three small crosses at a place called Hornby Point.

The beach at Hornby Point runs from sand to platter-size stones. Shaped by exuberant springtime floods and polished by the abrasives of time, they've been sorted by the Thelon, leaving the fines near the waterline, the gravels higher and the boulders beyond it all, bulldozed high by rafts of ice.

Rocks roll beneath my feet as I climb toward a tiny opening at the edge of the trees—a clearing so small that even those who search for it often pass it by. In fact, as I step from the stones to the spruce-scented taiga, I begin to think that I've erred. No crosses greet me. Neither is there a hint of the cabin, which is not surprising, considering its ruinous state thirty years ago. But as I advance into the tiny clearing, I spot first one cross, then two more lying on a carpet of caribou moss, their flaking, dull white paint almost hidden by masses of russet needles and rotting leaves.

In 1968 the weathered crosses stood at odd angles near the entrance to a tiny shack. On a later visit, they wore a fresh coat of white—a tribute from passing canoeists who had come to explore Hornby's beloved sanctuary.

The cabin's roof had fallen in, lying broken within a small, knee-high rectangle of moss-covered logs that once were walls. As I stood beside the graves, the Hornby story came flooding back, filling me with sadness as I sensed the sorrow and quiet desperation that these walls had witnessed during a long, harsh winter that began in 1926.

In 1904, John Hornby, having failed his exams for the Diplomatic Corps, bade his parents goodbye and sailed from England at the age of twenty-three. Moving west from Montreal, he tried farming near Edmonton. When it held no appeal, he headed north, where he surveyed, prospected and hunted the barrens, becoming a resourceful, hardy individual who could persevere when old hands quit. As Hornby's trapper friend Jim Cooley put it, that fellow Hornby "could travel further on a diet of snow, air and scenery than a Lizzie [a model T Ford] can go on twenty gallons of gas."

At five foot four and a shade over a hundred pounds, Hornby was surprisingly fit. George Whalley, the author of *The Legend of John Hornby*, recalls that Hornby once "ran one hundred miles from Edmonton to Athabasca Landing in under twenty-four hours."

Hornby quickly learned the lessons of the bush, including how to tolerate starvation and began to prefer to live off the land like a native. As Whalley observed, "Hardship and starvation seemed to take on a positive value for him, as though they were the only substantial values left, as though an ascetic and masochistic spirit were driving him to some impossible consummation with the country he loved."

That consummation was predicted by his friend, D'Arcy Arden, who warned Hornby, "You go where there are no Indians, Jack, and you'll die. Every time you've starved, Jack, an Indian has come to your assistance. You get away from those Indians and you'll die like a rat." Hornby just smiled.

In the spring of 1926, having just returned from England with his cousin, a lad of seventeen named Edgar Christian, Hornby headed north from Edmonton with Edgar, accompanied by a twenty-seven-year-old Royal Air Force veteran named Harold Adlard. They arrived at the eastern end of Great Slave Lake during the long summer days of June.

With the arduous, three-and-a-half-mile, five-hundred-foot-high portage into Artillery Lake finally behind them, the trio began a leisurely trek across the barrens toward Hornby's beloved Thelon River, which they expected would carry them to the long chain of Beverly, Aberdeen and Schultz Lakes. After paddling the lakes, they'd ride the last miles of the Thelon to overwinter at Baker Lake.

Little is known of their journey across the barrens from the time they left Great Slave until October, and by then it was early winter. Lacking suitable clothing and knowing that the lakes leading to Baker Lake had already begun to freeze, Hornby decided that attempting to cross the remaining two hundred miles of open wind-swept tundra would be suicidal. Besides, he loved the Thelon valley. The river held fish, the forest provided shelter and he expected a surfeit of game.

By mid-October, the three adventurers had completed a one-room, dugout/log cabin in a spruce grove on the Thelon's northern shore, and young Edgar had begun to make regular entries in his neglected diary.

That fall, when the Hornby party failed to arrive at Baker Lake, few expressed concern, for Hornby's reputation as a skilled hunter, trapper and survivor led to the conclusion that the party had holed up on the Thelon and would arrive the following year.

Spring came, then summer. Weeks passed after the big lakes west of Baker had shed their sheaths of ice—time aplenty for the party to reach Baker Lake if they weren't disabled or dead. Searchers traveling as far west as Aberdeen Lake found no one, and a scarcity of aircraft and weeks of poor weather prevented a search farther west.

A midsummer party of canoeists following Hornby's route found a rock cairn near Deville Lake and in it a note from Hornby: "About August 5, 1926. Owing to bad weather and laziness, traveling slowly. One big migration of caribou passed. Expect to see you all soon. J. H."

Although travelers in the area had been urged to be on the look-out for the Hornby party, no one noticed the little cabin nestled in evergreens high on the Thelon's shore. Another year passed until, on July 21, 1928, four young canoeists finally spotted Hornby's shack.

Outside the cabin, the horrified men discovered two bodies wrapped in blankets. When their calls produced no response, they forced the door, which was secured from the inside, leading them to believe that another body lay within. There, illuminated by dim light that filtered through two tiny windows, lay a third blanket-covered body.

Kenneth Dewar, one of the canoeists, would later write in *The Beaver*, a Hudson's Bay Company publication, "The right hand bunk appeared to have something under the blanket, so I gave the blanket a slight pull. . . . With that little exercise, the bones of two feet fell off the foot of the bunk and the skull rolled off to the side." They belonged to Edgar Christian. Admitting later that a sort of panic propelled them, the men retreated to their canoes and began long days of furious paddling toward Baker Lake.

When the RCMP made a more thorough search the following summer, they discovered something that the distraught canoeists had missed: On the top of the sheet-metal stove lay a discolored note that read "WHOEVER . . . LOOK IN STOVE." There, they found a grim account of inch-by-inch starvation in the diary of Edgar Christian.

According to Edgar, by the time they had reached the sheltering spruce thickets of the Thelon valley, they were very late indeed. The plentiful caribou that they'd failed to hunt, thinking there would be hundreds more, had moved far off to the south. As the weeks stretched into months and the days grew short, Edgar Christian read and reread a loving and prophetic last letter from his father: "We think of you with hope & love & I know you look forward to success. But life is full of disappointments & disillusionments & things very seldom turn out as we hope."

As carefully rationed supplies slowly disappeared, their deprivation oscillated between serious and extreme. They managed to shoot or trap a few ptarmigan one week plus a fox or a wolverine in another, and by scavenging their dump for discarded caribou guts and fishheads, they persevered through the stingy light of winter in temperatures of fifty below. And though they took turns hunting, Hornby bore the brunt, repeatedly exhausting himself on ill-clad forays in the energy-sapping snow.

January came and slowly went. The warmest day was minus ten, the coldest, minus forty as Hornby further reduced his rations, having decided to sacrifice himself in the hope that the others might live.

February passed slowly, followed by the equinox with its increasing light and warmth. Edgar's diary: "Hope to god we get caribou soon as nothing seems to get in the traps ... we are grovelling around for rotten fish."

On April 2, though too weak to hunt, Hornby took advantage of a spell of mild weather to struggle out to where Adlard had killed a small caribou and collected "a little blood which made an excellent snack."

Having arrived late in the fall, they had stored what little dry wood they could find. To conserve their supply, they tried green wood, which burned poorly and surrendered little heat. Finally, on April 6, when none had the strength to venture out, they burned their last scraps of dry wood. Four days later, Hornby wrote his will, bequeathing his all to Edgar Christian.

Edgar's diary: "16th April. Between us have prepared a meal of hide. . . . Jack still breathing but unconscious. . . . April 17. At 6:45 p.m. last evening poor Jack passed away . . . determined to pull through and go out to let the world know of the last days of the finest

The author's Tundra Cub, a 1947 Piper PA-11 Cub Special.

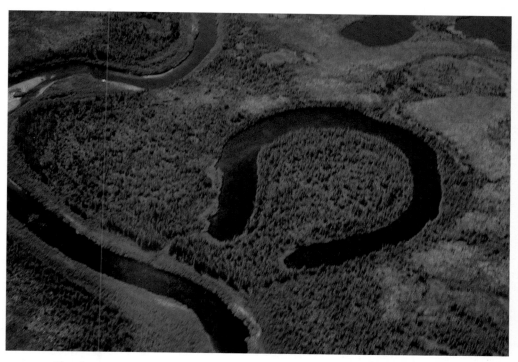

Erosion cuts through the stem of land, lays a sandbar across the channels,
and forms an oxbow lake near Manitoba's Owl River.

The freighter *Ithaca*, aground near Churchill, Manitoba.

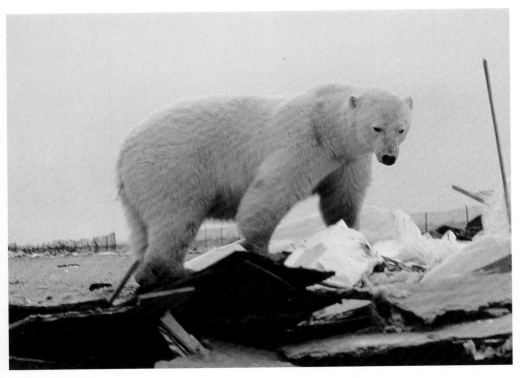

Searching for hors d'oeuvres at the Churchill, Manitoba dump. PHOTO: DALE WALKER

A polar bear swims gracefully in Hudson Bay. PHOTO: PETER COLENBRANDER

The author's innovative and productive lures.

One hand grips a *kikivak*, a three-pronged trident-like spear at Chantrey Inlet, Nunavut.

Fanning out across the Thelon River's broad beach, the caribou plunge into the current.

A lunch-size trout from Lockhart River, NWT.

Another pilot's unlucky landing on the shores of a remote lake in the NWT.

PHOTO: ELDON SORENSON

Crossing the Continental Divide, northwest of Fort Ware, B.C.

Soaring above snow-laden cirques and azure ponds in Northern B.C.

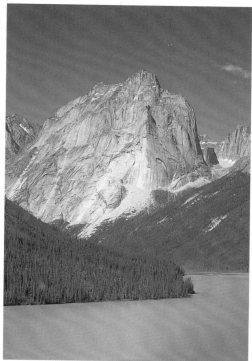

(left) Juneau's popular Mendenhall glacier towers above Mendenhall Lake, Alaska
(right) Glacier Lake leads the way to Mount Sir James MacBrien, NWT.

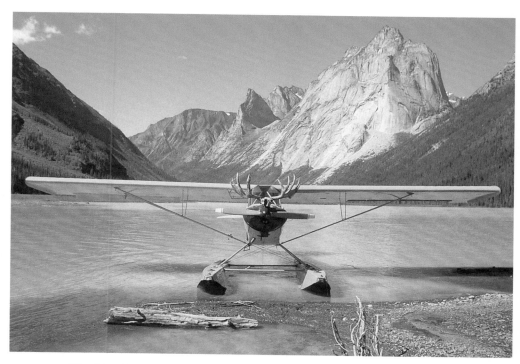

The Tundra Cub finds a novel hood ornament at Glacier Lake, NWT.

The Tundra Cub contemplates the Nahanni Range at Little Doctor Lake, NWT.

Communing with Unok beneath a black subarctic sky, Indin Lake, NWT.

man I have ever known and one who has made a foundation to build my life upon. Snowstorm all day. 20 degrees.

"May 4th. At 10:30 p.m. dear Harold passed away. . . . I cannot hunt, as walking around in soft snow is beyond my powers now, and the weather is bad."

Despite his weakness, Edgar somehow managed to wrap Adlard in a blanket and drag him outside. When Edgar crawled back into the silence of the spruce-log walls, Harold Adlard lay a few yards east of the cabin door beside the body of John Hornby.

"May 7th . . . as thin as a rake about my rump and my joints seem to jerk in and out of position instead of smoothly. This I believe to be exactly the same thing as happened to poor Jack and Harold. . . . May 17. If I cannot get grub tomorrow must make preparations. . . . Now June 1st. Yesterday I was out crawling . . . found fish guts. . . .

On June 2, as a bright spring sun flooded the tundra with warmth, blossoms and birds, Edgar wrote, "Weaker than ever . . . food on hand, but heart petering. Sunshine is bright . . . Make preparations now."

As Whalley later wrote, "Making preparations had been Hornby's term for doing the last things before death." In Edgar's case it meant writing separate letters to his mother and father in which he praised Hornby, writing, "Please don't Blame dear Jack."

Whalley continued, "When the fire had died out and he had decided that he would never light it again, Edgar Christian placed his two letters in the cool ashes of the stove, together with Hornby's will . . . and his diary. On the top of the stove he left his note."

"He was wearing a heavy gray sweater over a khaki shirt, gray flannel trousers held up by a silk handkerchief, a muffler around his neck, and winter moccasins with puttees. He turned in to his bunk and pulled two, red Hudson's Bay blankets over himself, covering his head." In the warmth of presolstice sunshine, Edgar Christian died in the solitude that Hornby had loved and that all three had come, too late, to respect.

Prior to setting out for the Thelon, Hornby had recommended in his Caribou Report that a sanctuary be created for musk oxen in the Thelon River District. In June 1927, shortly after Hornby died, but before his body had been discovered, the Thelon Wildlife Sanctuary was created to protect the remaining musk oxen and all other game as well.

Still thinking about the fallen crosses, I turn and head back to the Cub. Part of me says to leave them where they lie, while the other argues that the travelers deserve a marker. I stop briefly, undecided, then climb back to the clearing. Knowing that no matter what I do, nature will have its way, I brush away the debris and drive the crosses into the ground with a hefty river-worn stone.

When I untie the Cub, I spot a skipping stone beside the river's edge. Flat and well rounded, it fits perfectly within the arc of my thumb and fore-finger. As I send it bouncing across the Thelon, I think of Hornby, who hopped across the North like a stone skipping water, defying its pull for twenty-two years. After kissing the smooth-flowing river again and again, my stone encounters an unexpected ripple and, like John Hornby, Harold Adlard and Edgar Christian, quietly disappears into the depths of the Thelon Sanctuary.

The midafternoon sun pouring through the windshield demands a pair of sunglasses to mute the beautiful diamond-littered Thelon. Raising my camera to frame the river, I close one eye, rotate the polarizing filter—and everything goes black!

I sight through the camera again—still black. Turning the polarizer farther admits more light, but not enough. Has my camera failed—a near-disaster at this stage of the trip?

Removing my sunglasses, I carefully examine the Nikon while holding the stick with my knees. Nothing seems amiss, so I sight through the camera again. The lighting is now perfect, the windshield reflections gone as the Thelon gleams a sinuous, sequined blue. Puzzled, I stare at the camera as the Cub drones along, then notice my sunglasses lying in my lap and remember that they, too, are polarized. The answer's so obvious that I laugh out loud.

Polarized sunglasses reduce light in two ways: by their tint and because they are scored with tiny, invisible, parallel lines that admit light that "vibrates" in only one plane. When I first looked through the camera, the lines on the polarizing camera filter and the lines on my sunglasses happened to be aligned. Light that could pass through my glasses could also pass through the filter, just as a letter could pass through two closely aligned mailbox slots. But when I rotated the filter ninety degrees, the light it admitted arrived at right angles to the lines on my sunglasses, which wouldn't allow it to pass. In turning one of the mail slots, I'd stopped the sparkling panorama when it was halfway through.

Suddenly, a canoe flashes beneath my wing. Within it, two men frantically wave arms and paddles as if in distress while I circle to land.

As I drift up to their beached canoe, I examine the voyageurs. Scruffy beards proclaim two to three weeks in the bush. They're both in their fifties, and one of them sounds and looks exactly like Lee Marvin, the actor. Sunburned, sagging and semiclean, they introduce themselves while I try not to stare.

Their problem: the Thelon is too boring. Farther upstream they'd run a few challenging rapids, but for the last 150 miles, the river's millpondlike flow has been driving them mad. They'd originally planned to paddle up one of the Thelon's tributaries, then portage over to the Back River, but an early spring and a drier than normal summer has turned their tributary to a trickle, condemning them to the Thelon. Weary of its easy temperament, they ask me to arrange for a plane to fly them out when I reach Reliance.

"I could do that," I say, "but if I'm delayed or decide to follow a caribou herd I might not get to Reliance for three or four days. By then, you'd be halfway to Baker. Besides, no charter pilot is going to come looking for you on my say-so unless he's paid in advance." That stops them.

Actually, I have little sympathy for them. If they'd done some reading about this beautiful country, they'd have had other interests to follow when their much-anticipated contest with a lion became a stroll with a lamb.

As I push the Cub back into the current, I remember to ask if they've seen any game. "We sure did." One responds, "About fifteen musk oxen near Warden's Grove, and two days ago we ran across a God-awful herd of caribou."

The Cub's Continental barks to life as caribou fill my mind. Could the paddlers' herd have been the main migration? Two weeks from now, perhaps, but even that would be early. At any rate, finding that herd is unlikely, for two days of travel would have taken it well to the south of my route.

Grassy Island has always produced caribou, but this year's herd is disappointingly small—fewer than a hundred animals. Like leaves caught in a whirlpool, they circle in response to the orbiting Cub until I roll back on course to follow the millions of hoofprints that litter the Thelon's shores.

Far ahead, cloud shadows cast Rorschach patterns across sunlit sandbars. The shadows merge, becoming funnel shaped near the river. Wait a minute. Those aren't shadows—definitely not shadows. They're the lobes of an immense herd of caribou streaming down from the hills to the north. Fanning out over the Thelon's wide beach, the caribou plunge into the current, drifting sideways as they cross—like the Cub in a crosswind. On the opposite shore, they surge from the river, shaking rainbows of spray from their coats, then regroup into a wide column that extends as far as I can see. Like an immense swarm of procession caterpillars, the insects that travel head to tail in an endless game of follow the leader, the herd heads for the southern horizon. I stay with the herd for fifteen miles, and there's still no end in sight. As I roll into a 180, the herd plods on like a single-minded living carpet, drawn to the south by memories stored in their genes.

The Thelon falls behind as the Cub descends toward a Steel Lake island that will lower the odds of a midnight encounter with tundra grizzly bears.

Except for a tiny beach, the island's a confusion of frost-shattered rock. I secure the Cub to a stunted spruce and set off to search for a campsite. When I'm halfway to the top of the island, a fist-size chunk of rock nestled in a dark green bed of bearberry leaves catches my eye. On one glistening angular surface, a single inch-wide lichen lifts its face to the sun.

I hunch down on my knees and elbows like a Muslim at prayer to fill the Nikon's viewfinder with its yellow-on-maroon beauty mark of patient life. Delicate-looking but tough, these amazing life-forms endure summer's searing heat and the worst winter's cold to decorate the tundra with patches of mauve-gray and pink, with orange, red and black.

What a subarctic paradise! Blossoms speckle the tundra; fluffy, sheeplike cumulus clouds graze skies of royal blue; to the southwest, a straw-colored esker enlivens the horizon. Looking like the back of a giant lizard, the esker separates Steel Lake from Helen Falls and Dickson Canyon, two Hanbury River hazards that thin the ranks of migrating caribou.

Every spring, when the swift-running Hanbury bears rafts of ice, migrating caribou are swept downstream into a meat grinder of ice blocks and boulders called Dickson Canyon. Those that somehow survive the canyon plunge over Helen Falls to an almost certain death. In the placid water below the falls, however, caribou can cross with ease, swimming obliviously past the drifting bodies of their kin to graze away the short subarctic summer.

Drawn by the faint, characteristic clicking sound of caribou ankle bones, I turn to the northwest. The clicking fades, then returns more strongly, carried on the wind. A set of antlers rises over the crest of the island as a caribou bull grazes into sight. Approaching from upwind, he's unaware of me. I raise my camera to center him in the viewfinder—and discover a forest of antlers behind him.

When the bull is forty feet away, he spots me, snorts loudly and stops. Head tilted, he stares as he lifts his nose to the wind. He advances ten feet and stops again, legs spread in the characteristic alarm stance of caribou, then sidesteps around me, as others follow in a tympani of clicking and clacking hooves. They inspect me with their large round eyes, but not a one takes alarm when they pass downwind. Have I no meaning to them? Not being a grizzly, a wolf or a fox, am I, for all my human vanities, just an irrelevant collection of nonscents?

Brushing aside the insects that they've kicked out of the brush, I follow the herd until they slip into the lake and fan out behind the buck. They're soon halfway to the mainland, propelled by huge hooves and buoyed by coats of hollow hair and the summer's accumulation of fat. In their wake, a coating of caribou hair calms the wavelets of the Steel, bringing to mind a Hudson's Bay Company maxim: "If it doesn't have a caribou hair, it's not a proper cup of tea."

As I carry my tent to the island's only decent campsite, I'm suddenly strafed by a screeching bird. Whirling around to confront my assailant, I come face-to-face with an arctic tern that's beginning another pass.

When I scan the ground for the chicks that she must be protecting, I discover two fluffballs huddled beside a clump of arctic cotton just as their parent performs another wing-over and comes back like a dive bomber. I retreat to the Cub, clamp on a hat, retrieve my camera and catch the tern in midattack, its wings a blur of acceleration. Switching to telephoto, I lie down about twenty feet from the chicks for two quick photos.

Within a few weeks, these clumsy chicks will ride record-setting wings, for the arctic tern is the greatest traveler of all living things. Weighing just four ounces, these globetrotters "winter" in *southern* South America before returning to the Arctic for every northern spring.

Once supper is out of the way, I contemplate a quick bath. Unlike white-tail fawns, which are said to emit no predator-attracting scents, I'm awash in avgas, insect repellent, bacon grease, crushed insects and sweat. But my hands, still aching from washing dishes in the frigid water, protest that even ravenous grizzlies would be repelled by my malodorous melange. It's said that the wind goes to bed with the sun, and today is no exception. Within an hour, the breeze falls away, its sighs replaced by the annoying, high-pitched mating call of female mosquitoes as they summon mates with their vibrating wings. Seduced by the Joni-one-notes, the eager males take wing to find true love.

Mosquitoes, the Arctic's all-day suckers, pass through several stages before becoming adults: eggs yield larvae; larvae repeatedly shed their skins and become pupae; the pupae, bursting with energy, split down the back and out crawl miniature *aliens*. Chock-full of hormones, pheremones and eager to emit other moans, mosquitoes mate at the first opportunity. The females then search for blood, homing in on our warmth and our carbon dioxide-rich exhalations before laying eggs after every meal. Some species can survive mild freezing; a few can produce several generations on plant nectar alone, but all prefer blood, for its rich store of protein boosts egg production a hundredfold.

A mosquito alights on the back of my hand and becomes a tiny drilling rig, but luck is not with her. Finding a dry hole, she pulls the pipe, moves to one side and begins to drill at a slant like a wildcatter angling under his neighbor's property line. When her gusher comes in, she injects an anticoagulant, protein-laden saliva to prolong the flow. (It's the proteins that cause the itching and swelling.)

Back inside the tent, I try to focus on Diane Ackerman's *A Natural History of the Senses*, but I'm distracted by the horde of insects that are probing the netting in search of a meal. One queen-size mosquito repeatedly thrusts her "stinger" through the mesh, tempting me to grasp it between my fingernails, but, Gandhi-like, I decline. Another wobbles past. Overloaded with blood, she staggers through the air and lands on the *inside* of the netting, revealing that she too has supped—on me. Backlit by the lowering sun, she glows ruby red, a translucent, winged jewel.

I'm unwilling to have my blood fortify another horde, so I smear her vital cargo into a crimson B-positive streak. To my surprise, the blood fails to interest her relatives, who wander across the netting, oblivious to the treasure at their feet.

Returning to my reading, I begin the chapter on touch, with its captivating references to lovers and sexuality, only to be distracted by the sounds of snorting and snapping twigs. Through the tent's rear window, I spot several caribou heading for the river. The first pays the tent no mind, but the second stops, casting a maze of antler shadows across its yellow nylon walls. Turning its head, the caribou licks the tightly stretched fabric with its rasplike tongue. In the midst of its third lick, I curl a pointer finger into my thumb and give the tongue-depressed fabric a snap. The shadow leaps skyward and disappears in a clatter of hooves.

What a turnabout! A few hours ago, I had almost given up on caribou, and I'm again immersed in their flow. But now that the wind has dropped, this herd is beset with mosquitoes and flies. Tails flicking, their heads shaking and their backs shivering, they head for temporary relief in the lake.

Barren Ground Caribou are larger than Santa's Lapland-type reindeer, which dwarf the near-white, Peary's caribou of Canada's Arctic islands. These names, however, are white man's names. The Inuit, whose fortunes rose and fell with the herds, called their provider Tuktu—"the traveler." To them, Tuktu was a storehouse of vital food encased in an insulating hide that could shelter and warm their bodies and could be cut into useful ropey strips.

Tuktu is a marvel of evolution. Each spring, pregnant cows lead the trek north, arriving at the windswept barrens about a month ahead of the bulls. There they deliver calves that can stagger after their mothers within minutes of birth. A few days later, they'll out-run a human.

The fall retreat to the semishelter of the taiga is led by mature bulls carrying up to thirty pounds of back fat that serve as a reservoir of calories against the coming winter. For added protection, caribou muzzles are furred to reduce heat loss when they search for food beneath the snow.

As for the "caribou moss" that sustains Tuktu through the winter, it's not a moss; it's a lichen, and caribou are not the only ones who have prized this hardy plant-and-animal blend. Because lichen absorb and retain scents, tons of these symbiots were shipped to Europe during the eighteenth and nineteenth centuries, where, after being dried and packed in flowers, their finely ground remains brought enduring fragrance to sachets and powdered wigs.

With the exception of humans, caribou have only three enemies: grizzlies, wolves and insects, and because grizzlies and wolves feed primarily on the injured and aged, they're not a serious threat to the herd. And although it's hard to believe, even the millions of mosquitoes and blackflies are minor problems compared with the threat of two agile insects that can easily tolerate wind—and the caribou know it.

As a herd grazes lazily through a lush subarctic meadow, a caribou suddenly shakes its head violently and bolts, running wildly, as it flees from one of two villains, or possibly both: the warble fly and the nose bot fly.

Warble flies prefer thin, lightly furred skin on which to lay their eggs: the inner surface of a caribou leg or the soft hide of its belly. After hatching, the tiny saw-toothed larvae burrow into the animal's hide, then migrate through the flesh to the warmth of its well-furred back, where they overwinter in a fibrous sack. By spring each has become an aqueous grub about the size of a jelly bean. In June, two hundred or more grubs emerge through their often-infected breathing holes, which not only attract blowflies, but riddle the hide so badly as to render it worthless. Fortunately, the holes slowly close, making late-fall and winter hides useable.

Falling to the ground, the grubs pupate into warble flies, their life's ambition dictated by their genes: find a caribou leg or a belly and perpetuate your kind. Some of the grubs fall prey to birds, and, not surprisingly, to the Inuit, because, as survivors in a difficult climate, the Inuit developed eclectic tastes.

Gontran de Poncins in *Kabloona*, once shared these details about Inuit hors d'oeuvres: "They skinned the beast, and then one of them took the flesh in his fingers and pinched it sharply. Two enormous lice—worms, more truly—jumped out of the carcass . . . one after the other Kailek squeezed the worms out with his thumb and popped them into his mouth. I, who was determined to try anything once, took one up, shut my eyes, and put one in my mouth. It was sweetish inside its surprisingly fuzzy, raspberry-like skin, and I spat out the skin and had another, while Kailek sat with a heap of them before him on the snow."

While the warble fly attacks the caribou's legs and belly, the bee-like nose bot fly invades their nostrils, laying eggs that hatch into irritating larvae in the pharyngeal mucus of the animal. There, the wriggling mass restricts breathing, making the severely afflicted easy prey for wolves and bears. (In *People of the Deer*, Farley Mowat wrote of removing "one hundred and thirty of these giant maggots, each an inch long, from the throat and nostrils of a single doe.") Coughing and sneezing, caribou find relief only after the mature larvae return to the nostrils and fall to the ground, where they pupate into flies.

The last caribou departs, leaving only the hum of insects and the cry of a distant wolf. For a moment, I consider leaving the tent to howl a reply, but I'm dissuaded by the bugs. As the howling fades and the mosquitoes hum an endless reprise, I recall the thought-provoking words of Canadian biologist and author George Calef: "Like the caribou, the buffalo and the passenger pigeon were prodigious, gregarious species that made annual migrations. . . . Both are long gone, under the impact of fences and firearms, the ax and the plow."

As civilization moves ever northward, must the caribou herds go the way of the carrier pigeons and bison?

Leaving the Thelon Sanctuary behind, the Tundra Cub heads west across hundreds of miles of drumlin fields. Formed from glacial debris dropped behind resistant outcroppings of bedrock, the teardrop-shaped drumlins line up like compass needles, their tails revealing the direction of the last glacier's flow.

I've always had marvelous fishing where the Lockhart River tumbles into Artillery Lake, so I veer a bit to the north, and an hour later, the Cub bounces across the turbulent Lockhart and drifts to shore amid a swarm of blackflies. Here, where the river rushes down staircase rapids into a rippled backwater, blackfly larvae thrive.

Unlike mosquitoes, blackflies rip out a crater of flesh, then lap up the bloody flow. Mindful of their ferocity, I anoint my hands and wrists with repellent, tuck my pants into my socks and clamp on a hat and head net, taking care to cinch the net around my upraised collar. Only then do I open the door.

Beneath the floats and along the shoreline, every subsurface rock bears a mossy coating of blackfly larvae. At the water's edge, I cup my hands about my eyes and lower my face to the surface. In the seething nursery below, tiny, wormlike larvae cling to stones, straining nutrients from the passing water with iridescent, antennaelike filters mounted atop their heads.

Some have already encased their bodies in a tiny but growing bubble of air that will soon lift them free of the larval mass. As each bubble pops to the surface it ruptures, launching another hungry humpback into flight. But even as they mature, others are seeking them out, for trout and grayling fingerlings have a taste for blackfly larvae.

Clipping on a Daredevil, I send the red-and-white lure spinning out over the rapids, trapping the reel under my thumb as the lure strikes the water. The lure, restrained by twenty-pound line and pulled along by the Lockhart's flow, arcs shoreward as it's carried downstream, then enters a foam-laced eddy below several Volkswagen-size boulders.

I'm expecting a strike, but even so, a tremendous jerk almost rips the rod from my hands. This is *not* a grayling. It's a trout, and a big one that surprises me by heading upstream, leaving the calm water below the rapids to challenge my line in the river's fast-flowing core. As the trout drags me upstream, I slowly release line, afraid of losing him. When I'm down to a few yards on the reel, he pauses. I cannot move him, but neither can he move me. And then, when I'm almost convinced that my line is trapped beneath a boulder, the strain eases. Like a poker player who has seen one too many raises, he folds.

A minute later, a huge trout rests at my feet. I don't dare to lift him the way one might lift a smaller fish, so I drop to my hands and knees and scoop him into my arms. Staggering to my feet, I face my tripod-mounted camera and lift my head net to prove that this is me. Bad move.

Before I can lower the trout and replace the netting, the black-flies have found my face. I crush them against my skin, but a few escape the assault, leaving welts that will itch for days.

Working quickly, I measure the trout with my pocket tape. Thirty-two inches from his sour-faced jaw to the tip of his tail, he's thirty pounds for sure, maybe more. I slip him back into the river, then hold him upright while his wide mouth opens and closes, pumping oxygen-rich water past his gills. Sleek-finned and flecked with yellow, brown and gold, his streamlined body quickly broadens, then tapers to a lean and flexible tail that suddenly flicks—and he disappears.

Boosted by the fast-flowing river, the Cub leaps back into the air. Midway down Artillery Lake, a small resort sits astride the tree line. To the north lie the barrens, and a few miles to the south, the beginnings of the boreal forest. At the lake's southern end, where the Lockhart tumbles five hundred feet into Great Slave Lake near a settlement called Reliance, I begin to wonder if the barge has arrived with my fuel.

When I taxi in, I spot good news at the end of the pier—a fifty-five-gallon drum of avgas bearing an approximation of my name— "Erenson"—but what do I care? Were it labeled "Beelzebub," I'd claim it as my own.

As I roll the three-hundred-pound barrel to the Cub, a smiling man with a Kenny Rogers beard and a Willie Nelson body offers to lend a hand. On a shirt that's soon to see the rag bag, an embroidered pocket introduces me to Jake.

"So you're the one who ordered the fuel," says Jake. "Where're you heading?"

"West to Yellowknife," I reply.

"Uh-oh," says Jake. "I've got bad news for you. The weather that way is terrible. To the northwest, it's even worse."

"Well," I respond, "I suppose I'd better run up to the station anyway and talk to the weatherman."

"You already did," says Jake. "He's me!"

10

Reliance to Fort St. John, British Columbia

All men have stars, but they are not the same things for different people. For some, who are travelers, the stars are guides. For others, they are no more than lights in the sky.

— ANTOINE DE SAINT-EXUPÉRY,
The Little Prince

IN THE EARLY 1900S, a Norwegian scientist named Vilhelm Bjerknes theorized that great domes and valleys of air circle the earth, changing the weather as they pass. Today, we call them "highs" and "lows." As new stations gradually filled in the gaps between distant reporting points, Bjerknes's son envisioned the cold and warm fronts that our weather maps now portray.

While weatherman Jake and I alternate on the wobble pump, whooshing a pint of avgas into the Cub with every stroke, Jake describes the classic low that's squatting over Yellowknife. On its western side, the counterclockwise winds that circle every low are driving dense arctic air southward, lofting thunderstorms along a four-hundred-mile cold front.

On its eastern side, between Reliance and Yellowknife, the same counterclockwise flow sweeps moisture-laden air up from the prairie provinces. Overrunning the milder northern air, the moist mass condenses, lowering ceilings and dropping visibility with rain, drizzle and fog. And though neither Jake nor I mention it, we both know that a forced landing in bad visibility opens the door to injury and death.

Accompanied by the distant throb of the weather station's diesel-driven generator, I tell Jake of an irrepressible friend who flew his Beechcraft Bonanza into the ground while searching for a Worthington, Minnesota, runway on a fog-shrouded summer night. The plane was found by a farmer when the fog lifted. His injured wife and two other passengers survived, but my friend was slumped cold and lifeless over the controls.

I've often wondered if his confidence began to erode as he orbited the airport, dropping lower with each revolution. Did his stomach churn, his guts turn greasy as his altimeter slowly unwound? Did his reason scream for a change of plans or did he descend serenely, only to have his optimism shattered by the blow that crushed his chest?

"Why don't you come up to the station for a cup of coffee while you decide about the weather?" suggests Jake.

As I finish my second cup, he asks, "Well, are you going to try for Yellowknife?

"Jake," I say, "I hate head winds, but waiting for Yellowknife's weather to change suits me even less, so I guess I'll angle south." Extending my hand, I add, "See you next year."

"Not here, you won't," he replies. "The station's closing. They'll probably have some sort of automatic reporting system, but there won't be any staff."

Nodding, I add, "And no free lunches, either."

Weighted down with sixty-five gallons of fuel, the Cub labors onto the step, hammers across a six-inch chop and rises from Great

Slave Lake. I circle to wave my thanks to Jake, who has promised to change the destination on my flight note to Fort Smith, which lies 240 miles to the southwest.

Except for the head wind, I'm pleased with the change of plans. Yellowknife can wait, and the detour might allow a stop at Snowdrift, Canada's most northerly Chipewyan settlement. Better yet, my course will follow Great Slave's spectacular East Arm, which is part of a 150-mile escarpment that's called the McDonald fault. Like the more famous San Andreas fault, the McDonald is visible proof that the earth's crust is webbed with globe-girdling cracks.

Between those cracks, and above the dense, semisolid mantle below, the lighter continental plates slowly perform a geological version of a bump and grind. Were they to be examined every million years or so, as with time-lapse photography, their sluggish wanderings would become the casual dance of the continents.

The plates are also fractured, one of the most obvious being the McDonald fault, where the Great Slave domain of the North American Plate grinds against the Churchill domain. In Christie and McLeod Bays, shorelines rise straight up for close to a thousand feet, creating vistas that moved George Back (of Back River fame) to write, "The scenery increased in grandeur and boldness; and never, either in Alp or Appenine, had I seen a picture of such rugged wildness."

Today, every well-educated person knows that the continents have been shuffling about for millions of years, but that now-well-proven theory received little but scorn when it was proposed by an early twentieth-century German astronomer-turned-meteorologist named Alfred Wegener, who became fascinated with geology while in Greenland. Wegener, in his 1915 book *The Origins of the Continents and Oceans*, proposed that the continents began as a single land mass that he called Pangaea, meaning "all land," which eventually split into several migrating plates, the continental plates that we speak of today. In so doing, Wegener challenged the science of the day, which claimed that continents and mountains arose from the wrinkling of a cooling, contracting earth. Poor Wegener—

he was derided as an outsider and told to stick to meteorology.

Perhaps Wegener had read that in the sixteenth century Sir Francis Bacon had noticed the fit of the Americas with the western coast of Africa, a fit that's even more precise when one uses the true borders of the continents, the margins of the continental shelves. Wegener's mass of evidence correlated the Cape Ranges of South Africa with comparable mountains that extend into Argentina, noted similar fossils on the opposing African and South American coasts, and included similarities in the Indian and southern oceans. He argued that the massive coal deposits in China and North America, which form from tropical forests, must have originated near the equator.

Finally, Wegener pointed to measurements suggesting that Greenland and Europe were slowly moving apart. Had he known of the fossilized forests in the Arctic islands, he'd have had further proof of our continents' wandering ways.

Though Wegener's *Origins* elicited little but yawns from his fellow Germans, it met a storm of criticism abroad. Harold Jeffreys, an eminent geophysicist, flatly stated that Wegener's proposals violated the laws of physics. "Continents," said Jeffreys, "cannot possibly plow through the earth's rocky mantle, which everyone knows is solid." Refusing to retreat, Wegener answered their objections in a second and third edition of *The Origins* and attended the 1928 American Association of Petroleum Geologists, where his work received a thorough pasting.

In 1930, Wegener returned to his beloved Greenland to study its glaciers. A few months later, after a successful 250-mile struggle in horrendous weather to bring supplies to two stranded members of his expedition, Wegener, on his fifieth birthday, set out with a companion to return to base. Neither was seen alive again, although Wegener's snow-covered body was eventually found.

Fortunately, science is a self-correcting discipline. By the fifties and sixties, most geologists favored Wegener, won over by the barrage of evidence from radiometric dating, from the discovery of the midocean ridges where upwelling magma drives the continents apart, and from the magnetic pole reversals recorded in the ridge-paralleling bands of hardened magma.

When lava is ejected onto the ocean floor it's much too hot to be magnetic, but as it cools, its iron particles align themselves with the earth's magnetic field. When radio-dating of rock became possible, surveys of the ocean floor revealed the chronology of the magnetic reversals. On each side of the midoceanic ridges, the history of the spreading ocean floor is revealed in bar code–like images of pole reversals trapped in the rocks—the code on one side of the ridge being a mirror image of the code on the other.

As Wegener had predicted, the oldest rocks lie far from the mid-ocean ridge. Like Agassiz, Wegener relied on the evidence, challenged the orthodox view and proved it wrong.

Chewing through the twenty mph head wind, the Tundra Cub finally reaches Snowdrift, but its piers are slick with spray. I'd like to stop, but since I've plenty of fuel, I decide not to risk the hazards of an unnecessary rough-water landing and an unprotected pier.

McDonald Lake crawls into sight. Dropping close to the foam to make my progress seem faster, I flit along the fault's ruler-straight escarpment within fifty feet of the soaring spruce that cling to McDonald's steeply rising shore.

I love the drama of vertical country. Its headlands, spires and chasms charm my flatlander eyes as I cruise past their battlements, ramps and towers, their massive shoulders of stone. Like a child fascinated by the glittering tinsel of a long-awaited Christmas, I'm dazzled by nature's ornaments. For thirty miles, I soar beside the fault, then turn south to head for Smith, and leave the fault behind.

The farther west I travel from Chantrey Inlet, Churchill or Minnesota, which lie south of *both* the geographic and magnetic poles, the larger my compass "error" becomes. Although compasses point to the more southerly *magnetic* pole, the *geographic* pole is the navigator's constant, and from my westerly perspective the two now lie

25 degrees apart. Consequently, to fly south, I need a compass heading of 155 degrees. Were I to fly a 180-degree heading, I'd miss Fort Smith by almost a hundred miles.

I'm weary and saddle sore. Except for fishing, fueling and eating, I've flown all day, and with Fort Smith still far away, I decide to camp. Besides, I'm surrounded with gorgeous campsites, while the country gets boggy near Smith. I scan my well-worn chart, searching for a pencilled *S* (for sand) alongside a T-shaped lake that I've visited once before.

I was also tired that day, when, after a long flight, I shook myself alert and lined up to land on T-bone lake. The lake, wide enough for two landings, was dead calm as I descended nose high with partial power, waiting for the floats to touch the invisible surface of T-bone's mirror-flat, invisible water. Like others before me, I was so confident that I could "put 'er where I want 'er" that I landed directly toward shore instead of parallel to it, which would have allowed an abundance of room.

Still airborne as the shoreline grew large in my windshield, I realized it was too late to add power and climb over the trees. The Cub touched down sixty yards from the beach, then skipped toward shore. I instantly shut down the engine, dropped the water rudder, shoved the stick left and the rudder right, doing everything I could think of to create drag. Planing into the shallows, the Cub slid to a stop with the tips of the floats overhanging the beach.

Were I inclined to deceive myself, I might call my landing a precision maneuver that few pilots could match. In fact, weariness had swayed my judgment, and I was lucky not to have damaged the Cub. Oddly enough, that same summer, another Minnesotan flying in the same area made the same mistake with more serious results.

Although they were flying similar aircraft, "Roger" had made fewer glassy-water landings than the pilot in the accompanying Cub. Moreover, their skills were not comparable. On seeing his partner make a successful landing directly toward the shore, Roger followed his example. Roger, however, carried a tad too much power, which extended his descent, and by the time his Cub touched down, he was rapidly closing on the shore.

Still planing along on the step, the Cub slid up the beach and jammed the tips of its floats into the ice-raised berm that rims so many northern shores. The aircraft's momentum lifted the tail skyward and stood the Cub on its nose as the prop bit into the brush. Fortunately, seaplane floats extend a foot or two beyond the prop, and the Cub came to a stop while pointing straight down—with the float tips resting on the beach and the prop on the berm—a perfect but unique three-point landing. Poised vertically, the Cub stood like a monument to all unlucky pilots—an obelisk with wings.

After Roger calmed down, the two pilots made a tripod from spruce trees, and with a rope sling, carefully lowered the tail. Fortunately, the Cub was undamaged except for the end of one propeller blade, which was slightly bent. But by roping a stout tree trunk to the blade and levering the tip forward, they soon had it tracking the same as the undamaged tip.

When the time came to fly his aircraft out, Roger lacked the nerve, for although the prop was fairly straight, it caused a disturbing vibration. The two pilots switched planes and flew to the next town, where they installed a new prop and continued on their way.

As I taxi toward my old campsite on the eastern shore, expecting nothing but sand and solitude, I spot a small shack set into the edge of the bush. A battered outboard protrudes from beneath an overturned boat. Behind the cabin, a moose hide is stretched on a black spruce frame.

After kicking aside a scattering of pinecones, I pitch my tent and rummage through my freeze-dried food for one of my favorites: beef stroganoff. I've finally learned to curb my impatience when cooking freeze-dried foods, so I force myself to stir the bubbling pot for the required time while savoring its scents and the sound of distant loons.

By the time I've scrubbed my dishes and pumped the fuel from floats to wing tanks, it's almost nine o'clock. I'm bone tired, but it's time for clean clothes and a bath. I strip, grab a bar of soap and run full speed into the dying whitecaps of T-bone Lake. The lake's not as cold as the Thelon, but it's frigid enough, and I emerge pink, goose-bumped—and quickly.

Later, dry and warmed by the southerly wind, I lean against a towering spruce as sparks from my campfire drift across the lake. Climbing like stars into the nighttime sky, they dance in the rising air, then flicker and die.

When the ancient Sumerians looked to the stars, they envisioned eternal lights that returned to the east by way of an underground river. Other cultures saw in the tiny lights the campfires of their ancestors. To Egyptians, the sun and stars rode courses not far above the canopies of their tents, and similar thinking led Chinese and Middle Eastern astronomers to scale stone towers to bring themselves closer to the heavens.

Anaxagoras, a fifth-century B.C. Greek philosopher, disagreed, lofting the sun to a height of some four thousand miles. A century later, Aristarchus, who had already proposed that the earth moves about the sun while spinning on its axis, reckoned the distance to the stars at approximately what we'd now call one light-year, an astoundingly perceptive conclusion in an era of astronomical ignorance.

Given such a promising start, one might expect that the science of the ancient Greeks would have flourished. It should have, and it could have, had it not been overcome by a new and powerful religion that, for centuries, opposed intellectual pursuits. Believing that the end was coming *soon*, early Christian leaders declared that it mattered not if the earth were round or flat, as it was already corrupt and doomed. As St. Ambrose put it, "To discuss the nature and position of the earth does not help us in our hope of the life to come."

Monks, acting on the orders of St. Cyril, stripped the living flesh from the woman geometer and librarian Hypatia with oyster shells and burned her corpse. Religious zealots plundered the famous half-million-volume library at Alexandria. When the Roman Emperor Justinian shut down Plato's Academy, scholars fled to the safety of a more tolerant Byzantium. Devoid of science and intellectual pursuits, Europe plunged into the Dark Ages, and the heavens, ruled once again by churchmen who saw the universe not as a stunning, lofty sphere, returned to the tent roofs of old, across which angels drove the stars.

A thousand years later, when men like Copernicus *again* proved that the earth orbited the sun, the Vatican's earth-centered theology began to crumble. And when observers noticed that the stars' brilliance remained unchanged despite our moving toward and away from them by the diameter of the earth's orbit (183 million miles) during our trip round the sun, the stellar lights returned to their rightful place. Today, no one believes that climbing a ziggurat will improve one's view of the stars.

In 1834, British astronomer Thomas Henderson used the diameter of the earth's orbit as a baseline to triangulate the distance to Alpha Centauri, which he thought was our nearest star. (Proxima Centauri is a tad closer.) His results, though half the true distance, lofted the stars even farther. Science, unfettered by dogma, was finally marching on.

Now, as soft winds whisper through the jack pines to fan the embers of my dying fire, I'm left to wonder which stars are titillating astronomers with evidence that they, too, have planets.

With so many to choose from, I turn to the child's game of "Star light, star bright, first star I see tonight." Which star should I wish upon, and for what should I wish? Certainly not a self-centered request like health or wealth. Perhaps world peace? An end to greed? A stable world population? Still not satisfied, I rummage through the alternatives and choose omniscience. Then, realizing that downloading omniscience might take a while, I lean back and let my imagination run while I wait. No longer superheated balls of gas, the stars become fireflies, sparks and Christmas lights, bits of radium glowing bright and astral clocks that light the night.

A southwesterly breeze confirms that yesterday's low still squats over Yellowknife. By 9:00 A.M., I've eaten and emptied the floats of the few cups of water that seep in every night. It's too long since I've thoroughly checked the Cub, so I examine it inch by inch, checking every cable and hinge. Opening the cowling, I examine the fuel lines and plug wires. As usual, a few of the cylinder head cover bolts are a quarter turn loose. I tighten them, then turn to the carburetor that hangs below the engine.

The Cub's carburetor is almost identical to the old Marvel-Schebler carburetor that once fed "Allis," my grandfather's tractor. Reliable and semi-efficient, my carburetor stems from an atomizer that caught the attention of a fledgling German automaker. After replacing the perfume with gasoline and making a few changes, he used this primitive carburetor to feed his first automobile, which he named for his daughter—Mercedes.

Satisfied that all is well, I fire up the Cub, and within the hour cross the Slave River near Fort Smith, just north of the Alberta border. Launch your boat here, in the heavily silted Slave, and thirteen hundred miles of deep-river water will carry you to the Arctic Ocean. Just upstream lie thirteen miles of rapids, followed by the equally navigable Slave, Athabasca and Peace Rivers.

As pelicans scoop whitefish from the rock-strewn eddies of the Slave, I think of a local guide who likes to tease his river-running guests. Before they enter the rolling foam, he relates how each set of rapids received its name. After explaining Mountain and Cassette Rapids, he says, "We call the third rapids Pelican, because it's the most northerly breeding ground for pelicans in North America. And then there's the Rapids of the Drowned." He waits.

When someone finally can't resist asking about *that* name, he replies, "Well, we call it that because every year some tourist dies while trying to run it, and no one's drowned in it this year—yet." He smiles for a moment, and then delivers the truth: the rapids found its name in 1786, when five canoeists perished after mistaking a hunter's volley for the OK signal of one of the party members who was scouting the river downstream.

Canada, like most countries, has many towns that are named for individuals: Fort Smith, Churchill, Gillam, Thompson, and so on. My favorite place-names, however, are those that spring from optimism. Some, like Fort Enterprise, Fort Reliance, Fort Confidence and Resolute ring of determination. When optimism waned, Fort Good Hope and the Bay of God's Mercy fell onto the map, while those beset with troubles left behind Dismal Lake, Repulse Bay and the Funeral Range.

As I taxi up to the pumps, a Beaver pulls away from the Loon-Aire docks. I'm still long on fuel, but I need to add oil, and I want to call my wife. Having passed up the radio-telephone at Reliance in my rush to depart, I have not spoken to her since I called her from Baker Lake.

Peace River, my next stop, is only four hours away, so I empty the gas bags into the mains while Scott adds a liter of oil. Knowing that I'm an American because the Cub bears registration numbers (Canadian aircraft use letters) he asks where I've come from. When I explain he erupts: "My God, man, that's fantastic."

He slides a hand along the Cub's cowling. "I tell you," he says, "someday I'm going to buy one of these little beauties. I'll take off for two weeks straight—no, I'll take three—and see the country. God! I'd give anything to go along with you."

Laughing, I say, "I don't want to hurt your feelings, but a nice-looking gal back at Red Lake said those exact words, and I passed her up, so you know what the odds are for you."

As Scott fills out the charge slip, I ask if I can make a credit card call. "Sure," he replies. "Just go through that door and down the hall. The phone's in the first room on your left—under Georgia."

"Come again?"

"On your left under Georgia."

Figuring that they have a wall map of the United States with a pay phone over Florida, I head for the office, where I discover that Georgia is a gorgeous *Playboy* centerfold. "Wow!" I exclaim to the grinning clerk who's watching me, for I can't be the first to be stopped in his tracks by this eye-popping Georgia peach.

I stare at her. A bath towel V's suggestively upward from between two perfect legs to end conveniently an inch below her breasts. Her hazel-eyed gaze is direct and slightly inviting. She's stunning—a modern Rubens or Venus without the fat.

"Think you're man enough for her?" asks the grinning clerk as he eyes my graying hair.

"Sure am," I reply, and as my eyes sweep Georgia's curves, I tell him about the elderly gent whose friends expressed concern that bedding his bride of twenty-eight might become too much of a strain. "What the hell," he replied. "If she dies, she dies!"

While Georgia watches and the clerk listens, I try to call my wife. But the operator claims ignorance of my long distance phone company, and I'm forced to call collect.

"Hi, it's me," I say, forgetting that the operator has already told her. "I'm in Fort Smith."

"Where's that?"

"Northern Alberta," I respond, deliberately turning my back to Georgia, for I'm uncomfortable talking with my wife while my eyes cruise Georgia's curves.

"I thought you were going to Yellowknife," she says.

"Well, the weather forced a change of plans, so I'll probably stop there on the way back. I should reach Peace River today and Fort St. John—that's in British Columbia—tomorrow. You getting along OK?"

"Oh sure. You too?"

"I'm fine. Beautiful country north of here, you know."

"I suppose."

I pause, trying to think of something that might interest her, but she's heard it all before. Though our worlds intersect in many rewarding ways, flying isn't one of them, and as our conversation dwindles, I decide that the clerk and Georgia must think I'm terribly dull.

"Well, I'd better be going. I'll call from Fort St. John."

"OK. Take care. Good-bye."

"Miss you," I quickly add, telling myself that I *am* sincere and not just responding to Georgia's scenery. I wait for a response, but my wife is gone.

When I return to the Cub, a smiling Scott asks, "Did you find the phone?"

"Sure did," I reply. "I bet you have guys flying a hundred miles out of their way just to use that phone."

"Wouldn't be surprised," he says.

As I wipe a smudge from the Cub's yellow cowling, I think of Jim Kimball, my friend who fished for grayling in the fog at Baker Lake. After watching Wes and me fuss over our Pipers day after day, he claimed that pilots' wives would have a right to be jealous of the attention we heap on our planes.

"Think about it. You treat them like lovers, touching them, adjusting and loooooobricating them," he said, drawing out the word with a leer. "You fuel them, polish them and fly off together, then do it again and again."

At the time I thought that Jim was either a little nuts or that he'd been away from home too long. But as I slide a hand along the Cub's rounded cowl and strap her idling, vibrating frame to my body, I wonder if maybe Jim wasn't right, and I'm the one who's been gone too long.

The Cub levels off over Wood Buffalo Park, Canada's largest national park, a wilderness puzzle of spruce islands, bogs and salt flats that straddles the Alberta/Northwest Territories border. In 1922, the Canadian government set aside 17,300 square miles for the protection of the last remaining herd of wood bison, then later imported some seven thousand plains bison with which the wood bison have interbred. Although the herd was reduced by an outbreak of anthrax a few decades later, it remains the largest concentration of bison in North America.

The overcast thins and disappears, revealing a veil of cirrus clouds. Far below, the fifty-mile-wide Peace River valley separates the domed plateau of the Birch Mountains from the slightly more prominent Caribous. To the east, Lake Athabasca, the sparkling tiara that joins northern Saskatchewan to Alberta, trails two hundred miles of glitter into the midday haze. To the south lie the Athabasca tar sands, which Alexander Mackenzie visited in 1789. Strip-mined like coal and then heated, the sands surrender thousands of barrels of petroleum products every day.

At age fifteen, Alexander Mackenzie began decades of service with the North West Company, the efficient rival of the stodgy Bay. Formed from independent French trappers when France lost Canada to the British, the North West Company quickly spread posts across southern and western Canada—posts that prospered under energetic, foresighted men like Mackenzie.

Mackenzie believed that the company's success depended on expansion and set off in 1789 to explore the Slave River, which flows north from Lake Athabasca. Misled by an optimistic map provided by his predecessor, a hot-tempered three-time murderer named Peter Pond, Mackenzie believed that the Pacific lay just two hundred miles west of Lake Athabasca and had good reason to hope that his voyage would reach those shores. He could hardly have been more wrong. As Mackenzie would eventually learn, the Pacific was seven hundred miles distant, with the Rockies in between.

Although Mackenzie's downstream two-thousand-mile "float" to the Arctic Ocean has been compared to Samuel Hearne's arduous journey from Churchill to Coppermine, Mackenzie's voyage was more like a cruise. Leaving his Lake Athabasca post (Fort Chipewyan), Mackenzie drifted down the Slave past today's Fort Smith to Great Slave Lake. Not knowing where the huge lake's outlet lay, he hired native "conductors" when he could and kidnapped them when he couldn't.

Mackenzie, depressed by the Slave's long northward run, took heart when the river ran west from Great Slave for all of three hundred miles. But then the natives' Deh Cho ("Great River") turned north, and as Mackenzie's hopes for a Pacific terminus began to fade, he named the watery highway the Disappointment River. In mid-July the river finally dissolved into the maze of channels, and the explorers camped on a low piece of land known as Whale Island. There, a rising midnight tide washed away any doubts that they'd reached the Arctic Ocean.

Undeterred by his failure to reach the Pacific Ocean via his Disappointment River, Alexander Mackenzie left Fort Chipewyan again in 1792, headed up the Peace, and overwintered near the site of Fort St. John. After an epic struggle, his party finally reached the Pacific in 1793, only to beat a quick retreat with hostile natives in pursuit. In so doing, Mackenzie crossed the North American continent twelve years before Lewis and Clark, who carried with them Mackenzie's account of his travels, *Voyages from Montreal.*

Unlike John Hornby, Mackenzie had no love for the North, saying, "I think it unpardonable in any man to remain in this country who can afford to leave it." He was knighted by King George III, purchased a substantial interest in the North West Company and retired early to Scotland. He died in 1820 at the age of fifty-six.

Because I've had nothing to eat but an OHenry and some fig bars since breakfast, four o'clock brings hunger pangs, but I'm too close to Peace River to stop. The Highway 2 bridge slips beneath as I radio the airport to have fuel delivered to Cardinal Lake. I'm sure I have enough gas for the 120-mile hop to Fort St. John, but I want to play it safe.

The fuel truck arrives, driven by Mack, a fellow pilot who brims with information—the best place to eat, where to stay and which pub has the best entertainment. As the tanks fill, Mack switches from his current events to history: "Bet you don't know how the Peace River got its name."

"I've no idea," I respond.

"Well," says Mack, "the natives around here had been at each other's throat for years. But the Bay needed trappers, not warriors, so they arranged a peace treaty not far from here. And that's why it's called Peace River."

Mack offers a ride to town, where, within minutes, I attack a chicken-fried steak. A cab ride later, the Cub and I head west in search of a small lake between Peace River and Fort St. John. On its western shore lies a tiny campsite that's highly recommended by a fuel-truck driver named Mack.

Skipping along the northern edge of farms lush with the radiant yellow beauty of canola (rapeseed) fields, I begin to daydream about author Richard Dawkins's "gently spinning, green and gold harvest festival of a planet"—and almost miss Mack's Shangri-la. At first glance the lake seems much too small, but flying its length at ninety mph takes eighteen seconds, so it's almost half a mile—plenty of room—especially since there are no obstructions at either end.

As the Cub drifts to a stop, I sense the campsite's charms. Unlike many farm country lakes that ground seaplanes in muck five yards from shore, Mack's small beach rises abruptly from the depths, marches inland fifty feet and disappears in a haze of willows and birch.

A solitary thunderstorm rumbles in from the west as I stow the last of my gear, bringing introductory mists, then droplets and a brief deluge, each phase backlit by the evening sun. The storm passes, trailing two rainbows, one nestled within the color-reversed arms of its contrarian mate while the soft light of evening sets buds and branches aglow.

The Cub's thermometer reads eighty-two degrees—just right for laundry and a swim, as I'm wearing my last clean clothes. Laden with an armful of sweaty garments and a bar of nonphosphate soap, I wade into Mack's lovely lake.

I sidestroke away from shore, savoring the lake's soothing, sensuous fluidity, blowing bubbles as cool currents caress my shoulders and thighs. Still too warm, I dive toward cooler bottom water, sending crayfish scuttling to safety. For twenty minutes I cavort like an otter, then turn to my laundry.

Later, dry and refreshed, I look around before turning in. To the west, Venus slowly descends toward distant Rocky Mountain peaks. I wonder if her nine-month orbit of the sun, a duration equal to that of a human pregnancy, is the reason that Venus is called the Goddess of Love?

Beyond the Cub, which is so festooned with drying laundry that it seems to be shedding its skin, a rising moon silhouettes a distant grove of tamaracks.

Edmond Rostand's nineteenth-century creation Cyrano de Bergerac suggested ascending to the moon by tying bottles of dew to the traveler, who'd be drawn aloft by the rising vapors. As an alternative, he considered tossing a magnet into the air from a light iron chariot, expecting the chariot to be pulled upward. The voyager would then catch the magnet and hurl it upward again, hauling himself to the moon by his gauss straps. (Even serious Isaac Newton might have smiled at that.)

Although my tent is shaded, it's still too hot for clothing and much too warm to even think of lying on my foam mattress or sleeping bag, so I shove it all aside, stretch out naked on the satiny tent floor, clasp my bands behind my head, close my eyes and turn my already moonstruck mind to a metaphorical tale from American author Diana Brueton's story collection *Many Moons.*

According to Brueton, certain aborigines believed that the moon was once an exceptionally fat man who truly loved women. Failing to attract any because of his size, he became very lonely. Night after night he'd sing to fair young girls and plead for a ride in their canoes.

Finally one pair relented. Swimming alongside, they towed the canoe to midstream, where they played for a while—and then upset it. The moon sank into the river, glowing faintly as he fell. Eventually, the moon climbed ashore and rose into the sky where, to this day, he beams down wistfully at the women of the world.

Five

FORT ST. JOHN
TO FORT SIMPSON,
NWT

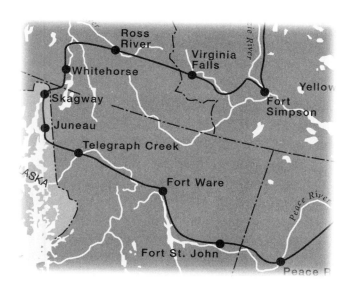

11

Fort St. John to Juneau, Alaska

The Tree which moves some to tears of joy is, in the Eyes of others, only a Green thing that stands in the way.

– WILLIAM BLAKE

INE O'CLOCK! I chastise myself for wasting a beautiful morning, then suddenly realize that I've found an excuse to delay breakfast: Fort St. John is just an hour away, so someone else can do the dishes. Still, even though I hop to it, it's almost ten by the time I taxi to the eastern end of the lake.

When the Cub pivots into the wind for takeoff, I'm surprised to discover a western horizon bulging with storm clouds. Figuring that I can reach the seaplane base before the deluge arrives, I pour on the gas, but twenty miles later, the Cub shudders into a wall of wind, and a semi heading to Fort St. John slowly leaves me behind. As lightning leaps from cloud to cloud, the British Columbia lion replaces Alberta, the lamb.

Determined not to return to Mack's lake, I red-line the Cub, then switch on my radio.

"Fort St. John, this is Piper 4745 Mike."

Silence.

"Fort St. John, this is Piper 4745 Mike."

More silence.

Realizing that my transmitter might be working, but not my receiver, I press the mike button and report: "Fort St. John, Piper 4745 Mike is a Piper PA-11, twenty east of Fort St. John for landing Charlie Lake."

Suddenly, I realize that I'm not getting any feedback in my headset. Either the entire radio is messed up or my batteries are dead. I try a few other frequencies without response. Probably batteries.

As the distant Rockies twist the wind into knots, the Cub, like a just-roped stallion, begins to leap and dive. I throttle back to reduce the stress on the Cub, then counter with stick and rudder as we struggle through turbulent air.

By the time Charlie Lake finally appears, the advancing squall line is already pummeling the far end of the lake. And as the Cub descends toward the whitecaps, I remember that eleven soldiers drowned just here while building the Alaska Highway in 1942–43.

I land close to the beach at the lake's southern end. If the breakers damage a float, or the wind and waves upset me, I'll be in shallow water, drifting toward the beach. But the same wind that churns the lake also cuts my landing speed, and after two jolts, I'm down and pitching on the waves. I momentarily consider drifting back to the beach, but without tie-downs the Cub would be at the mercy of the oncoming storm.

Pitching from crest to trough against the gusting wind, the rocking Cub makes little headway until I increase power. But the Cub's engine falters on the lake's spray, so I pull on carb heat, which directs cowling-protected spray-free air to the engine, and its gasps subside.

The tiny seaplane base isn't much more than a slot in the shoreline, but it looks like the Promised Land. After taxiing into its tree-rimmed shelter, I secure the Cub, then investigate a nearby house. When no one responds, I grab my bag and hit the road as rain drops like overripe grapes splatter down. A half minute later, a Chevy pickup stops and the passenger door opens. As I leap inside, the driver says, "Nice day, eh?

"From here, it's gorgeous," I reply, raising my voice above drumming on the roof, "but fifteen minutes ago it didn't look so good, and it's great to be on the ground."

"You need gas?" he asks.

"Just enough to top the tanks," I answer, "but I couldn't find anyone at the base."

"Rex is gone," he says. "I'm his neighbor, sorta. I saw you come in and figured you'd need a ride. I had to go to town anyway. If Rex isn't here when you come back, just gas up and leave a note with your name and address. The pump'll be on."

After turning down a cup of coffee, he drops me at the Coachman Inn, where I ask for a top-floor room so that nothing but rain can dance on my ceiling in the middle of the night.

A bed—a real bed. I stretch out on it, savoring its uniformity. No hidden pinecones here, no knuckled roots or unseen stones to jab my hips. And not just a bed, but television, a shower *and* a tub. Unable to resist it, I postpone eating, adjust the mirrored bathroom door so I can see the TV and slip into the steaming tub. To my great surprise, within a few minutes, the station turns to one of my heroes, a man whose work assisted Alexander Mackenzie: Galileo Galilei.

In 1609, when Galileo learned of the telescopes being demonstrated in Holland, he quickly grasped the principle and made not one but several telescopes. Although the ingenious, contentious and rather self-centered Galileo possessed an open mind, nothing could have prepared him for seeing mountains on the moon, a spotted sun or, perhaps most of all, for Jupiter's multiple moons.

The following year, Galileo published his observations in his book, *The Starry Messenger*, which created a sensation throughout Europe.

The Catholic Church, however, could no more abide spots that marred the perfection of the sun than they could accept Buddhism, Hinduism or Islam. Nevertheless, Galileo's sightings supported what Copernicus had feared to reveal: that the earth was *not* the center of the universe, an annoying fact that disproved the geocentric theology of the day, reaffirmed the sun-centered solar system of the pre-Christian Greeks and reduced our importance in the Grand Celestial Scheme. (Knowing that Cardinal Bellarmine had condoned, if not arranged, the murder of Giordano Bruno for defending the Copernican theory, Copernicus entrusted his *De Revolutionibus Orbium Coelestium* to Andreas Osiander, a Lutheran cleric, for publication after his death. *De Revolutionibus* was condemned by Rome, and by Calvin and Luther, who stated, as some fundamentalists still do, that "Joshua commanded the sun to stand still, and not the earth." The manuscript was placed on the Index of Prohibited books, a move that delayed its influence for more than a hundred years.)

Galileo, who was convinced that the evidence in his telescope outweighed biblical literalism and the speculations of theologians, soon ran afoul of the Church. When he was warned to stop teaching his "theories," he instead wrote a whimsical play in which the Church position was advanced by a rather dull character named Simplicius. In response, the pope ordered Galileo to appear before the Inquisition, where he was threatened with torture if he failed to recant.

Remembering the fate of Bruno, Galileo confessed to error. He was condemned to spend the rest of his life under house arrest, where he lost his eyesight from age and studying the sunspots that the Church said didn't exist.

Fort St. John, with a population of twelve thousand, is too large to inspect on foot, especially since the Coachman's on the fringe, so I strike up a conversation with Carla, a waitress who could easily work for the Chamber of Commerce.

"Well, first of all, we're the oldest settlement in B.C. If you want shopping, go to the Totem Mall. We've got a bunch of tour outfits that go to the mountains and Williston Lake, and if you like golf, there's the Country Club. Downtown we've got a new cultural center and the world's largest glass beehive."

"Really!" I exclaim, then dare to ask, "How do you know it's the largest?

"I dunno," she replies with a toss of her head, "but it is."

She pauses, then adds, "Oh, yeah, there's a museum at the Bennett Dam with lots of fossils they dug up while making the dam and there's a mastodon trunk." Giggling at her mistake, she clasps a hand to her mouth and says, "I mean tusk."

One customer advises me not to miss the W.A.C. Bennett Dam, claiming that it backs up the world's largest reservoir, Williston Lake. Apparently a long-time resident, he ends many of his sentences with the stereotypical "eh?"

Resuming my role as visiting skeptic, I ask if he's certain that the reservoir is the world's largest, mentioning those created by the Hoover, Grand Coulee and Aswan Dams.

"Just a minute," he says, then yells to a uniformed woman seated at the far end of the counter. "Hey, Ruthie, isn't Williston the biggest reservoir in the world?"

"Yeah," says Ruthie.

As Carla hands me my bill, she says, "I just thought of something else. You might want to see the derrick."

While I wonder if the derrick is also the largest in the world, the cook shouts, "Carla!" and she dashes off.

Assuming that the derrick is an oil-drilling rig, I ask the cashier for directions. With a jerk of her thumb, she says, "Go that way a few blocks and you'll see it."

The derrick turns out to be a midsize drilling rig adjacent to the tourist bureau/museum/bookstore. The museum is small, but its collection of pioneer memorabilia and photographs of the construction of the Alaska Highway trap me for more than an hour. By restraining myself, I manage to leave the bookstore with just two volumes: Dick Turner's *Nahanni* and Shirlee Matheson's *Flying the Frontiers*.

I phone the weather bureau, which promises blue skies by morning, then call my wife to let her know I'll be in Juneau in a couple of days. "Miss you," I say, and this time she hears.

As the sky opens up and thunder booms, I flip on the television, belch a hint of Canadian bacon and open Ms. Ackerman's book to the chapter on *taste*.

It's clear. In the distance, mountain peaks rasp the base of a deep blue sky as I check the Cub, then top the tanks and leave Rex a note with my name, address and the amount of fuel I pumped.

Aided by cool, dense air that adds power and lift, the Cub leaps from Charlie Lake and climbs into a northwest breeze. What a difference! Yesterday, a sky wrenched with seizures. Today, a gently rolling swell. I love it, and the Cub loves it, too, for as I cross the Alaska Highway and head for Bennett Dam, the Continental has never sounded so smooth.

Scenic though it is, the Canyon of the Peace offers more than rugged peaks and wildlife. Beyond the dam, the Peace River coal block disappears beneath Williston Lake. Mined for more than a century, the coal now lies undisturbed, abandoned when immense reserves of cheap, clean-burning natural gas and oil were discovered near Fort St. John. Even so, energy still flows through Hudson Hope, generated by turbines in the concrete stopper that restrains Williston Lake, the largest reservoir in *British Columbia*.

When Williston Lake rose behind Bennett Dam, it inundated 640 square miles of farm and forest. Flooded-out homesteaders were relocated to areas of equal value. Whites whose traplines were submerged received consideration, and a method was even devised to provide substitute habitat for moose. But when it came to compensating the Sekani Indians who had hunted and fished the newly drowned valleys for centuries, nothing was done.

As the British anthropologist Hugh Brody wrote in *Maps and Dreams*, "Their reserves were destroyed; they were dispossessed of the entire area of their traditional homeland, expected to move along, make do, or somehow disappear."

Many of the Sekani moved up the Finlay River to a settlement called Fort Ware, the site of my next fuel stop and, according to folks at Fort St. John, the community with the highest murder rate in Canada. Bigotry and exaggeration, I tell myself. Prejudice of the worst sort. Still. . . .

Because Alexander Mackenzie knew that accurate maps were essential to the success of his employers, he carefully charted his travels by relying on star and sun sightings to determine his latitude (his north-south position). But when he needed to determine his longitude (his east-west position) Mackenzie was hampered by a less-than-reliable chronometer. In its place, he often substituted Galileo's infallible timepiece in the sky: the planet Jupiter and the clocklike regularity of its moons: "I had another observation of Jupiter and his satellites for the longitude . . ."

To understand why explorers had to know the time in order to determine their longitude, let's envision a popular fruit, an orange.

With your imagination, strip away the peel and cup it in your hand, stem end up. The stem end is the North Pole; the South Pole lies in the palm of your hand. Now draw a horizontal line around its belly—an equator. On the far side of your darkened room, a flashlight beams—the sun.

Your orange, for our convenience, has twenty-four wedges instead of the usual dozen or more. Lines drawn from pole to pole, like the lines between the wedges, are called meridians, or lines of longitude. Since the earth makes one revolution each day, it follows that the sun illuminates a new wedge every hour. Thus, each wedge equals a time zone of one hour, and because the earth is some twenty-four thousand miles in circumference, each of the earth's twenty-four wedges spans about a thousand miles *at the equator*.

If we could turn our orange as slowly as the earth revolves, we'd see that the time required for the flashlight beam to cross a single wedge/zone remains one hour *even to the north or south of the equator, where the wedges narrow on their way to the poles*. Although the wedges taper toward the poles, the number of degrees (fifteen) *in each zone and the time each zone represents remain the same*. Since the sun transits one wedge/zone every hour, and an hour equals fifteen degrees of longitude, time is related to distance. Consider now the fabled explorer Vasco da Swenson, two days out of Portugal in search of the legendary McDonald Islands and their Arches of Gold. If he sails north, the sun will move lower in the southern sky and the north star will rise higher; the farther he sails, the greater the change. Knowing that the earth is some twenty-four thousand miles around and by relying on sightings taken with an astrolabe, Vasco can pretty well fix his north/south location, his *latitude*. (Over the years, astrolabes shed superfluous parts, becoming quadrants, then sextants then octants, and now, thanks to GPS, obsoletants.)

But Vasco also needs to know his longitude—how far west he's travelled. And as Shakespeare so wisely observed, "Ay, there's the rub."

Out of sight of land, and with winds and currents of varying strength and direction, has poor Vasco averaged a hundred miles a day or two hundred? Depending on his fortunes with wind and wave, a week under sail could carry him a thousand miles from Lisbon's cantinas or as little as a few hundred. In which of those one-hour wedges is he located when the sun rides high at noon? Fortunately, there's a way out for Vasco, because even though he can't measure his east/west distance, we're going to let him measure its equivalent—time.

For a moment, let's present Vasco with a gift: a spring-driven chronometer from two hundred years in his future. So accurate is this timepiece that it varies less than a second per month. Unlike the inaccurate spring-driven clocks of Vasco's day or pendulum clocks that became useless when moved about, Vasco's chronometer is happy on pitching deck or jolting wagon. As the science writer Dava Sobel so vividly describes in her book *Longitude*, the chronometer was built over a period of forty years by John Harrison, clockmaker, in response to a British promise of a £20,000 reward. His eighteenth century timepiece could rival the best wind-up clock of today.

Because Vasco (the diligent) has taken care to keep his chronometer wound, it still tells Lisbon time. Three days out, under his first clear skies *with the sun directly overhead*, he checks his chronometer, which reads 12:20. Vasco, who is no dummy, quickly realizes that he is twenty minutes (five degrees) west of Lisbon.

Were Vasco on the equator, he'd have travelled 333 miles. However, since his westward course from Portugal crosses time zones that have narrowed to less than 1,000 miles, he first determines his latitude by observing the angle of the sun above the horizon. With his latitude known, his charts reveal that the zones at his latitude are only 780 miles across. Vasco therefore knows that he has sailed west for 260 miles.

With his old clock, which often varied by two minutes a day (most were much worse), he could be off by as much as a hundred miles—and in which direction, east or west? Having solved his problem, Vasco heaves a huge sigh of relief—and hides our miraculous clock.

Poor Vasco. That which we give, we can reclaim. However, to replace his treasured clock, which we cannot leave behind, we'll give him a celestial clock, the clock of Galileo's moons, the same moons relied on by Mackenzie in a world beyond Vasco's ken.

When Galileo trained his "optical tube" on Jupiter, he found four moons circling the planet with clock-like precision. Once their relative positions were carefully recorded, the "Galilean moons" became a universal clock that all could see at the same instant *regardless of their location*. Given a steady deck and a clear sky to grant good viewing, if Vasco's telescope shows the same arrangement of Jupiter's moons at 11:52 p.m. that the Lisbon tables show for midnight, he knows his old unreliable clock has lost eight minutes and must be reset. Periodically corrected by Galileo's moons, Vasco's clock can now be used to determine his longitude with greatly improved precision.

Within a decade of his death, Galileo's method for determining longitude had become widely accepted, especially on land, which always provided a stable platform. Thus equipped, geographers promptly set about resurveying the world—moving islands and shrinking nations. (Upon being presented with an updated map of his kingdom, King Louis XIV complained that he had lost more of France to the astronomers than to his enemies.)

Due in part to national pride, captains who sailed from London referred to London time, those from Venice to Venice time, and so forth. Fortunately, after a few centuries of printing different tables for every port, an international agreement finally named the meridian that runs through Greenwich, England, the Prime Meridian— zero degrees. Since then, all longitudes are measured from the "prime," as are times for navigation, which are given in Greenwich Mean Time, or GMT.

We now return to Vasco, who, with the aid of Galileo's celestial clock, finally reached the American coast, where he had a horrible nightmare in which huge garbage barges kept dumping their loads at sea. Disgusted with what the future might hold, Vasco turned south and came upon the Cayman Islands, where he established Los Bancos da Swenson to escape the taxes of his avaricious king.

Sprawling across the land like a recumbent T, Williston Lake begins at Bennett Dam. Seventy miles to the west, where the stem of the T joins the crossbar, I turn to the north, surrounded by malachite mountains that rise from Williston's chop. Far below, a tugboat strains against hundreds of chain-bound logs, heading south to Mackenzie's mills. A glance ahead reveals their source: entire mountains plucked bare.

Forests are renewable resources, but I fear the consequences of replanting them as single-species forests, which are more prone to disease and support a much smaller range of animal species than mixed forests. How sad it is that every day, almost everywhere, for our short-term convenience, we are shoving other species aside and driving them toward extinction.

Masquerading behind names that include the words "green," "environment," and "conservation," too many companies are following the lead of the Wise Use movement, a devious organization that talks "green" while opposing environmental concerns. In Alberta, where one pulp mill is expected to discharge twenty million gallons of questionable effluent into the Athabasca River every day, the provincial government has already leased a fourth of the province to clear-cutting pulp operations, most of them foreign owned.

Now, having denuded thousands of square miles of southern British Columbia timberland, industrial-strength clear-cutters have set their sights on the forests of the coastal range. According to a Canadian government report, at present cutting rates, all of the commercial old-growth forest will disappear in fewer than ten years. Meanwhile, the timber companies promise gifts and jobs, but common sense and experience tell us that the companies will leave when the trees are gone.

Yielding to summer's slow ascent, the higher peaks of Williston's northern arm bear shrinking robes of snow. Rivulets of meltwater pour from beneath their ermine mantles, joining to cascade down slopes laid bare. Clear streams that once watered verdant valleys dirty themselves with torn-up soil and stain the bays below. How much of this, I wonder, really stems from need? How much from waste?

Why should forests fall for junk mail? Why should trees be pulped for individuals, businesses and governments that refuse to use *both* sides of a sheet of paper? I envision Henry Thoreau and

Aldo Leopold grieving over prime forests and protesting the level-
ing of the few old-growth stands that remain. I recall my grandfather
describing the white pine forests of Michigan, Wisconsin and Minnesota that were expected to last for centuries but disappeared in
less than Lincoln's four score and ten.

Though I fly though grandeur, I hear chain saws and see the falling forests of Malaysia and Brazil. I remember the words of Renatas, a Tanzanian park ranger quoted in William Calvin's *The River
That Flows Uphill*: "After I be dead, others will follow. If people be
killing killing, there will be no more buffalo, no rhino. If they be cutting cutting, there will be no more trees, no oxygen, no rain. Like a
desert. What will my daughters think? They will come and there
will be nothing. Our father was stupid, they will say."

Like Renatas, Thoreau railed against the abuse of nature: "most
men . . . do not care for Nature and would sell their share in all her
beauty. . . . It is for the reason that some do not care that we need to
protect all from the vandalism of the few."

The Tundra Cub leaves Williston Lake behind and follows the
Finlay River to a remote Sekani settlement set deep in the Wolverine
Mountains. According to the *Water Aerodrome Supplement*, a publi-
cation listing seaplane bases and the services they offer, Fort Ware's
avgas is reserved for emergencies, but the Cub can burn car gas, so
I'm really not concerned.

Although the *Supplement* advises landing upstream *into* the
Finlay's twenty mph current, I line up with the current to reduce the
sudden drag of touchdown, then drop between the towering evergreens that line its serpentine banks. Engine muted, the Cub's noisy
slipstream becomes a whisper. Swissssh. Piece of cake.

I turn upstream, then angle toward the shore, wincing as I slide a
float firmly onto fist-size rocks. With the engine running to keep the
Cub grounded, I climb onto the float, cut the ignition, then leap off
and rope the Cub to a tree.

Just downstream, several natives are lounging near the center of
a bridge that spans the Finlay. A dog romps at their feet. Suddenly,
one of them scoops the animal up and tosses it over the side. As the

dog falls, kicking, into the Finlay and struggles toward shore as the current sweeps it downstream, they laugh uproariously. I'm disgusted, but I'm also aware that this is a good place to mind my own business, so I lock the Cub and add another rope.

Thinking that a show of concern for the Cub might give them ideas, I avoid looking back as I jog toward the airport. When I find nothing that looks like a fueling site, I hail down a speeding three-wheeler.

"Who do I see for gas?"

"Over there," he says, pointing to a small building.

Inside, I discover what appears to be a store. The shelves along one wall are half-full, while those that line the rest are close to empty. In the center of the room, surrounded by benches strewn with books, clothing and personal gear, a white man sits, packing boxes. When he looks up, his face fills with surprise, then pleasure at seeing a stranger.

"Hi, there" I begin. "They say you're the man to see for gas."

"That's right," he replies.

"I've got a Cub on the river that could use about fourteen gallons. If you can't spare avgas, car gas will do."

"Sure, sure—I'm Andy," he says, extending a hand. Where'd you come from?"

"Fort St. John," I reply, "on my way to Juneau."

After looking around to make sure we don't have company, I tell Andy about the Indians who threw the dog in the river and ask if things are as bad as I've heard. With a voice tinged with anger, Andy begins.

"Well, I don't know what you've heard, but it's bad enough. The death rate for babies here is the highest in Canada. Accidents and violence among teens and adults are four times worse than elsewhere. As for tossing dogs in the river—that's called fun. He sighs, then adds, "In a month, I'm outta here. I thought this job would be a great getaway but it's been more like a sentence. "Look at me," he continues. "A month to go, and I'm already packing. Says it all, doesn't it?"

A woman passes by the open door. Andy waits a few seconds, then says, "That woman—that's Nettie—one of the Sekani elders. She's so disgusted with things in town that she's moving back into the bush."

When I pick up a can of corn, my eyebrows rise at its price. Andy notices my reaction. "Food costs here are the highest in British Columbia," he says. "And there isn't much money to begin with. The natives earn a little from trapping and fighting the odd fire, but a lot of it goes for booze."

As I fuel the Cub, I ask Andy what lies beyond the bridge, since I hadn't seen any roads on my way to Fort Ware.

"Oh, there's a road, all right," he answers. "But it's pretty well hidden. I've never been down it, but I hear it ends near Mackenzie at the south end of Williston Lake."

When the fueling is done, Andy holds my wing while I fire up the Cub. I yell, "Good luck!" then pour on the gas. The Cub fights the Finlay's current as it struggles onto the step. I glance to the side. We're already planing across the water, but the shoreline hardly moves. Nevertheless, as her ninety horses wind up and her wings begin to lift, the Cub slips back into the sky.

An hour later, the Tundra Cub crosses the Continental Divide and soars above the snow-filled cirques and aquamarine ponds on Mount Cushing's northern face. On either side, fluted pinnacles of stone rise like giant organ pipes, bringing to mind bits of Grieg's piano concerto, then *Finlandia* and the soaring centerpiece from Saint Saen's organ concerto.

Two hours out of Fort Ware, I measure the remaining distance to Juneau. It's almost three hundred miles. If all goes well, I could make it without a fuel stop, but if I run into head winds, or if coastal weather forces a return to Telegraph Creek, I'd be in trouble. Besides, the *Supplement* reports a "very strong current" in the Stikine River, which cools me on Telegraph Creek.

I head instead for Iskut, a tiny settlement on Highway 37 with a seaplane base just south of town. Nice long lake. Flat water. No current. And when I taxi in, no base. A passerby informs me that it's been moved south to the next lake. "Just fly along the shore," he says, then adds the inevitable "You can't miss it."

Ten minutes later the Cub noses onto a wooden ramp adjacent to the Stewart-Cassiar Highway. I add a quart of oil, then fill the tanks while the base operator suggests a campsite on nearby Kakkidi Lake.

"It's a lovely spot," he says, "with a beautiful beach and maybe even some char."

I decide that Juneau can wait.

As the Cub rounds the steep flanks of Tuktsaada Mountain, I slip a wide-angle lens onto the Nikon, open the right window and maneuver close to the trees. Leaning out into the slipstream, I capture steeply wooded slopes that leap skyward from one wing and plunge away from the other, then throttle back, and the Cub soon coasts to a stop at a gently sloping beach rimmed with yellow flea-bane. When I open the door, the wonderful silence seems magnified by the quiet tick, tick, tick of the Cub's cooling engine.

A nearby river as wide and smooth as a city street flows out from Kakkidi Lake. Clipping a Meps spinner onto my line, I follow a set of moose tracks to the river and, with a sweep of my arm, toss the spinner across the stream.

The water erupts in an explosion of spray, as a troutlike fish shakes its head, scattering sunlight from the whirling spinner, then dives and heads downstream. But it's a small fish, easily overcome, and I soon reel in a foot of red-speckled beauty—a Dolly Varden char. By the time the sun has slipped beyond the mountains, I'm sampling my first nonarctic char.

While searching for a pack of raisins, I come upon a pocket radio that I'd tossed in on a last-minute whim. Little bigger than a cigarette pack and cheaply made, it's probably useless here. Nevertheless, I thumb up the volume and begin to cruise the dial. Static mingles with beeps and yowls until, at 580 khz, the music of a bigoted but hugely talented German composer named Wagner rasps from the set. How can this be? With only one station, I'm favored with Wagner! Lying back, I walk my fingers back and forth to the march from *Tannhauser*.

Wagner finally fades away, and as the brightest stars begin to shine, I am reminded of Tycho Brahe, whose passion was astronomy.

Brahe, an excellent observer, began to doubt Ptolemy's earth-centered solar system (which we know had the support of the Church) when he discovered errors in his Ptolemy's work.

When Brahe's benefactor, Denmark's King Frederick II, drank himself to death, Brahe moved to Prague, where he hired a very unlikely assistant: Johannes Kepler, a neurotic, sickly, self-critical man. Kepler, however, had one saving grace: he was brilliant—so brilliant, in fact, that Immanuel Kant called him "the most acute thinker ever born."

The two despised each other, but Brahe needed Kepler's fine mind to unify his data into a comprehensive theory, while Kepler could do nothing without the precise observations that Brahe had so carefully amassed. In 1601, time, the salve that cures all ills, intervened when Tycho Brahe died. Suddenly granted unlimited access to the data that Brahe had been slowly sharing, Kepler set out to complete the task that Brahe, thinking it an impossible one, had assigned to him: determine the orbit of Mars.

For eight frustrating years, Kepler studied dozens of circular orbits, creating almost a thousand pages of calculations before he thought to try an ellipse, which worked beautifully, and not just for Mars but for all the planets as well. In vindicating Copernicus, the sickly, unappealing Kepler proved the Church and Ptolemy wrong and set the heavens right.

A few years later, in 1618, hatred between German Lutherans and German Catholics catapulted Europe into the bloody Thirty Years' War. Soldier-borne smallpox killed Kepler's son, Friedrich, age six. His wife, already stunned by the soldiers' atrocities, contracted typhus and died. His mother, accused of witchcraft, was narrowly acquitted, and then only through the intervention of the "imperial mathematician," her son. She died within six months.

To escape "the barbaric neighings" of religious intolerance, Kepler fled to the country, taking pains to avoid itinerant prophets who proclaimed the end of the world. Unable to collect money owed him or to find work to feed his children, he died at the age of forty-eight in the midst of the war he hated.

Although the Thirty Years' War put a premature end to Kepler's genius, a century later, another war, the Seven Years' War, persuaded a nineteen-year-old military-band oboist named William Herschel to turn from carnage to the cosmos and sail for England. There he set music aside and began to study the stars.

Within a decade, Herschel was producing Newtonian (mirror) telescopes without peer. He discovered Uranus, which doubled the diameter of the known solar system and garnered a grant from the king. With money in hand, Herschel sought a foundry to cast a thirty-six-inch mirror with three times the light-gathering ability of previous mirrors. When all refused, he decided to cast it himself.

After constructing a circular mold from densely packed horse manure in his basement, Herschel fired up his furnace and proceeded with the pour. The mold cracked. When he tried again, the furnace cracked, sending a fiery stream of molten metal flooding across the floor—and Herschel abandoned the casting business.

A few years later, the king's foundry finally provided a forty-eight-inch mirror for Herschel's new reflecting telescope. When the king invited the archbishop of Canterbury to the dedication, he reversed their usual roles, telling the archbishop, "Come, my Lord Bishop, I will show you the way to Heaven."

For breakfast, it's char for protein, pancakes sweetened with fresh blueberries for carbohydrates and vitamins and bacon for fat—a balanced meal, or close enough.

Under clear and windless skies, the Cub's unchanged altimeter proclaims a high-pressure dome that should take me to Juneau with ease. Before I depart, I spread out the Atlin chart and draw a course line from Kakkidi Lake to Telegraph Creek, then extend it west to Juneau's Tracy Arm. Thirty minutes should take me to Telegraph Creek, two more to Juneau.

While the Cub idles across the lake, I search my chart for the name of the mountain that towers above my camp: Edziza. Near its seven-thousand-foot level, I spot some eye-opening names: Williams Cone, Eve Cone and Cocoa Crater. I'm in Volcanoland!

Eager now, I feed in full throttle and climb toward Williams Cone. From a distance, both cones look like four-hundred-foot anthills—like the cinder cones of southern California. But up close, their thirteen-hundred-year-old mix of ocher, russet and black cinders speak of sulfur and iron compounds that escaped from deep in the earth.

It's Cocoa Crater, however, that really catches my eye, for Cocoa's more than a cinder cone, it's a crater where lava once leaped and splattered before hardening like wax in the crater's throat and on its flanks. As I circle Cocoa, sunlight dances across its glittering slopes.

My course briefly overlaps the valley of the Stikine River, the birthplace of the Raven, who in Tlingit lore is the creator of the world. I follow the rolling river downstream to the tiny town of Telegraph Creek. Built to serve a never-completed telegraph line between North America and Europe by way of the Bering Strait, the town clings to the steep north bank of the Stikine, lingering on, its future in communications severed by the transatlantic cable.

I flip my radio to 123.2 mhz, then lift the mike to ask Telegraph Creek to advise Juneau customs of my arrival time—a notification required, in part, by our endless war on drugs.

"Telegraph Creek, this is Piper 4745 Mike."

No response.

The feedback in my headset indicates that my new batteries are good, so I try 126.7, then 122.2.

Still no response.

Damn!

I'm unwilling to use the emergency frequency, because this is no emergency, but if the customs agent makes me empty the plane or dumps a fine on me, it will be. Switching back to 123.2, I keep calling as Telegraph Creek falls mutely behind.

At full throttle, the Cub climbs to eighty-five hundred feet, then levels off above a panorama of mountain peaks enrobed in snow—the white lava of the Alaskan Coastal Range. To my right, the Sawyer Glacier smothers whole mountains like a huge albino octopus, its gravel-striped tentacles slipping along rocky slopes to probe the valleys while I gawk at a thousand square miles of peaked meringue, or is it divinity, so pure and white?

The Continental abruptly loses two hundred rpm, then steadies. Probably carburetor ice. I pull on carb heat, flooding the carburetor with warm air from inside the cowling. Because warm air holds less oxygen than the same volume of cold air, the engine drops another hundred rpm. But, minutes later, the ice is gone and we're back to twenty-one hundred rpm. With the carb heat off, it rises to twenty-two.

I cruise across heaps and valleys of frozen cream while eyeing their graceful slopes. If I had to, I could land almost anywhere, as it's not that different from landing a seaplane on grass, which I've done many times. Once down, I'd flip on my Emergency Location Transmitter and wait for a chopper or ski plane to fly in a mechanic. For the takeoff, it's aim downhill, keep the nose up a tad and pour on the power.

The engine stumbles again, dropping to nineteen hundred rpm—not good, but enough to hold altitude if I raise the nose a bit. Carb heat on again—and I wait. With the peaks a thousand feet below, and the valleys even farther, there's plenty of time to melt the ice—and to cuss myself for not leaving the carb heat on until I'd flown into warmer air. I've left the dry inland air behind, and entered maritime air. Instead of being surprised, I should have expected ice.

The turquoise waters of Whiting Lake, British Columbia, lead to Alyeska, the "Great Land" that W. H. Seward, Lincoln's secretary of state, purchased from Russia for $7.2 million. In 1867, Seward's jeering critics promptly dubbed the purchase "Walrussia" and "Seward's Folly," and *The New York World* complained that "Russia has sold us a sucked orange." They couldn't have been more wrong, for Alaska's been more plum than orange. Twice as big as Texas, and with only 3 percent as many people, Alaska has barely been nibbled upon, let alone sucked dry.

Admiralty Island, a hundred-mile-long battleship of an island with mile-high peaks and a brown bear population of one per square mile, emerges from the Pacific haze as the Cub glides down the Sawyer's crevasses and soars over Tracy Arm, where, on truck-size slabs of swell-damping ice, harbor seals relax, safe from their chief predators—orcas, which we also call killer whales.

Surrounded by the waterfalls, I flit past a ship rimmed with waving sightseers, then turn up Stephen Passage. Suddenly, a dark form erupts from the ocean, focusing my panorama-scanning eyes on a single point as a breaching whale hangs briefly above the swells, then falls back in an explosion of spray. It's much too large for an orca, most likely a humpback whale that's returned from Hawaii to restore its forty-ton body in Alaska's krill and herring-rich waters.

Beyond the Cub's right wing, the advancing tongues of Taku, Norris and Wright Glaciers lick the waters of Taku Arm. The Taku glaciers, unlike most Alaskan glaciers, are considered "healthy," having advanced as much as eight miles since the turn of the century. Elsewhere, our warming climate has been more than a match for most of the world's glaciers, which are melting at a rate that exceeds their steady flow.

I send out a call to the Juneau tower.

"Juneau tower, this is Piper 4745 Mike."

No response.

I can hear the tower's more powerful transmitter directing other traffic, but they still can't hear me. Finally, as I pass Taku Harbor, Juneau responds, requests a call back on a one-mile final approach and confirms my request for customs.

Juneau clings to a narrow strip of land, hemmed in by Gastineau Channel cruise ships on one side and steep mountains on the other.

Descending, the Cub crosses the channel-spanning bridge that connects Juneau to West Juneau and the slopes of Douglas Island, then follows the channel north toward a long, two-hundred-foot-wide water-filled ditch—the seaplane waterway that parallels Juneau's main runway. A Boeing 727 descends from the opposite direction as if coming to meet me, its lowered gear reaching for the ground like the outstretched feet of a landing goose. When it touches down I pick up my mike.

"Juneau tower, Four five Mike is on one mile final."

"Four five Mike, cleared to land. Taxi to far end of the waterway. Mooring area will be on your left."

When I'm a half mile from the waterway, my peripheral vision picks up a huge blue-green wall—the terminus of the Mendenhall Glacier, one of the most visited glaciers in the world.

OK, I tell myself, let's not get distracted—gawking can get you killed. Carb heat already on. Fuel selector to fullest tank. Mixture already full rich. Power near idle. Trim the nose up until she slows to fifty-five, then fifty, then forty-five. With a prolonged hiss of keels kissing water, the Cub touches down and idles past a long row of colorful seaplanes, the taxis of the North.

Dropping the water rudder, I turn toward the mooring area while gawking at the glacier and ignoring the control tower now that I'm down. As I'm about to shut down the engine, I decide to taxi in a circle to photograph the glacier through the Cub's windshield.

"Four five Mike! You are crossing an active runway! Turn left immediately!"

Oops. Dumb move. (If I'd been paying attention, I'd have heard the tower clear another seaplane to land.)

Glancing to my right, I spot an Otter about to touch down. Fortunately, there's plenty of room, but my unauthorized 360 wasn't very bright—a legacy of operating from remote lakes and uncontrolled airports for far too long.

U.S. Customs officials require pilots to stay with their aircraft, but my bladder demands a quick trip to the bushes, where I meet an astonishing change. Ten feet from the asphalt ramp, I'm engulfed in evergreen-shaded, ankle-deep emerald green moss, the product of 130 inches of rainfall a year.

When the glowering customs officer finally arrives, clipboard in hand, he ignores me while he scans the Cub and writes down its registration number, then asks for my name, address and phone number.

"Why didn't you give us the *required* one-hour notice of arrival?" he asks.

"I tried to. But Telegraph Creek wouldn't respond to my request to relay the message. I tried all the frequencies except 121.5, but nothing worked. Then I couldn't raise Juneau until I was close because of the mountains."

He glares at me. I have broken a rule. He could fine me. He could make me unload every item from the plane and open every float compartment just to be difficult. He delays and ponders, playing me like a fish while I wonder if I will be released or tossed into the frying pan.

"Well," he finally grumbles, "You did *one* thing right. You had the tower call us before you landed."

Turning silent again, he collects the yearly $25 fee that private aircraft owners must pay for the privilege of returning to their own country and walks away. I'm free!

The Aero Service fuel truck brings a change of attitude: a friendly face, pleasant conversation and avgas at $2.54 a gallon—half the price at Fort Ware. Still, that's 60 cents more than I pay in the lower forty-eight.

I settle my bill while the driver calls Taku taxi, and within minutes a well-used Chevy arrives, driven by a loquacious retiree named Harry who's still got a grip on the spirit of the North. It's a good eight miles to Juneau, but Harry, prompted by my many questions, makes like Hubert Humphrey all the way.

"It's gold that got Juneau going, you know," says Harry, whistling his *S*'s between a gap in his teeth. "The story is that a couple of prospectors named Joe Juneau and Harris found it back in 1880, [but the truth is that they were led to it by a Tlingit chief.] Why, just one of Juneau's mines has already coughed up ten times as much gold as the whole damn state cost! We're the capital, you know. Might've made sense when they did it, but it's a piss-poor idea now. They ought to move it north instead of dragging everybody down here. Prices are nuts, too. You'll see."

"I thought they decided to move the capital up near Anchorage. Whatever happened to that?" I ask.

"You're right," says Harry. "They voted to move the whole works back in the eighties. But when the time came to pay for the move, they wouldn't do it. How dumb can you get?

"Bald eagle perched on that crane," he remarks, jabbing a finger toward the channel. "They're here year-round, especially in the winter—after the salmon, you know. A bit north at Haines they have more eagles than people when winter sets in.

"There's the Gastineau fish hatchery," he adds. "Want to stop?"

I glance at the meter. I'd like to stop, but not with the meter running. Sensing my problem, Harry swings into the parking lot and shuts off the meter. "Tell you what," he says, "I'll take off a little time and show you through."

The Gastineau hatchery sits at the end of a stair-stepped fish ladder that switchbacks into the plant. A large window in the side of one of the ladders provides an underwater view of the salmon that are heading "upstream." Expecting to see just a few fish, I'm amazed to find dozens of huge chum and sockeye salmon lazing in swirls of dancing bubbles, while silver-sided cohos weave in and out of sight. Instead of spawning and subsequently dying, which is the fate of all Pacific salmon, the females will be stripped of up to ten thousand eggs, which are promptly fertilized with milt (sperm) squeezed from the males.

"What happens to the meat?" I ask.

"It's used for bait. Sometimes for dog or cat food or it's dumped into the channel.

"Why not for humans?"

"Well," says Harry, "you gotta remember that ready-to-spawn salmon stop feeding when they enter the rivers. The meat goes bad as they use up their bodies for energy."

"OK, but why not just let them spawn naturally? Why all this?" I ask, momentarily forgetting that my Minnesota Department of Natural Resources strips walleyes of eggs and sperm.

"Because the nursery gets a 90 percent hatch rate, but Ma Nature gets just 5!

"Wow."

Inside the hatchery, Harry pauses beside a cylindrical ceiling-high aquarium stocked with oceangoing fish. As the fish weave in and out of sight, he helps with their names.

"That's a sockeye," he says, pointing to five-pound red salmon. "When it comes to value, the sockeye's number one."

"And I suppose that's a silver," I add, as a chrome-plated salmon pauses, hanging eye-to-eye with me.

"That's right," says Harry, "but we call them cohos."

After pointing out the pink (humpbacked) salmon, Harry locates a dog salmon or chum, the least valuable of all.

"What about king salmon?" I ask.

Harold circles the aquarium. "Don't see any," he says. "The grown-ups'd be too big for this tank anyway. We call 'em Chinooks, you know. They run up to a hundred pounds."

A replica of a fish wheel draws me to a picture window overlooking the Gastineau Channel. Powered by river currents, fish wheels tirelessly scoop up migrating salmon and deliver them to adjacent holding pens via internal inclined ramps. As I examine the fish wheel, I'm reminded of another device that found use along this coast: a machine that was insensitively advertised as "The Iron Chink." Introduced in 1903, the revolving mechanism processed a salmon every second, replacing fifteen overworked and often underpaid Chinese.

As we return to the cab, I ask Harry to recommend a hotel, explaining that I'll take anything that offers beds without bugs. His first choice, the Prospector, has no vacancies. His second, the Alaskan, is also full, as is the Driftwood, but the Baranof will accept me for $132. Being tired and desperate, I settle up with Harry and sign in.

The Baranof takes its name from Alexander Baranof, the heavy-handed manager of the Russian American Company prior to 1817. Baranof, the "Lord of Alaska," drove his men to scour the coast for fur so thoroughly that by the end of his tenure, fur-bearing animals had almost become extinct. In his single-minded pursuit of furs, Baranof treated the Tlingits badly, practically enslaved the Aleuts and is said to have ordered a Russian shot for spreading rumors of gold.

In Juneau, price and quality don't always go hand in hand. The Baranof's main restaurant, the Gold Room, glows with a lushness appropriate to its pricey menu, but my $132 room is well-worn and only semiclean. Perhaps to compensate for its sixties furniture, its drab draperies and dated light fixtures, the bathroom bears a modern touch, the silly but obligatory strip of paper spanning the toilet seat "for your protection."

When the blast of a horn announces the arrival of another cruise ship, I raise my fourth floor window to watch it dock, only to be diverted by loud barking from across the street. Moments later, the door of the Taku Cab office opens and a malamute emerges. A hand slips his leash around the doorknob and disappears. Seconds later, the malamute lifts a leg to a nearby light post and emits a seemingly endless stream that flows down the sloping sidewalk, perversely avoiding the gutter as it trickles past four businesses before finally disappearing into a sidewalk crack. When I look up again, the ship has docked.

I consider a late lunch at the Red Dog Saloon but put it off in favor of checking out one of the cruise ships. I strike up a conversation with a couple heading toward the gangplank—just another happy camera-toting passenger heading home. Once inside, I realize that I forgot to read the ship's name. Oh well, if I'm questioned I'll just look blank and ask, "Isn't this the *New Amsterdam*?" the ship docked just ahead.

Without a floor plan, I don't know whether to head up, down, right or left. Up wins, as I want photos of Juneau's wharves from the upper decks. I wander through the immense ship from bow to stern and deck to deck until I come upon a huge, elegantly decorated dining room, the Coral Room, where I learn it's but one of three. I contemplate asking for a tour of the engine room but decide not to push my luck and head instead for the ramp.

The *New Amsterdam* lies beside the wharf like an enormous elongated beehive. On its Gastineau side, an endless procession of float-equipped Otters, Beavers and Cessnas buzz up to an opening in the hull near the waterline. Passengers leaving the aircraft gesticulate wildly, their words lost in the rumble of idling radial engines. Four, six and eight at a time, they're replaced by eager tourists ready to gawk at the sights of the Taku and Tracy Arm glaciers.

Having skipped lunch, I'm ready to treat myself to a seafood supper, no matter what the cost. The Fiddlehead, a highly regarded restaurant, has a prohibitively long waiting line, and another restaurant within walking distance won't open for an hour, so I return to Fisherman's Wharf, where I settle for a $16 seafood sampler, which arrives at my plastic table on a plastic plate, accompanied by plastic utensils. My scallops, fish, clam strips and potatoes arrive so over-fried that they make the plate seem tempting, but I console myself with the knowledge that I won't have to worry about undercooked food.

While drizzle drips from the Wharf's shed roof into the channel, I grind away at the least brittle morsels while feeding a one-legged gull that begs from the railing beside my table.

"Here," I say. "You take it." He does.

When I return to the Eagan Street shops, the command "Repent" reaches my ears. A tall evangelist is holding forth beside a raised planting of petunias, nasturtiums and marigolds. As if numbed by his presentation, a city worker patiently waters the smiling pansies at his feet while it rains.

With boyish certainty, the young evangelist gushes gospel at indifferent passersby, rails against the "devil's doctrine—evolution" and urges all to "turn away from Hell and seek, instead, divinity." Smooth-faced, with his hair combed like Ralph Reid, he is Reid writ large as he fervently pitches a mixture of Jesus and Armageddon.

When he can't draw a crowd, I conclude that by ignoring him, passersby are obeying his admonition to reject the profane.

While the evangelist derides evolution, I think of Cornell University scientist Carl Sagan, who wrote in *The Demon-Haunted World* that much of the resistance to the fact of evolution "derives from our difficulty in imagining the passage of millennia, much less the aeons. What does seventy million years mean to beings who live only one millionth as long? We are like butterflies who flutter for a day and think it is forever."

The biologist William V. Mayer put it more bluntly: "Arrogance comes in a variety of forms. The arrogance of great wealth, the arrogance of great power, the arrogance of great beauty, and the arrogance of the great master are bearable because they rest on an acknowledged and measurable base. The arrogance of ignorance, however, is unbearable because it is rooted in the smug satisfaction of being isolated from the facts of the case. The anti-evolution plank in the platform of Christian Fundamentalism is a classic example of the arrogance of the know-nothings." Eager for a change of atmosphere, I spend a rewarding hour with the displays and photographs of the Alaska Museum, then head for its bookstore, where I promise myself that I won't buy more than one book, then begin to browse. Thirty minutes pass without notice, then forty-five. With four books in hand and the museum about to close, I force myself to choose just one—a lovely photo/essay book called *Searching Home: Pacific Salmon, Pacific People* by Natalie Fobes, Tom Jay and Brad Matsen.

In a nearby art store, I'm drawn to a bronze mottled-green statue of a standing polar bear that's a bit too large for the Cub. And at $4,400, it's also too big for my wallet. Still, I'm entranced by its graceful contours, its benign, inquisitive pose. Moving on, I buy cards and books for my wife, sons and grandchildren, then backtrack to the statue, not knowing that before leaving Juneau, I'll return again to stare.

It's already dusk by the time I get back to the Baranof. In the harbor below, the cruise ships have lit their rigging—a lovely sight marred only by the buildings that partially block my view. Thinking that I might get a better photo from higher up, I head for the top floor and start knocking on doors.

The first, already vibrating before I knock, opens onto a raucous party.

"*May I take a picture from your window?*" I shout over the din.

"*Sure. Go right ahead,*" the host bellows back.

In less than a minute, I'm back in the hall. Half of me wishes they'd asked me to stay, but the half that hates chaos is relieved.

As I slip a new roll of Ektachrome into my camera, I remember passing a one-hour photo shop. They won't be able to process my slides, but they could develop the print film from my backup camera. Ninety minutes later, while the celebrants on the top floor keep their neighbors awake, I spread the photos across my bed, revisit my Steel Lake caribou and feast my eyes on the whipped-cream topping of the coastal range.

Following a delicious Baranof breakfast, I catch a Gray Line bus to the Mendenhall Glacier, only to be disappointed that the road ends a mile from the glacier's face. Fortunately, a paved walkway to Mendenhall Lake cuts the mile in half, and I'm soon gawking at the mountain of frozen Aqua Velva that rises from Mendenhall Lake. When someone mentions a trail leading to the glacier, I return to the starting point at the tourist center, locate the trail and head out.

According to the park map, I should be able to reach the glacier in about twenty-five minutes, snap a few pictures and be back in time for my bus. But what the map doesn't reveal is that the trail makes innumerable switchbacks, climbing some five hundred feet before descending to the glacier.

As I trudge upward through a soggy forest decked out in lichen and moss, my initially swift ascent slows. Forty minutes after leaving the tourist center, I puff to a stop at a river that cascades into Mendenhall Lake just as a returning group of hikers appears.

"How much farther to the glacier?" I ask, but receive only apologetic looks and a few words in German. Three hikers later I learn that the trail, which has been pretty good, gets worse. If I go on, I'll surely miss my bus. If I turn back now, I might catch it. I hesitate, then give up. I want to leave Juneau today, and if I'm late for the bus, that might become impossible.

Later, having missed the bus despite turning back, I stop for a final look at the glacier just as a pinnacle of ice crashes into the lake with the roar that the Tlingits call "white thunder."

With neither cabs nor buses in sight, I hike down the road, hoping that my cameras will help me look benign while my upraised thumb pleads, Brother, can you spare a ride? No one stops.

The road parallels a tributary of the Mendenhall, and when I stop to rest my legs, I'm surprised to find the stream swarming with jut-jawed salmon. Atlantic salmon can reproduce year after year, whereas spawning for Pacific salmon is a one time fling. In the river's gravelly bed, the fertilized eggs become "alevins," then "fry," ready to feast on nature's insect- and crustacean-rich cornucopia. Those who survive return in two to seven years, depending on their species. Guided by the chemistry of the stream in which they hatched, they journey upstream to spawn and die in the cradle where they were born.

As cars and tour buses hurry by a few feet from my back, hundreds of green-headed, russet-sided sockeyes weave back and forth in the final dance of their days while the tattered bodies of their spawned-out kin drift slowly back to the sea.

When a spawning female drives another salmon away from her "redd" (nest) of fertilized eggs, I suddenly find myself blinking back tears. What's going on here, I wonder. Why am I so moved? Do others feel this way?

Later, co-author Natalie Fobes's description of her first visit to a salmon run provides the answer: "A streak of crimson split the seams of the waterfall; I leaned forward to clear the fence from my sight. And then—a sockeye salmon floated in the air.

"Even today it is hard to describe the jumble of emotions I experienced during those moments. . . . I remember slowly turning to my father. His face had a look I had never seen, and before he turned away I saw his eyes were full of tears."

A car pulls over, its occupants curious to see what I'm photographing. As if fearful that talking would break some magic spell and they'd disappear, I silently point to the salmon. More cars stop—the beginning of a traffic jam. When I finally ride off with a couple from the *New Amsterdam*, I count myself lucky to have missed my bus and to have been denied a ride until I'd witnessed the spawning of the sockeye salmon.

12

Juneau to Whitehorse, Yukon Territory

Gold is a living god.
— PERCY BYSSHE SHELLEY

"Juneau Tower, Piper 4745 Mike is ready for takeoff.
Request north departure with a right turn.
Four five Mike cleared for north takeoff. Right turn approved.
Four five Mike cleared north with right turn."

SETTING the Cub's altimeter to ten feet, the elevation of the waterway, I advance the throttle. The Cub almost leaps into the sky, assisted by dense sea-level air.

A right turn quickly brings the Cub to the Mendenhall's gullied surface, where I hug the Nugget Mountains, leaving room for a quick turn if the glacier's slope begins to rise faster than the Cub can climb. Rolling from side to side, I photograph blue-green crevasses while wishing I'd done this yesterday, when the sun was still in bloom. When I've had my fill, I reverse course and glide toward the Lynn Canal, the ninety-mile-long fiord that leads to Haines and Skagway.

To my left, the navy blue waters of Icy Strait roll a gentle swell; on the right, Herbert Glacier pushes a frigid tongue toward a harbor brimming with gillnetters and seiners that can, at the height of the salmon run, net a fisherman $2,000 a day. In their midst I spot a few trawlers—boats that Harry despised: "Those goddamned bottom trawlers," he'd erupted when I asked about trawlers. "They crush and bury everything. What they don't catch they maim or kill. Compared to those damned trawlers, seiners are a just bunch of kids with dip nets."

A shaft of sunlight enlivens the pastel blues of Eagle Glacier as a column of rain descends on the Chilkoot Mountains. The closest drops will make their way to the Lynn Canal, but those that fall just a few miles inland will feed the Yukon River, with two thousand miles to travel to reach the Bering Sea. Dead ahead, an oncoming cruise ship tows a mile-long wake to Juneau.

A rapid hammering interrupts my reverie. The gauges read normal, but the hammering continues. Then my eye catches a blur at the front of the engine cowling where one end of the rub strip that fits between the cowling and the nose bowl is flailing against the cowl. It's not dangerous, but I'm not willing to let it go, so I land, locate a small roll of duct tape and begin to make repairs.

Just as I close the cowling, I'm interrupted by a loud whoosh, then several more. Spinning around, I'm surprised to see several four-foot-tall dorsal fins heading straight for the Cub. It's a pod of orcas.

I hurriedly retrieve my camera while my mind fills with stories of orcas upsetting rafts of ice to devour basking seals. I know that orcas are primarily salmon feeders and that kayakers routinely paddle among them, but even so, I chicken out and stay inside the Cub.

Feeling foolish for my retreat because if they wanted to they could easily sink the Cub, I raise the camera, then discover that I need to change the film.

The last orca in the pod lifts its head above the water and seems to examine the Cub. With eye patches of white, the black slick-skinned whale looks playful, the raccoon of the cetacean world. Close, yet worlds apart, we eye each other. I'm filled with wonder, but I'm also embarrassed to be part of the species that's imprisoned, maimed and murdered his kin. (At least a fourth of the orcas captured for aquariums during the sixties and seventies bore bullet wounds.) Does this orca know our past, I wonder. Would his thoughts make sense to me? Would mine to him?

Assisted by a strengthening tailwind, the Cub flits past one of the Alaska Marine Highway's many "blue canoes," the five-thousand-ton ferry *Matanuska*, which has just departed from Haines, her hull crammed with cars, buses, campers and semis, her railings lined with passengers bound for Juneau and Ketchikan.

By the time I reach Skagway (from a Tlingit word meaning "windy place"), the harbor is leaping with waves that are much too large for the Cub, so I fly on toward the ghost town of Dyea (pronounced Die-ee) where the wave-muting Taiya Inlet might permit a landing. If it does, I'll search out the Chilkoot Trail, the Gold Rush Highway to the Klondike.

Gold is a self-loving metal. Unlike gregarious carbon, which combines with other elements in half a million ways, gold consorts with just a few, and even then reluctantly. Conceited gold mimics Narcissus, the youth ensnared by his own reflection on the surface of a forest pool. But unlike the mythical waters that trapped Narcissus, water can set gold free.

In 1896, when a prospector named George Washington Carmack found flakes of placer gold near the Klondiuck River, a tributary of the Yukon, he set in motion a stampede that would enrich a few and impoverish many, build and destroy friendships and bring out the best in some and the worst in others.

Of the three main routes to the Klondike fields, the easiest was an all-water route through the Bering Sea to the tiny town of St. Michael. There, the stampeders boarded a sternwheeler and steamed up the Yukon to Dawson's fields of gold.

The remaining two routes involved a climb over one of two mountain passes—either Skagway's White Pass, which came to be known as Dead Horse Pass, or Dyea's Chilkoot Pass, which had a final ascent that was much too steep for horses. Although Chilkoot Pass stood six hundred feet higher than White Pass, prospectors had four good reasons to choose the Chilkoot: it was shorter by ten miles; it was open year-round; Dyea was safer than corrupt Skagway and, in the warm months, the Klondikers escaped the stench of the three thousand rotting horses that had died on the White Pass trail, "the pack animals' hell."

During the winter, packers struggled up fifteen hundred icy steps to the crest of the Chilkoot Pass, paying $1 a trip for their use. From dawn to dusk, a continuous line of gold seekers plodded carefully upward in the "Chilkoot Lock-Step." If an exhausted stampeder collapsed while climbing the "Golden Stairs," he could face an hour-long wait for a chance to get back in line. With the pass attained, some tobogganed back down on a shovel, but most rode the seat of their pants.

Faced with packing a ton of supplies over the pass (which the RCMP required to prevent starvation) prospectors had two choices: tote it themselves or hire natives who were quickly becoming rich. In addition, natives who had become Presbyterians refused to work on Sunday. Worse yet, halfway up the pass, some would set down their loads and "renegotiate" the rates.

When Skagway's George Bracket finally built a toll road twelve miles up White Pass, many were eager to use it, but no one was willing to pay, so he sold out to a pair of railroad men named Thomas Tancred and "Big Mike" Heney, the latter having bragged, "Give me enough dynamite and snoose and I'll build a road to hell."

Two years and 450 tons of explosives later (and an unknown amount of snoose, or chewing tobacco), Heney made good his boast. But by then, the Rush was over. Nevertheless, the White Pass and Yukon railroad guaranteed that Skagway and the steamboats of the upper Yukon would make money for many years, while Dyea's days of glory would quickly fade.

During World War II, the WP&Y supplied most of the materials for the Alaska Highway. But when metal prices tumbled in the eighties, many Yukon mines shut down, taking the railroad with them. Today, the WP&Y is back in limited business, hauling loads of Skagway tourists to the summit of Dead Horse Pass.

I can't find Dyea. I'm beginning to think I've missed it, when I suddenly realize that the rubble passing below my wings is all of the town that remains.

To avoid taxiing into the last few spike-studded remnants of the mile-long wharf that had connected Dyea to saltwater, I land on the Taiya River, which is flush with salmon, the brown bears' food stamps, then set off across the tidal flats toward a wall-like stand of hemlock trees resplendent with bald eagles. Drawn by the spawning runs of chum, coho, sockeye and humpbacked salmon, the eagles' annual gathering of three thousand exceeds the population of Haines and Skagway combined.

As I stroll through Dyea's grassy remains, I can hardly believe that a town of five thousand once stood just here, with a main street two miles long. In the silence, I envision throngs of hopeful Klondikers hauling their gear past the clamor of Healy's Trading Post and crowded saloons until the bubble burst, replaced by the sighing wind and the cries of eagles and gulls. Now all ghost and no town, Dyea lies buried beneath fields of wavering goosegrass and lavender lupines.

Spotting a violet-rimmed mound of trash, I set my camera aside and, accompanied by the hum of bees, begin some prospecting of my own. Beneath scraps of deeply rusted iron, crumbling asphalt shingles and rotting wood lies a bed of broken glass, a handful of metallic slivers that once were nails and the disintegrating remains of corroded cans. As I carefully scrape aside each layer with an old strap hinge, my eyes search for the gleam of a long-lost $20 gold piece.

By the time I reach ground level, I'm down to the residue of a fire that must have died well before the shingles were dumped on top. Shaving off a quarter inch at a time, I sift through the ashes and toss them aside. Minutes later, something gleams—not gold, but silver. A key.

Its pitted nickel plated shaft bears a sculpted oval at one end and a small lock-engaging T at the other. Perhaps it's a skeleton key, the master key to old door locks. With no one to dispute me, I decide that it must be a skeleton key, having risen from Dyea's bones.

Pocketing the key, I head north through a scattering of blue-flag iris. The trail divides. One branch turns toward the western mountains, perhaps to join the Chilkat Trail, a little-used alternative to the Chilkoot. I explore it briefly, hoping to stumble onto an abandoned trapper's shack, but find only a lush patch of waist-high salmon-berry bushes. Because grizzlies enjoy these large raspberry-like fruits too, I carefully scan the meadow for fifteen-hundred-pound mounds of fur, then pick a handful of the delicious-looking but disappointingly flavored berries.

A mosquito probes my wrist, reminding me of a Tlingit legend that tells of the sister of a chief, who, despite being told that she would never bear a child, soon became pregnant. The baby, born much too early, bore a heavy coat of hair and a mouthful of very sharp teeth. Growing rapidly, the child began to kill, for pleasure, every animal that crossed its path.

Because the child was related to the chief, no one dared to intervene. Finally, in desperation, the chief himself threw the incorrigible child into a roaring campfire. As the flames consumed the creature, a voice rose from within the flames, promising that it would drink human blood for a thousand years. The fire shot up, sending millions of ashes high into the sky, and each one became a mosquito.

Retracing my steps, I return to the gravel road that connects Skagway to Dyea, and follow it north toward the Chilkoot Trail until I come upon a sign that reads "Dyea Cemetery."

Although I prefer cremation, the soft, cool shade of the deeply wooded cemetery appeals to me. Sitka spruce and towering hemlocks spread layers of evergreen boughs over graves surrounded by nodding ferns, bunchberries and bell-blossomed pyrola. Their lofty branches whisper tales to the wind, but at ground level it's still and hushed.

Most of the wooden markers read "April 3, 1898"—Palm Sunday— the day that a Chilkoot Pass avalanche snuffed out sixty lives. On that day, a woman named Anne Maxon was struggling up the pass. Glancing up from beneath her load, she gasped as the onrushing avalanche swallowed the shouts and bodies of the fleeing stampeders above. Within seconds she, too, became trapped in the tumbling mass. Minutes passed as she grew cold. Her breathing became difficult; her cries for help weakened.

As she was about to lose consciousness, something poked her side, followed by shouts and frantic shoveling. Freed from her white coffin, she fled just as a second avalanche broke loose. The whirling mass roared downhill, caught the woman and again entombed her in a snowy shroud of white. Anne Maxon's good luck, however, was the equal of her bad. Once more she was discovered and quickly set free again.

Hailing from distant Maine, California, Minnesota and a host of other states and countries, the dead stampeders share their resting place with native graves surrounded by wooden fences. One granite headstone bears a finely detailed engraving of a beaver above a listing of those interred: Tagish Johns and his kin; Dyea Johns and his. At its base, ruby red strawberries mingle with the lacy ladderlike foliage of horsetails.

A glance at my watch persuades me to forgo the Chilkoot Trail. If I find it, I'll want to climb for at least an hour. Add the return trip and, if I still can't land at Skagway, I'd be late getting into White-horse. As I return to the road, I pause to pick a pyrola loaded with blossoms, then add a horsetail and slip the cluster into my shirt pocket—my Dyea boutonniere.

Horsetails, unlike much of the foliage that surrounds us, are truly ancient plants. Having found a niche that suited them well, they've changed very little from their fossilized ancestors, saying, in effect, "We're fine as we are."

Charles Darwin might have been surprised at such behavior, which seems to dispute evolution. Such arguments, however, miss the point, for evolution doesn't demand anything, including change. It's just what happens when nature comes upon a more efficient way.

When Darwin boarded the *Beagle* in 1831, he was a strict cre-ationist who reckoned the age of the earth at around ten thousand years. Imagine, then, his turmoil when he realized that millions of years must have been required to shrink volcanic islands to coral atolls and to write of the detailed fossil record that supported the suddenly obvious process of evolution.

As I retrace my steps down the rain-forest path, I imagine a wide-eyed Darwin clambering over Canada's richly fossilized Burgess Shales or ascending from the Grand Canyon's mile-deep floor. In its depths he'd find ancient rocks devoid of life. A third of the way up, near the four-hundred-million-year-old limestones, he'd marvel as fossils appeared—first shells and worms, all of them aquatic and primitive, without backbones, then, higher up, vertebrate creatures like armored fish. Climbing toward the younger two-hundred-mil-lion-year-old strata, he'd encounter the mineralized remains of rep-tiles and air-breathing fish, advanced forms of the aquatic life he'd seen below. With great luck, he might come upon the remains of a dinosaur. But he wouldn't find fossilized mammals.

Unfortunately, even the upper levels of the Grand Canyon are too old to record the onset of mammalian life. For that, he'd have to find younger sedimentary rocks that time hasn't worn away. Were he so fortunate, he'd notice that dinosaurs disappeared from the fossil record some sixty-five million years ago and that humanoids arrived just two or three million years in the past.

Darwin, who was an excellent observer, might also notice a thin, odd-looking layer of clay near the last dinosaur fossils. Below that layer, dinosaurs and a large variety of tiny creatures called foraminifera thrived, but above it, all evidence of the dinosaurs disappeared, and only a single species of foraminifera survived.

In 1978, a U.S. physicist named Luis Alvarez and his geologist son Walter decided to have the clay analyzed. To their great surprise, they learned that the layer was rich in iridium, an element that's rare on earth but common in meteorites. When subsequent studies revealed that the off-white stratum occurred worldwide, they proposed that the band was composed of dust from a huge meteorite strike that altered the earth's climate enough to end the reign of the dinosaurs.

Darwin's *The Origin of Species...*, like the man himself, was so well-organized and logical that his conclusions struck most readers as self-evident. In *The Origin...*, Darwin demonstrated that reproduction, being imperfect, creates offspring with varying assets and liabilities. Those equipped with traits that prove advantageous to survival produce more offspring than those not so well equipped in a process he called "natural selection."

Fearing a storm of religious opposition, Darwin set his book aside for years, finally going public only when another scientist, Alfred Russell Wallace, contacted him with similar material that he planned to release. There, in 1859, the story should end, but it doesn't.

After sixteen years of ridicule and criticism from religious conservatives, Darwin answered back in a rather genial autobiography (to be published after his death) that included his personal beliefs. Speaking of his early years, Darwin confessed that "it never struck me how illogical it was to say that I believed in what I did not understand and what was in fact unintelligible," and concluded that "the Old Testament, from its manifestly false history of the world . . . was no more to be trusted than the sacred books of the Hindoos, or the beliefs of any barbarian."

Unfortunately, Darwin's devout wife censored his autobiography, and the public remained ignorant of his thoughts until seventy years later, when his granddaughter discovered the original manuscript and ordered his words restored.

When I return to the Cub, I scrub my newly found key in sparkling river water. Then, struck by the contrast between its nickel plating and the emerald green algae-coated pebbles, I lay the key in the shallows and bring my camera close to capture another memory.

The sun, muted by a raft of cirrus clouds, becomes a pale yellow moon while I examine my key and search for the stories it holds. Did it open the door to Meyer's Saloon or secure John Healy's goods? Did the soft hand of a dance-hall girl enfold it as she locked a Palace Hotel door against yet another night? Did it rest in the cleavage of a prostitute? If so, had she come to her occupation by choice or was it a last resort? As I admire its still-gleaming patina and catenary curves, I wonder, was this nickel-plated keeper of secrets hanging on a nail when the fire came, or did it fall from burning clothing as its owner fled the flames?

The wind that sped me to Dyea becomes a head wind as the Cub struggles back to Skagway. It's not likely that the wind has shifted enough to let me land, but I press on anyway, for I'd really like to spend the night in Skagway.

On Skagway's infamous White Pass, the longer but lower of the two rival routes, the cost of getting a man's gear across the mountains often included the life of a horse. The adventurous author Jack London wrote, "Horses died like mosquitoes in a first frost. . . . From Skagway to Bennett, they rotted in heaps." Fortunately, the White Pass and Yukon railroad (and the dwindling gold rush) brought the carnage to an end.

At White Pass, as on the Chilkoot, the Mounties admitted only those with enough supplies to last a year. Without help, a man might need three months to haul such an outfit over the pass. Worse yet, every time he returned to Skagway, the Klondiker faced a different sort of hazard—a corrupt city run by a crafty con man named Soapy Smith.

Jefferson Randolph Smith picked up the nickname "Soapy" in the gold fields of Colorado, where he ran a bunco game using bars of soap with a $20 bill tucked under the wrapper. A few accomplices bought the marked bars, then flaunted their "good luck." Soapy, on hearing of the Klondike gold rush, promptly headed north, predicting that he would become Skagway's mayor. He also became its dictator.

Operating first out of Clancy's Saloon and later from Jeff's Place, Soapy and his congenial con men employed a multitude of schemes to separate the greenhorns from their money. Need to send a message home? Mr. Smith had a telegraph office. Never mind that it had no wires, no lines to anywhere. Just pay $5 and come back later for your reply, which (of course) always arrived collect. Freshly composed in the back room by Soapy's swindlers, the reply always included a desperate plea: wire money.

At Soapy's saloons, card sharks and watered whiskey whittled away a stampeder's reserves. If an alert gambler withdrew, a few drugged drinks or a mugging would follow.

On one occasion Soapy's "agents" solicited $35,000 (perhaps $200,000 in today's funds) in Skagway's bars, gambling halls and bawdyhouses to build the new pastor a church. Soapy, with great show, turned the money over to the preacher, then had him robbed while he slept.

Soapy, who had bought off the law, reigned supreme while Skagway paid the price. Warned that the town had become a stinkhole of crime, hundreds of stampeders bypassed Skagway's eighty saloons and sailed on to a quieter Dyea. Finally, when a group of vigilantes sprang to life, Soapy's days were numbered.

Emboldened by their swelling ranks and a common cause (the return of $2,600 in gold dust stolen from a prospector) they moved against Soapy, who packed two pistols and a rifle, and went to meet his fate. In the ensuing face-off, a vigilante named Frank Reid shot

Soapy, who died on the spot. Unfortunately, Reid also received a fatal wound, and twelve days later followed Soapy to the grave.

The wind at Skagway has indeed shifted—for the worse. Some other year I'll visit the Trail of '98 Museum that I can see so well below. Perhaps I'll lunch at Red Onion Saloon, its lusty past neutered by a large neon *Pizza* sign in its window. The women of the Red Onion, which was once a bordello, designated their availability by placing dolls bearing their names on a downstairs rack—upright for available and supine for engaged.

Lifting the Cub's nose with power, I head up the Skagway River as the WP&Y tourist train pulls out of town. With the highway on one side and the railroad looping to and fro on the other, finding the White Pass town of Fraser is simple, and after a quick stop at Canadian Customs, the Tundra Cub charges into the sky and heads for the first flat stretch of the prospectors' highway, the shining expanse of Bennett Lake.

In the spring of 1898, at the height of the Klondike Gold Rush, a sea of white canvas tents overspread the shores of Bennett and Lindemann Lakes. There, thirty-thousand gold seekers hammered and lashed together seven thousand rafts and boats, using green lumber whipsawn from trees on nearby mountain slopes. Each bore a number assigned by the Mounties, who kept a corresponding list of passengers.

One of those boats was captained by Lars Gunderson, the organizer of the sixteen-man Monitor Gold Mining and Trading Company. Mostly Norwegian Minnesotans, they arrived at Dyea from Minneapolis on the last day of January 1898.

The Monitors, as they called themselves, had expected to have the Chilkoot behind them within two weeks. But despite their diligent labors, three weeks of constant toil found them only halfway up, and three more weeks would pass before the last of their outfit topped the pass. Two weeks later, as they hauled the final load into their Bennett Lake camp and began to build their boats, they learned of the Chilkoot avalanches and the loss of sixty lives.

When 150 boats disintegrated in the Yukon's Miles Canyon, the Mounties began turning back unseaworthy and undermanned boats. Women and children were ordered to portage the Five-Mile Canyon and to leave the boats again at Squaw and Whitehorse Rapids.

At the tiller of one square-sailed skiff stood Jack London, who, after boasting that he could "outpack any Indian," had shouldered his gear over Chilkoot Pass without assistance. Moving downriver with spring toward a single, almost fatal, winter in the Yukon, he sampled the river's indifference and the dramas that lined its shores.

The following year London left the Yukon without a single regret, his pack loaded not with gold but with books by Darwin and Milton. Having learned firsthand the meaning of cold and scurvy, he left the Klondike gold behind and wrote his way to fame.

The Monitors, after surviving Miles Canyon and Whitehorse Rapids, floated on to Dawson, where they scraped their claims down to bedrock. When pay dirt failed to appear, they staked more, then survived by working for other miners. In August 1899, the Monitors disbanded. Most of them returned to Minnesota, but Lars Gunderson, the group's organizer, stayed on and became the U.S. commissioner and recorder for mining in the Seward Peninsula. The reward for their trials was paid not in wealth but in lifelong friendships. Like Jack London, they never found more than pocket-change gold.

The Cub slips through Bennett Valley on air like liquid glass. On either side, five-thousand-foot peaks hewn concave by glaciers reach up to touch the sky. At Carcross (caribou crossing), the sun returns to highlight the Caribou Hotel, the home of Polly, an alcoholic parrot that had been taught to sing "Onward Christian Soldiers" and to respond to queries of "Polly want a cracker?" with "Go to hell!" (Polly's death occasioned a special burial in the Carcross cemetery, a trainload of mourners from Whitehorse and a monumental wake at the Caribou Hotel.)

Turning north at the "smallest desert in the world," the Carcross desert, the Cub follows an emerald green string of marl-bottomed lakes north to the Alaska Highway and Whitehorse, the capital of the Yukon Territory—population sixteen thousand.

The reservoir formed by the Northern Power Commission dam swallowed the foaming horsetails and whitewater manes that inspired "Whitehorse Rapids," the source of the city's name. A fish ladder climbs the dam's eastern flank. Switching back and forth like a mountain highway, it shepherds salmon past the final obstacle on their two-thousand-mile odyssey from the Bering Sea to the streams of the Chilkoot Range.

Although evading nets and fish traps seems enough of a challenge, today's salmon face industrial pollution and spawning beds fouled by Yukon miners who are exempt from the Fisheries Protection Act. Not surprisingly, environmentalists and Canada's beleaguered salmon industry argue that the exemption has given the miners a license to pollute.

In response to shortsighted policies that depleted the stock of Newfoundland's Grand Banks and left fifty thousand Canadians jobless, and to claims that Alaskan fisheries are harvesting too many Canadian-spawned salmon, the Canadian government loaded its ambassador to the U.S., Raymond Chrétien, aboard a destroyer in 1995 and sent him off to discuss the salmon problem with Alaska's governor, Tony Knowles. Despite the military overtones, the meeting was cordial, but no one had expected a solution, and none was reached.

A year later, Canadian fishermen blockaded and egged the Alaskan ferry *Taku*, when it arrived at Prince Rupert, B.C. In 1997, an even larger group prevented the *Malaspina* from leaving port for several days.

Despite the decline in the Oregon, Washington and Canadian salmon harvest, which was caused by dams and the clear-cutting of forests, a burgeoning Alaskan "crop" in the early nineties sent prices tumbling. The temporary abundance, however, was due not to nature but to the success of the Gastineau-like hatcheries and to multinational salmon farms that feed so many fish in pens that half of the salmon consumed today are raised like chickens—in captivity. In Alaska, however, salmon farms have been banned since 1990, partly because the surrounding waters become polluted with high levels of excrement. Fish farms, though temporarily successful, fail to address the real problem: a warming biosphere and too many mouths. Unless we curb appetites that are taking giant tuna to the brink of extinction, the now-declining Alaskan harvest is doomed to share the fate of Newfoundland's once Grand Banks and California's near-barren fisheries near Monterey.

Whenever humans and nature have come into conflict, nature has usually lost. Will the salmon be an exception, or will we play yet another reprise of "screw the owls, the frogs and the wetlands" by refusing to limit our numbers?

The Tundra Cub taxis past stands of sweet-stemmed fireweed, the Yukon's official flower, and drifts to a stop at the pumps of Tagish Air. While the Cub accepts its precious load, I chat with Andy Jensen, a college student bound for Dawson.

Fortunately, my trip's gone better than Andy's. Since leaving Fort St. John, he's had two flats, an alternator fail and a rock crack the windshield of his battered '82 Ford.

"Any chance of a ride to town?" I ask.

"Sure thing," he replies, as he extracts a bald tire from the passenger seat and jams it into the back. "Hop in."

Andy drops me off at the *Klondike II*, a 170-foot duplicate of the original *Klondike* sternwheeler that ran aground in '36. The *Klondike II*, the last paddlewheel boat of the British Yukon Navigation

Company, is now a Parks Canada museum, and I'm just in time for the tour. Within minutes, Rod, our genial full-bearded guide, invites a woman tourist to ring the *Klondike*'s gleaming brass bell to begin our landlocked tour.

Inside, Rod pauses beside a huge firebox door. "You," he says, pointing to a paunchy middle-aged man, "will be the fireman. By the time we reach Dawson, you're going to be in fantastic shape, because you're going to feed this boiler fifty cords of wood. And that's just a warm-up, because when we return against the current, we'll use 140."

On the *Klondike*'s second deck, an encompassing array of sunlit windows warm the wicker chairs and sofas of an attractive passenger lounge. Moving on, we enter a surprisingly elegant dining room that served the first-class passengers, whose cabins take up the rest of the deck.

On the third deck (this thing is huge) we find the captain's cabin, which is topped by a semicircular wheelhouse. As Rod demonstrates the engine room controls, he continues his spiel: "More than two hundred of these riverboats plied the Yukon before World War II. Each carried up to two hundred tons of cargo. But one by one they disappeared. Some were scrapped; a few were wrecked; others were left to rot.

"When the all-weather road to Dawson was finished in 1955, it snuffed out the last of their fires. Two of them, the *Casca* and the *Whitehorse* were hauled onshore right here in Whitehorse, and they'd still be there if the mayor's son and a few of his friends hadn't built a picnic fire on the *Casca*'s deck. When their fire got out of control, it took the *Whitehorse* with it."

The tour ends, and I head for the MacBride Museum, where, among exhibits of riverboat paraphernalia, I discover an old narrow-gauge locomotive that once chuffed up White Pass.

The Potbelly Restaurant (love that name) turns out to be deli-style, so I take my hunger to the hugely busy Talisman, where I wait twenty minutes for a table and another fifteen to order. The vegetable of the day is brussels sprouts—those yellow-green clumps of chlorophyll that should be fed only to convicted child molesters.

With my order finally accepted, I wait. Read paper. Ogle steaming platters of food destined for other diners. Reread menu. Speculate on the brown specks in the sugar dispenser. Level table with folded napkin. Food finally arrives. Damn fine sprouts. Hunger truly is the best sauce.

When a husky sixty-something man in an ill-fitting suit follows me to the register, I nod a greeting and ask, "You just passing through, like me, or do you live here?"

"I'm from Dawson," he replies, "but my son lives here. As soon as he's off work, we're hopping a plane to Las Vegas. Going to see the sights."

"I bet that'll set you back a couple of bucks!"

Smiling, he says, "Fortunately, money's not a problem. My wife and I had always planned to travel, but we never got around to it. A few years ago, she died, and now it's too late. Now, every day when I wake up, I wonder how I'm going to spend the money we saved. I don't want to make that mistake again, so now I take my kids."

Back at the seaplane base, a group of German tourists is having language problems with Bill, a local pilot who is trying to explain that he can't take them sight-seeing because he lacks a commercial license. Hampered by their limited English and his nonexistent German, Bill tries to explain that he'd like to but that by law he *can't*. With his point finally understood, the disappointed Germans head for their vans. As they depart, one of them mentions the Frantic Follies, a Gay Nineties stage show at the Westmark Hotel. I wonder what they'll make of *that*.

When I ask about a place to camp for the night, Bill purses his lips. "Well, lemme see," he says. "There's Fish Lake about twelve miles southwest. You'll find lots of grayling and a decent place to camp."

"That's great," I reply, "but I'm heading north, and I'd rather not backtrack."

"Gotcha," he says. "Thirty, thirty-five miles north of town there's a public campground on Fox Lake, just west of Lake Laberge—right next to the Dawson Highway. Just follow the Alaska to the Dawson Highway. When Laberge is on the right, Fox Lake'll be right on your nose."

As the Cub climbs away from Schwatka Lake, I scan the airport for the world's largest "windsock," a retired DC-3. Mounted on a huge pylon, the airliner still helps pilots make safe landings by pivoting into the wind, which, according to the forecast, is about to change. A deep low is moving in from the Gulf of Alaska. Fortunately, it's not due in Dawson for two more days, which is twice as long as I'll need.

A few miles north of Whitehorse, the Yukon River loops into Lake Laberge. There, when the cold breath of winter settles onto the lake's still water, ice forms more quickly than in the fast-flowing Yukon. And in the fall of 1900 the ice ensnared a steamer that was called the *Olive May*.

Hearing reports that the *Olive May* carried a miner dying from scurvy, a Dr. Sudgen hurried to the steamer but arrived a little too late. To dispose of the body, the resourceful Dr. Sudgen stoked up the *Olive May*'s firebox and used it as a crematorium. A few years later, a young Whitehorse bank clerk named Robert Service heard the story and promptly immortalized the steamer, the lake and the miner in "The Cremation of Sam McGee":

"... The Northern Lights have seen queer sights,
But the queerest they ever did see,
Was the night on the marge of Lake Labarge,
I cremated Sam McGee ...

In Service's poem, the *Olive May* became the *Alice May*, Laberge became Labarge, and the miner became a prospector bedeviled by the Yukon's cold. With the cremation supposedly finished, the miner's friends opened the firebox door. Inside sat a happy Sam, soaking up the heat. "Close the door," yelled Sam. "It's the first time I've been warm since leaving Tennessee."

As the Fox Lake sky turns crimson above the Miners' Range, I pour a steaming bowl of soup from my thermos, courtesy of the Talisman café. For dessert, it's fig bars and my last Mountain Dew. I should have bought more in Whitehorse. Oh well, I'll be in Dawson tomorrow.

13

Whitehorse to Fort Simpson, Northwest Territories

Three Laws of Thermodynamics:
You cannot win.
You cannot break even.
You must die to get out of the game.

– ANON

IT'S CLEAR TO THE SOUTH and east, but to the north, toward Dawson, rain clouds intrude. I reset the Cub's altimeter, which confirms the approaching low, then head for the derelict village of Lower Laberge, where the Cub rejoins the Yukon River.

When the Russians ascended the Yukon in the latter part of the seventeenth century, they used its Inuit name, the Kwikpak. But the Hudson's Bay Company, which arrived from the southeast, brought along its Athabascan name, the Youcon. The languages were different, but the meaning was the same—"big river."

From Laberge to Hootalingua, the Yukon twists through wind-polished canyons, hiding subsurface rocks that claimed twenty boats in a single day in the Rush of '98. In the notorious Thirty-Mile stretch, it loops so abruptly that sternwheelers winched their barges at an angle to the boat, then jackknifed their way through the turns. At Five Finger Rapids, Whitehorse-bound steamers had to winch themselves upstream with cables while their paddles churned the Yukon foam.

Split-up Island arrives. Legend says that here, incompatible Klondikers divided up their supplies and headed off on their own. One pair cut their boat in half, while another angry duo is reported to have sawed their only frying pan right down the middle.

The silt-laden Teslin River joins the Yukon near the abandoned RCMP post of Hootalingua, doubling its width. I'd planned to stop, but the decaying buildings persuade me to save the time for exploring a five-hundred-ton sternwheeler that's marooned downstream on Shipyard Island instead. Just when I begin to think I've missed it, I spot the sagging hulk atop an island not far from the western shore. She looks pretty good from bow to midships, but a giant has crushed her stern.

Skidding across gray-green Yukon water, the Tundra Cub noses into a dense stand of alders. The narrow trail that showed plainly from the air somehow eludes me, but after pushing through the alders, I'm soon standing beside the decaying sternwheeler that University of Wisconsin professor and author John Hildebrand described in *Reading the River*: "Its roof had slumped into the staterooms on the upper Texas deck and branches probed the pilot-house. The riverboat had been operated by two owners under different names, so *Norcom* had been painted above the water line on one side of the bow and *Evelyn* on the other—like a sailor with a tattoo for each romance."

Stepping carefully across her rotting deck, I explore the steamer's barren, half-lit interior. Strands of pale, sun-starved foliage struggle upward through breaks in her hull and quaking floor. Near midships, the scent of creosote spikes the humid air. Spotting a keyhole in an open door, I insert my Dyea key and give it a turn. The lock responds. How fitting—a skeleton key *should* work on a dead ship. Then, as I slowly enter the darkened, collapsing stern, the scent of a skunk turns me around.

Airborne again, I try to fly around the eastern edge of the advancing stratus. Ten miles pass, then twenty while the Cub cruises between peaks obscured by lowering clouds until I finally give up and turn east toward a brighter horizon and a town called Ross River. Dawson will have to wait.

At Ross River, the sun returns to highlight my skeleton key, which hangs, jittering, from the altimeter knob. Retrieving it, I turn it over in my hand. As the welcome sunlight slides along its shaft, I recall another sunny Ross River day that I'd just as soon have missed.

I'd been traveling with Stu Peel, one of the most gentlemanly traveling companions a man could want, and his son, Dan. Needing fuel, we decided to land on the river at the edge of the tiny town, where we'd fuel our Cubs with gas from a nearby station.

As Stu landed *downwind* and into the current of the swift flowing Pelly, I overflew the landing area, noting that the cables attached to the Canol Highway ferry ran straight up to pulleys near a suspended pipeline.

Seaplanes, with their long struts and tall floats, can nose over more easily than wheel aircraft during landing. Stu's Super Cub, with his 150-pound son on the rear seat and a pile of gear in the baggage, was considerably less prone to nosing over than my PA-11, which had little weight in the rear. Consequently, Stu had a good margin of safety when he landed *with* the wind and *into* the current to reach a sandy area just downstream from the ferry. After overflying the ferry to check the height of the cables again, I decided to fly upstream, turn around and land my Cub conventionally: into the wind and with the current. After landing, I'd just taxi under the pipeline to rejoin Stu and Dan.

Slowed by the head wind, the Tundra Cub settled gracefully onto the swift-flowing Pelly. Staying alert, I scanned the water for debris and obstructions while approaching the pipeline at fifteen mph, with about twelve mph provided by the Pelly's current and three by the Cub's idling engine.

I still don't know which I saw first—the thin, almost invisible second ferry cable hanging close to the water or Dan racing along the shore, frantically waving at me to turn around. As the rusty cable leaped into sight from its silty background, I stamped on the left rudder pedal and hit the throttle to hasten the turn.

As if trapped in a nightmare from which there was no escape, the Cub slowly began to turn in the suddenly molasseslike river, whose current, coupled with the Cub's beginning turn, hurried it toward the waiting cable. With the throttle and rudder pushed to the stops, I watched the woven steel approach. At fifty feet, the Cub, though turning, still drew closer to the snare. At thirty feet she finally began to point upstream. Two seconds from disaster, with her engine roaring and her propeller throwing spray across her shuddering tail, she finally held her own and snarled her way upstream.

Concentrating on staying in center stream, I pushed back images of my close call with disaster. Had I failed to see the cable or Dan's frantic signals, the river would have claimed the cable-ensnared Cub, riding up over her floats to pull her down. Had I been able to turn just ninety degrees before the cable rode up the sides of the float struts, she'd have gone under sideways. In either case, I'd have been scrambling out of the tumbling Cub and hoping to stay alive.

Minutes later, I soared above the pipeline, reversed course and followed Stu's example. For some reason, the seriousness of my close call hadn't sunk in by the time I nosed the Cub ashore. In fact, months passed before I really acknowledged how close I'd come to following the Cub through a slow and final roll beneath the river's swirls.

I dig out my Canada map and scan the country to the east. A few hundred miles away, on the Mackenzie River, I spot Fort Simpson. Now I'm more than pleased that I loaded extra fuel at Tagish Air. After crossing the Mackenzie Mountains, I'll intercept Canada's "Grand Canyon" of the South Nahanni River and land at Virginia Falls, a 315-foot-high spectacle that eclipses Niagara Falls. Perhaps I'll stop at Glacier Lake, a wilderness rival of Banff's Lake Louise, or, if the weather holds, camp beside a lovely beach at Little Doctor Lake.

The Cub climbs at full throttle toward the peaks of the Selwyn Range, where I cross the Continental Divide and return to the Northwest Territories. In dreamlike serenity, the Cub floats past 9,005-foot Mount Sir James MacBrien, soaring above sculpted snow fields as pristine as those of the Coastal Range until a glittering finger of water at Mount MacBrien's base finally slips into sight. I throttle back, letting the Cub slalom down to Glacier Lake, the crown jewel of the Ragged Range. S-turning through sweeping turns, the Cub and I descend through valley-cradled air.

As I coast to a stop beside a placid stream at the edge of a quiet beach, a stellar jay flits toward the mountain's vertical face. My eyes follow the jay, then climb six thousand feet of glistening rock to the pinnacles far above. At the foot of the mountain, a meadow bathes in sunlight, green and soft as a fantasy.

Spotting an odd-looking object protruding from the reeds, I remove my boots and socks, and wade through the frigid water toward what becomes a set of moose antlers. I'd love to take them home, but they'd never fit in the Cub, and they'd raise aerodynamic havoc if I strapped them to the floats. Still, I can't ignore such a find, so I haul the antlers back to camp and hoist them onto the Cub for a unique photograph. Backed by MacBrien's towering columns, the yellow Cub gleams at the edge of a sparkling stream, sporting a dark brown moose-antler hood ornament.

Although it's early, I decide to stay the night, so I stow my gear, push off into the stream and drift into Glacier Lake. I clip my church-key lure to the end of my line and send it flying. Something immediately strikes the lure, then shakes loose. Casting again, I retrieve my supper, a three-pound trout.

Immersed in mountain silence, I stand at the end of the float, trout in hand as a majestic array of snow-capped peaks spreads mirror images across the lake's opalescent green. At the head of the lake, the highest peak in the Territories guards the Cirque of the Unclimbables, an amphitheater of vertical faces that are sought by skilled climbers from around the world. Surrounded by such Macchu Picchu–like beauty, I understand why so many native Americans honored the land and rejected the white man's heaven.

An appallingly thin lynx walks into camp in the midst of my supper. Long-legged, with big feet and pointed Spock-like ears, the lynx strolls calmly past, not far from my hissing stove. It must be aware of me, but the scruffy animal hardly gives me a glance. Perhaps it had just passed through the depths of the endless ten-year-long boom-and-bust cycle of hare and lynx populations, and it isn't about to let pointless distractions sap its strength.

As mountain shadows creep across the valley, I grab a handful of dried apricots and head for the tent. When I pull back the netting, I notice a spider shuttling back and forth between the tent and a wild rosebush. With its outlining triangle already in place, the tiny eight-legged wonder links the sides with bracing, radial threads, then weaves concentric orbs. Fifteen minutes pass before the spider retreats to the edge of her web. Like the Ross River cable that reached for me, her imperceptible strands lie in wait for the careless, the hurried or the just plain unlucky.

It's cold. Without looking out of the tent, I know that Dawson's weather has caught up with me overnight. Vibrantly green just yesterday, the mountain slopes beyond the lake have been powder-sugared with snow.

While the Cub's engine warms, I plan my escape. Fortunately, the clouds are high enough to let me slip into the valley of the Slavey Indians' Nahedah—the "powerful river"—a much more appropriate name than the one on my map: the South Nahanni.

Unlike the Tundra Cub, which joins the Nahanni in its tranquil middle third, canoeists usually reach the headwaters of the river by car. After a long portage from the road to the Moose Ponds, they race through the Rock Gardens, a wild section of the Nahanni that drops one thousand feet in forty-four miles, providing what many say is the finest whitewater canoeing in Canada. Leaving the gardens behind, the exhausted river then winds through a broad valley, its slow descent revealed in looping curves and intertwining channels, briefly becoming a braided river, silted beige.

When the river's attained, I dig out my Park Use Permit, which allows me to land "at Rabbit Kettle Lake and Virginia Falls" and requests that I minimize "low-level flight over the river corridor or park features." Except for a brief river-scraping flight that I plan for Virginia Falls, I'll be pleased to honor their request.

The Cub flies itself through the still morning air while I search for Rabbit Kettle Hot Springs. Like Yellowstone's Mammoth Hot Springs, Rabbit Kettle's mineral-rich water drips from one rimstone pool to the next, building terraced tufa domes that rise well above the surrounding trees. The domes, already ten thousand years old, rise a tenth of an inch a year. And as the Cub orbits the highest terraces, lenslike pools gaze upward from the centers of the domes, their azure pupils staring into my camera as I circle round and round.

Before leaving Glacier Lake, I attached my camcorder to the Cub's wing strut just beyond the propwash, then covered it with a small plastic bag. Now, as the Cub approaches the billowing spray from the cascades that lead to the falls, I slow to seventy mph, trim the nose up a tad, open the window and slowly lower the door. Removing my seat belt, I stow my glasses, lock a foot beneath the seat, grasp a brace with my left hand and slide to the right until I'm sitting on the edge of the door frame. Slowly forcing my hand, arm and shoulder, then head and chest into the slipstream, I remove the bag and switch on the camcorder. Back inside, I replace my seat belt and glasses, and descend to within a few feet of the Powerful River.

The South Nahanni, a. k. a. the River of Gold, has as its prize nugget a massive limestone spire bisecting Virginia Falls. Aiming just to the right of the tall flat-topped pyramid, I flit above the tumult as the river smashes through the Sluice Box to explode into mist against house-size slabs of stone. When the Nahanni's roar overcomes the Cub's noisy engine, I find myself glancing at the tachometer to confirm that the Continental is still running.

The Cub darts between layered walls of limestone and shale, bobbing in turbulent air while the river gnaws at its banks and plucks evergreens from its slopes. When the Cub soars over the falls, I briefly shove the nose down to capture the plunging water on tape, then add full throttle to climb out of the deep and twisting gorge. Reversing course, I fly upstream and land, then aim the camcorder backward for a rear-facing view of the falls. After editing, the tape will begin with spectacular cascades rearing against the Nahanni's midstream monolith, then end with acres of free-falling foam plunging over the falls.

When the filming's done, I land and secure the Cub to an improvement acquired by the Nahanni's status as a World Heritage Site—a pier just above the falls. Years ago, with neither beach nor pier available, I'd been forced to leap into the opaque river with a rope tied to the Cub in one hand while grabbing for a branch with the other. Although I'd hoped that the river would be shallow so close to shore, I wet my ankles all the way up to my armpits.

Now, in addition to the dock and a helicopter pad, campsites with fireplaces nestle in spruce and tamarack groves. Where I once staggered down a slippery trail to the bottom of the falls, a boardwalk undulates through blueberry bushes, leaving visitors free to savor the Nahanni's sights and scents and sounds.

A mist begins to fall. As Sunblood Mountain, the vanguard of the Sombre Range, probes the clouds across the river, I head downstream with my rifle in hand in case of Mr. Grizz, then stop at an enameled Park Service plaque set well back from the canyon's rim. At the top of the plaque, a canoe load of voyageurs paddle across a map of Canada. The plaque reads:

> The South Nahanni is one of the world's great wild rivers. Its visitors are treated to a unique blend of scenic grandeur, wilderness adventure and solitude. Tumultuous rapids and meandering calm water have cut deeply into the Mackenzie Mountains, creating three towering canyons and Virginia Falls, twice the height of Niagara. Deep caves puncture the walls of First Canyon. Rabbit Kettle Hotsprings have built the highest tufa mounds in Canada. In recognition of this unique heritage, the South Nahanni River has been proclaimed a Canadian Heritage River.

Minutes later, I'm standing at the brink, watching fifty-foot spruce go tumbling over the falls. Far below, tree trunks trapped in the deluge spin round and round, their bark sluiced away by the pummeling river, their amber skeletons pirouetting in swirls of foam. It occurs to me that I wouldn't mind dying in such a place, but then an absurdity strikes me—I'd soon tire of the noise. Give me Glacier Lake instead.

As the Cub climbs away from the river, I look down at the falls, remembering the cascade-generated rainbows of other years that so colorfully portrayed the Nahanni's Jekyll-like nature. But as the mist turns to rain, it's the valley's grim history that brings to mind Mr. Hyde.

Since the turn of the century, at least twenty men have died within the Nahanni's confining walls. Some drowned near Pulpit Rock, a huge spire that towers above the whirlpools below the falls. Others perished in the Rapids That Runs Both Ways, while a few froze nugget hard on their winter traplines.

The ill prepared or unlucky starved. Two burned to death in their cabins. Others vanished into the depths of the Funeral Range.

One winter, when five poorly supplied prospectors began to starve, one man tied a stick of dynamite to his chest and touched it off. Two of the survivors tried to hike out and disappeared, leaving two behind to tell their tale. And though Death Lake denotes a fatal seaplane crash, the most colorful of the maudlin tales occurred in Deadman's Valley, a. k. a. Headless Valley, which is named for two brothers who actually lost their heads in a fruitless search for gold.

Frank and Willie McCleod entered the Nahanni valley in 1904, accompanied by a fellow Scot. When they failed to return, a search party led by their brother, Charlie, stumbled onto their decapitated bodies. Some say that the McCleods had been tied to trees. Their companion was never found.

One Nahanni trader, on receiving a friend's jubilant message that he'd finally discovered gold, hurried off toward the prospector's claim, where instead of gold, he found a burned-out shack and another headless corpse.

In 1927, a Minnesotan-turned-Canadian named Albert Faille probed the Nahanni to its source, becoming, over the years, a legend of the North. As Albert aged, he was succeeded by Gus Kraus, a trapper and prospector who'd been roaming the Nahanni for close to fifty years, building cabins at Little Doctor Lake and at a twenty-acre hot-spring-fed oasis beside the Nahanni River called Kraus Hot Springs.

Despite being so far north, much of the Nahanni Valley managed to escape the last ice age; below Virginia Falls, the canyon has been ice-free for a quarter million years. As a result, the canyon has retained the nearly vertical walls carved by the river's tongue.

With wind, rain and sun constantly picking at the Nahanni's cliffs, I wonder if the sound of the passing Cub might loosen a chip from its limestone lip, descending not in miles per hour but in millions of years per layer as it falls to the river below. In its brief plunge, would it transit layers of geological time that span ten million years? Forty million? More?

The Cub soars through the depths of Third and Second Canyons, then descends farther below the rim as I search for openings in the ribboned dolomite of First Canyon, the most spectacular of all. Here, waterfalls spring like magic from thousand-foot cliffs, for this is karst country, a soluble land of underground rivers, limestone pinnacles, sinkholes and caves.

The karst caverns may be realms of wonder to geologists, but they're deadly traps for Dall sheep: more than a hundred Dall sheep skeletons lie in Valerie Caves alone. Closed not for safety but to protect the caves themselves, Ice Gallery and the opalescent formations of Igloo Cave have been declared off-limits to all but official visitors.

Near the end of First Canyon lies George's Riffle, the understatement of the park whose bucking-bronco waves and rollers as high as corn shocks point the way downstream toward the Liard River, brighter skies and flat, uninspiring terrain. I'm tempted to continue east to the safety of good weather and mundane surroundings, but instead I turn north toward a lovely but distant campsite that I've used many times before. Rimmed with blueberries and yellow potentilla, the beach tugs at me from beyond the mountain-enveloping clouds.

As I leave the Nahanni behind and head up Fishtrap Creek, I write the time, one-fifteen, on my map, then measure the distance to Little Doctor. It's fifty-seven miles. If the weather holds, I should be taxiing up to the beach in thirty-five minutes.

Fifteen minutes pass as the ceilings slowly descend. Visibility drops to five miles. Mud Lake, the halfway point to Little Doctor finally falls behind. The Cub crosses the height of land and enters the broad Tetcela River valley as I press on amid memories of a wrecked aircraft that I'd once spotted just ten miles off to the west. Upon reporting the wreck at Fort Simpson, I was told that it was an "old crash site—nothing to worry about."

One-forty brings a lowering five-hundred-foot ceiling. Forward visibility, which is always reduced by prop-shattered rain, has dropped to two miles. To either side, it's three or four. Hemmed in by clouds above, by the Franklin Mountains on the left and the Nahanni Range on the right, I fly on, ready to return to Mud Lake if visibility drops to a mile.

I check my watch. Another minute gone and no lake in sight. Leaning forward in a mindless attempt to see better, I finger my skeleton key, then reach for the chart to compare its features to the convolutions of the Tetcela River. Surely two minutes have passed. I return to my watch. It's only forty seconds.

As the visibility drops, I think of Antoine de Saint-Exupéry. Lost at night over Egypt during an air race from Paris to Saigon, he descended through the darkness, searching for the lights of Cairo. Seeing nothing, he pressed his face against the window, tensely waiting for something, anything, to appear. "I was a man raking dead ashes, trying in vain to retrieve the flame of life in a hearth." He crashed—but survived.

Staying as high as possible, I scrape along the tattered underbelly of gray descending clouds. Another minute gone. Ceilings, 250 feet; visibility, two miles and shrinking. My hand complains, weary of crushing the stick in a snake-strangling grip. I change hands, then switch back, only to change again. Then, at one-forty-seven, thirty-two minutes after leaving the Nahanni, I see a light spot glowing through the mist. It's Little Doctor Lake.

Shaped like a round-nose arrowhead, the rain-stippled lake rams its tip through a three-thousand-foot cleft in the Nahanni Range toward a majestic beach. The Cub approaches tangent to the lake's curving lake shore, then slips between the treetops and taxis up to the beach.

Silence. Fresh from the tumult of Virginia Falls and the Cub's constant roar, I feel as if I've fallen into a feather bed. Under a nimbo-stratus blanket, the north country sleeps.

I hurriedly set up my tent, crushing spiderwebs bejeweled with mist. Later, with the flavor of vegetable beef soup still on my tongue and its heat comforting my body, I join the silence in sleep.

I awaken at six-thirty. It's still four hours until sunset, but the sky is almost dark. Only the steady hiss of rain assures me that the universe hasn't stopped. With my options reduced to reminiscing or reading, I turn again to Barbara Walker's revealing *Woman's Encyclopedia of Myths and Secrets*. An hour later, when the dwindling light censors my reading, it's still too early for sleep. Only memories remain.

When Wes Miller and I first arrived at Little Doctor, we had heard that Gus Kraus had built a tiny log cabin on the lake's western shore. However, since Gus spent most of his time in the Nahanni Valley, we were surprised to find not only Gus, but Mary, his Slavey Indian wife, and Mickey, their son. After introductions, I asked Gus how long he'd been roaming the Nahanni country.

"Maybe fifty years," he quietly replied as he hooked his thumbs in his broad suspenders, "except for a few months now and then in Fort Simpson."

Envisioning the long nights of the northern winters, I said, "I don't know if I'd be able handle a whole winter up here, but I might make it at those hot springs back in the canyon—if they're hot enough to make a difference."

"They are," replied Gus. "Even in January, the ground's warm enough to keep our cabin in the sixties. The snow across the river can be three feet deep, but we'll have bare ground outside. We only cut wood for cooking."

"How about gold?" I asked. "Did you ever find any gold?"

"No, I never did—but it's there. Someday they'll find it. Most likely a big outfit with a hired crew."

Then Wes said, "I've always wondered what it would be like to find gold. Not just a few flakes, you know, but some big chunks that would really add up."

"Me too," said Gus, as his weathered face stretched into a smile. "You want to know what I'd do if I stumbled onto a potful? Maybe get a new boat and motor." Then, with a sweep of his hand toward the Nahanni's peaks, he added, "But I'd never leave this."

That evening, as we watched the shadows creep up the sun-reddened Nahannis, Wes remembered Gus's suggestion that we use our binoculars to scan the range for sheep. Sitting on the beach, elbows on knees, he began the search. Within minutes, Wes said, "There they are."

Gus was right. Our ten-power binoculars easily transformed meaningless flecks into Dall sheep. And as the shadows climbed higher, we passed the binoculars back and forth, watching Dall sheep graze lofty meadows in the fading mountain light.

A few years after Wes died, the Tundra Cub again slid to a stop at the Little Doctor beach, this time accompanied by Ron Funk's Lake amphibian, a Piper Super Cruiser flown by Homer and Paul Bruggeman, and Stu Peel's Super Cub.

Earlier that day, as we crossed the rolling hills of Wood Buffalo Park, I'd radioed my companions, "Take a good look around, guys, and remember this when you're in the rest home!" Later, when someone complained that he was getting hungry, I urged him to fly another hundred miles, replying, "The weather's too good to quit. You can always eat, you know, but you can't fly in a rest home." Over the following hours, the rest-home line evolved into a standing joke as my companions listed additional delights we'd have to forgo when senility clipped our wings. That evening, we camped at Little Doctor Lake, ready to head for the mountains in the morning.

Daylight came. At five-thirty I looked out from my tent, saw no one and heard nothing but snores. Because we needed to get to Virginia Falls and back before the afternoon winds tied the mountain skies in knots, I noisily arose at six-thirty and began to prepare breakfast. When no one appeared, I yelled, "Come on, guys! You can sleep in the rest home!"

From inside one of the tents came the reply, "Not if you're around!"

Stu's packing philosophy and mine lie poles apart. Like John Hornby, I'm compulsive about traveling light. Do I really need this? Will A fit into B? As a result, I have less than Stu to carry, but I'm sometimes short on comfort.

Stu, on the other hand, packs all the refinements that I eschew. His cargo speaks of a wealthy trader, mine of an ascetic making do. Like Jonathon Jo's "wheelbarrow full of surprises," Stu's Super Cub seemed to me a cornucopia.

By the time we'd reached Little Doctor, I'd become accustomed to Stu's pulling his lawn chair up to his portable table beneath a sheltering tarp. Had he appeared in tails and addressed the evening's fillet with a glass of sauterne at his side, I wouldn't have been surprised. But that evening, Stu added yet another refinement, a tape player and a sampling of the classics. As a full moon climbed above the Nahanni Range, the soothing strains of Pachelbel's Canon in D rose above our campsite and wafted over the lake.

Thoughts of wine remind me of a treat in one of the floats—a twenty-five-ounce can of Foster's beer. With my Australian treasure in mind, I'd asked the Talisman's cook to hard-boil two eggs while I ate lunch. Then I sealed them in a plastic bag and stowed them away in a float compartment. Shaded by the wing and cooled by frigid lakes and rivers, my refrigerator-in-a-float works wonderfully well for up to several days.

I probe the darkness with my pocket flashlight. It's raining, but the drizzle doesn't dampen my passion for boiled eggs and beer, and after a quick dash to the shelter of the wing and back, I sit cross-legged, plate in lap, beneath a flashlight attached to the roof of the tent.

A tap or two on my knee and the eggs slip like wet ivory from within their shells. Before each bite, I touch them to a little mound of salt, though I know the extra salt will probably make my ears hiss, saying, I told you sssssso. One egg disappears, then the other, washed down with an abundance of beer. Twenty-five ounces, however, is more than I can manage, so I pour the excess out and enlarge the opening of the can with my pocket knife, knowing that during the night I'll need to return its contents. As barroom sages have observed from Nepal to Nairobi to Nome, "One doesn't purchase beer, one rents it."

Morning. Still raining. And *humid*. Visibility no more than a hundred feet. By ten o'clock, the fog has risen to fifty feet, but with the Cub's altimeter still unchanged, there'll be no flying today. Besides, I'd planned to stay for several days.

When the drizzle ends, I hike toward a stream that relieves Little Doctor Lake. I trudge along the beach, thinking about grayling until I come upon a string of bear tracks. Big as dinner plates, each print sports three-inch-long claws. Reversing course, I retrieve my Marlin rifle.

Before, I'd walked in silence. Now, I break into song, shattering the stillness with "Clementine," "The Beer Barrel Polka" and an occasional whistle. When I reach the river, I set the Marlin at the water's edge and toss my flip-top lure into its riffles.

The lure settles. I crank it in, then cast again and again. An hour later, I finally concede defeat and head back to camp, where I flip the lure fifty yards beyond the Cub's tail.

A fish shatters the surface with a twisting leap, stripping line from my reel as I walk along the beach to parallel its course. I'm sure it's a trout.

When the fish tires, I discover the largest grayling I've ever seen. Were it not for its sail-like russet-rimmed dorsal fin, its size alone might convince me that I'd found a new species. But it's definitely a grayling and, at over three pounds, a big one. Like all graylings, he wears the iridescent badge of his Arctic home, the aurora, but his colors seem to fade as I lift him from the lake. Were he smaller, he'd be my lunch. I let him go and opt for pancakes.

With coffee boiling and bacon sizzling on the stove, I dig out a container of mix, add water and a handful of blueberries, screw on the top and rhumba back and forth along the beach while shaking my batter like a James Bond martini. Fresh blueberry hot cakes, maple syrup, bacon and coffee. What a fantastic meal!

As I finish the dishes, a shower drives me back to my three-man tent, which really means two men if you plan to include any baggage. Rolling up my sleeping bag for a headrest, I finish Sagan's *Demon-Haunted World*.

Still raining. I sort through my gear while chuckling at myself for thinking that I, the proverbial rolling stone, could stay put for more than a day. I'm already becoming bored.

I lever the shells from the Marlin, insert a scrap of paper in the breech and sight through the barrel, pleased to see that the rifling's clean and sharp. Slipping my Bic pen into the Marlin's muzzle, I discover that Bic makes a .32 caliber pen, then drift into fantasy, envisioning a psycho writer using a pen-loaded pistol to dust off unfeeling reviewers who disdain his masterful works.

When the rain finally stops, I taxi to the base of the Nahanni Range. It's too wet for walking in the bush and, considering the bear tracks, maybe not too bright, but the lakeside edge of the rocky slope is almost brush-free.

Two weeks of flying have left me out of shape, so I take it easy. Even so, I soon puff to a stop. When I stretch out a hand to lean against a nearby pine, a blueberry squeezes from beneath its scaly bark. I check the other trees and find a scattering of berries. Something, perhaps a Canada or Stellar jay, has been stocking its winter larder.

Despite my complaining calves and quivering thighs, I delay resting until I reach the base of the clouds, which have risen some three hundred feet. Should I stop here, content to enjoy this gray yet marvelous view, or head farther up, perhaps high enough to break through the clouds into the pastures of the Dall sheep?

Since the Cub will be downhill and to the right when I return, I can't get lost, so I head into the clouds, taking care to angle away from the mountain's precipitous edge as I climb not so much into fog as into another world. As my vision is restricted, nearby evergreens leap into prominence. Every needle is sequined with dew. Spiderwebs sag, transformed by beads of moisture into strings of tiny seed pearls.

I climb for five minutes through the vaporous world, then stop to rest while my pulse pounds in my ears. How strange, I think, that the phenomenon that we call a "cloud" when we're outside of it, becomes "fog" when we're within. They're identical, of course, composed of billions of water droplets so fine that they float in billows. Then a new thought strikes me: Would radio-astronomy be the only possibility on a perpetually cloudy planet? What sort of eyes would evolve? How would we explain the seasons?

A flurry of sound upslope jerks me alert. Beginning as a rustle, it moves rapidly downhill, snapping twigs as it heads my way. Straining to see into the fog, I whirl around, thumb back the Marlin's hammer and point it toward the onrushing intruder. Crash! Thump! Splinter! Spotting motion in the mist, I raise my rifle as a boulder as big as a basketball comes barreling into view and bounces out of sight. I sigh with relief, then laugh out loud—I almost shot a rock.

The unseen rustling above continues, bringing visions of a busy wolverine or marmot. I consider climbing farther to see if I'm right, but I've had enough excitement. An hour later, in pouring rain, thunder rolls from peak to peak.

Toward evening, a lightening sky persuades me to build a fire. Since everything's soaked, I gather up a heap of wood, douse it with a cup or two of gasoline from the Cub, stand back and toss in a match. With an explosive *pow!*, the pile erupts into flame.

What a marvelous thing is fire. It lifts our sagging spirits, defeats the coldest morning and brightens flagstone skies. But the best fires are those that scent the air with the resinous vapors of pine, of tamarack or spruce. As if agreeing with me, my crackling blaze shoots off tiny rockets while it warms my face and paints shadows on the jackpine forest wall.

Too well rested to sleep and mesmerized by the dancing flames, I dredge up vivid camp stories of ravenous bears and narrow escapes, few of which probably happened.

My own encounters with bears include a hungry Yellowstone bear that climbed up onto my car, leaving a huge dent in the roof that I removed by lying on the back seat and pushing upward with my feet. Still, that's not the sort of bear that's on my mind. It's a young black bear that I shot a long, long time ago.

When I was sixteen, I bought a used 30-40 Krag, a relic of the Spanish-American War. That fall, when a bear came snooping around my parents' cabin, I ducked inside for the Krag. Then, after chambering a round with the rifle's unbelievably smooth, slick-sliding bolt, I slipped out the door.

The bear, some sixty yards distant and retreating, made the mistake of stopping when he heard the hinges squeal. Laying the sights on his chest, I touched the trigger. With a thunderous report, the rifle rammed my frame, digging its no-nonsense steel-plated stock into my bony shoulder.

The bullet caught the bear exactly where I'd aimed, throwing him, shrieking, ten feet into the brush. Still screaming like a human on a spit, he ran sixty feet and dropped. Rifle ready, I walked up to the gasping bear. Like Aldo Leopold, who, when young and "full of trigger itch," had watched the "fierce green fire" fade in a dying wolf's eyes, I was stunned. Accustomed to deer that obligingly fall without complaint, I'd expected a similar end. The bear's screams, however, stripped away my illusions and my isolation from the deed.

After peeling his hide from his suddenly gelatinous body, we sliced him into roasts and steaks. We ate the meat, but mine went down poorly. I sold the Krag. Tonight, sitting in my tent, as isolated as the last person on earth, I'm tempted to apologize like an Inuk, citing my need and respect. But, in truth, I was motivated only by "want" and, until the animal screamed had only felt indifference.

Fed up with bears, and prompted by a star glimmering through a tiny break in the overcast, I turn to a subject that surely must tantalize every lonely red-blooded male—Olbers' Paradox: If space is infinite and there are an infinite number of stars, as many propose, why is the night sky dark?

In 1823, Heinrich Olbers, a German physician and astronomer, reasoned that if space and the number of stars are infinite, the sky should blaze both day and night. However, as everyone knows, that simply isn't the case.

Scientists, philosophers and laymen offered solutions—most of them inferior to a theory that one gloomy American author proposed. In his *Eureka*, that writer suggested that the universe is still so young and the void so great that the light from the most distant stars has yet to reach us. Though we know him only as America's premier author of horror stories, Edgar Allan Poe's solution ranked with the best.

Later, others expanded on Poe, arguing that the unlimited but still empty universe surrounding the still-expanding star-filled universe within accounts for the paucity of starlight. Some postulated that in a fifteen billion-year-old-universe, many stars could have perished, leaving a void where once they gleamed.

What will happen, I ask myself, if a few billion years hence, our expanding universe slows to a halt, or, worse yet, begins to contract? As our skies brighten, what will we do with street lights, with headlights? What will become of the last drive-in movies? When the earth becomes a sauna, will our M&M's melt in our hands before they get to our mouths?

A shuffling sound wakens me—and it's definitely not a boulder. I quietly slip out of my sleeping bag, pull back the Marlin's hammer and point its barrel toward the approaching crackling. I expect the tent wall to bulge inward at any second, but the shuffling turns aside, then slowly moves away. I quietly slide to the front of the tent, ease it open and poke my head outside. Twenty feet away, a porcupine chews on a jack pine. I sag with relief.

"Hey, buddy!" I yell. "What are you doin', wakin' me up at this hour?" He examines me with his tiny black eyes.

Lowering the Marlin's hammer, I approach the porcupine and touch the rifle to his rear. Swat! His tail strikes out, scattering quills across the ground. I retrieve a few, then wrap them in duct tape—a gift for my grandchildren back home.

Preoccupied by the porcupine, I'm surprised to see clearing skies. Across the lake, the first sliver of a rising sun gilds the Nahanni Range as the last wisp of fog disappears and dew drips from the wings of the waiting Cub. Every bush is a liquid chandelier. Thousands of tiny spheres bejewel my tent. Unable to resist, I jar them into rivulets with a flick of my finger. Then, confronted with such a glorious day, I sail into a rendition of "Oh, What a Beautiful Morning..."

I glance at my watch. It's four o'clock! I could pack up and head for Simpson, but it's less than an hour away, and I'd end up sitting on the dock, waiting for the town to come to life. Besides, everything's wet.

Although I'm certain that my slumbers are done, I slip into my sleeping bag. As silhouetted beads of tent-wall dew coalesce before my eyes, I plunge back into sleep.

The Tundra Cub plows nose-high for a few seconds, then planes across the placid water of Little Doctor Lake. I lift one wing, letting the Cub skate along in a one-footed turn to follow the arc of the beach. The Cub breaks free, trailing tails of spray from floats and fuselage as it climbs into silken air.

Misty-eyed at leaving this Eden, I scan the lake, the forests and the surrounding peaks. Like a parting lover, I soak up every contour and curve and squeeze them into memory. Fifteen minutes later, the Nahanni Range lies miles behind, its bold peaks dwindling to dreams as they slowly disappear. After a third last look over my shoulder, I search the eastern horizon for a town by the name of Fort Simpson, just thirty minutes away.

Six

FORT SIMPSON
TO MINNESOTA

14

Fort Simpson to Coppermine, Nunavut

If a man would be alone, let him look at the stars.
— RALPH WALDO EMERSON

N 1804, THE HUDSON'S BAY COMPANY established the Fort of the Forks trading post on a long lens-shaped island near the junction of the Mackenzie and Liard Rivers. Renamed Fort Simpson in 1821, the town was until recently the end of the line for wheeled vehicles. But today, it's just a wayside stop, for the Mackenzie Road now follows the north-flowing river for another two hundred miles.

I tie up behind Simpson Air's multi-million-dollar twin turbo-prop Otter that's roped to the Mackenzie's riverside wharves. A flittering of dragonflies follows me to the top of the thirty-foot bank to search for a phone. Finding none, I return to the Cub and radio the airport, which relays my request for fuel. While I wait, the dragonflies patrol the riverbank, scooping mosquitoes out of the air as I contemplate the fates of two very different but related men who bore the name of Simpson. Both served the Hudson's Bay Company well, but one achieved wealth and acclaim, while the other died tragically, his character suspect.

As the winter of 1820 drew to a close, George Simpson, a polite, unprepossessing clerk at the Hudson's Bay Company post at Fort Chipewyan, could never have guessed that by year's end, thanks to his diligent work (and a lack of competition) he would have become Governor Simpson, the HBC's commander of all the North. Using tact, good sense and trust in his employees, the cherubic but demanding new governor promptly set out to ease old hatreds between the men of the just-wedded Hudson's Bay and North West Companies.

Simpson, by example and logic, persuaded former competitors who had even hunted each other to start anew. Aided by his excellent administrative skills and his open nature, Simpson would guide the Bay for close to forty years, a feat that earned him title of the Little Emperor, although never to his face. During Simpson's reign, and until the end of the nineteenth century, currency was virtually unknown in the North. Instead, the Bay used a barter system; one prime adult-size beaver pelt being the unit of trade—a practical solution that arose from the fact that in the beginning, the fur trade consisted almost exclusively of beaver pelts.

As other furs became popular, and a means of exchange based upon fractional values of a prime beaver pelt became necessary, the Company decided to "make a beaver" by establishing a smaller unit called a "Made Beaver" or MB. Near the close of the nineteenth century, one prime beaver pelt had a value of from ten to twelve MB. The standard in the lands farther north that lacked beavers was the pelt of a prime white fox.

After a trapper's pelts had been evaluated and their worth converted to an equivalent of Made Beaver, the trapper was paid with numbered disks made of ivory or shell or with quills (feathers or porcupine), depending on the post and availability. With these, he purchased whatever supplies he could afford, rarely leaving the post with any leftover MB, which, in most cases, could only be used at the issuing post. At various locations, "tokens" made of flat sticks, pieces of copper or lead embossed with the numeral 1 carried the value of one MB, but eventually, brass HBC tokens replaced them all.

Under this system, a large blanket might cost ten MB. Near the end of the nineteenth century, the same hatchet that Sears and Roebuck offered for 50 cents might cost one MB, and twelve could buy a rifle.

Guided by Simpson's frugal hand, Hudson's Bay stores remained cold long after stoves became available, for unheated stores saved money and were much less likely to burn. Furthermore, an unheated store not only discouraged loungers but also encouraged trapping. Damaged or worn-out boats were often burned to recover their nails, not so much as an economy measure but because nails were often in short supply.

Once relieved of the costs of competing with its old rival, the Bay quickly matured into an efficient, profitable company. During Simpson's time, dividends to shareholders always exceeded 10 percent, partly because the factors could charge whatever the traffic would bear, often exceeding the official Company rate of exchange by applying the "Factor's Standard." Simpson, who gradually turned the stodgy Bay into an upcoming giant, was knighted in 1841. He retired to a small town near Montreal, where he died in 1860.

Thomas Simpson, the governor's nephew, labored for the Company no less faithfully than his uncle, though often under miserable conditions. An excellent explorer and surveyor, Thomas canoed and backpacked the thousand difficult miles of Arctic coastline between Alaska's Point Barrow and Chantrey Inlet, twice enduring harrowing winters at a Great Bear Lake hovel called Fort Confidence. But instead of earning timely recognition that could have changed the course of his life, Thomas netted only a belated and useless reward.

After working faithfully for thirteen years, Simpson sought permission to explore the west coast of Baffin Island, a huge body of land lying well to the north of Quebec. The project carried his uncle's endorsement, but his repeated requests moved slowly through the London offices of the Bay.

Discouraged at the lack of response, Thomas in 1839 set out on a two-thousand-mile trek from the Arctic coast to Red River, a settlement near Winnipeg, Manitoba, where he hoped to receive a reply. Finding none, he snapped. With four companions, the embittered Simpson headed east for the nearest port. What happened next is still a source of debate. Within days, two of the five returned to Red River, where they claimed that Simpson had shot their two companions. The survivors fled, then retraced their steps after hearing another shot—and found Simpson dead.

If the survivors spoke the truth, Thomas Simpson died a murderer. If not, he was a tragic victim, murdered by those who returned to Red River, where, within days, a mail packet arrived. Within the packet, a letter addressed to Thomas Simpson approved his request and awarded him the Queen's Arctic medal with a life pension of £100 a year.

Coppermine, my next destination and the goal of Churchill's Samuel Hearne, lies five hundred miles to the north on an Arctic Ocean backwater called the Coronation Gulf. But today, I'll fly a dogleg course, first down the Mackenzie to Norman Wells, where I'll angle off to the northeast toward Coppermine.

When the Cub's finally fueled, I hike into town to Fat Daddy's Drive-In, where, undeterred, or perhaps spurred on by the diner's name, I pack it in. Outside again, I ask a native lounging against the building for directions to the Dene monument, only to have him slump to the ground. I'm about to call for help when I'm assailed by the smell of booze. (Just as the people whom we once called Eskimos prefer the word Inuit, the aboriginal natives of the northern provinces and the Territories have chosen the word Dene, meaning "the people.")

Fortunately, I've a pretty good idea where the monument is, and I'm soon standing before a low, platformlike marker that commemorates the 1975 gathering of the Indian Brotherhood. Here, three hundred delegates met to adopt the Dene Declaration: a demand for self-determination, world recognition as a distinct people, recognition of the Dene Nation and independence within Canada.

As I contemplate their goals, I consider the problems: in the Territories (where liquor consumption is 50 percent higher than in the provinces), the suicide rate for Inuit and Dene youths between fifteen and twenty-five is six times the national average.

The Cub overtakes a Northern Transport barge. Its decks are jammed with pipe, vehicles, crated snowmobiles, building supplies, appliances and construction equipment from Hay River, the three-hundred-mile-distant rail terminus on Great Slave Lake's southwestern shore. By the time the barge reaches saltwater at Tuktoyuktuk, she'll have been ten days en route. Pressing on through the foulest weather with the aid of GPS, navigation buoys and shore-mounted reflectors, this diesel-powered barge and its crew of three or four is a far cry from old sternwheelers like the SS *Mackenzie*, whose sixteen stokers fed her firebox a cord of wood an hour.

A deckhand waves. As I rock the Cub in reply, I hope that Canadians have learned a lesson from our sewering of the Mississippi, which we now labor to restore. Thirty minutes later, the river becomes Mackenzie's Disappointment River when it turns north at Camsell Bend.

Bored with flying down the wide superhighway, I make a torpedo run at Berry Island, then set my sights on McGern. McGern Island, being much larger than Berry, is more stubborn, absorbing five of my mental torpedoes before it slips beneath the waves. Then, as Jones Landing falls behind, I lower the nose and hurtle down the Mackenzie a few feet above the waves, seeking the thrill of low-level seaplane flying that the English adventurer Sir Francis Chichester described in *Ride on the Wind*: "I was only a foot or two above the water . . . The exhilaration of the flying stimulated and excited me til I felt half intoxicated with it. It was an almost incredible delight . . . and it left the once considered marvel of landplane flying as a dull old sow."

Cranking in a bit of nose-up trim as a safety measure, I counter the trim with a touch of forward pressure on the stick. (If I get distracted and release the stick, the nose-up trim will automatically cause the Cub to climb.) For twenty miles, the Cub roars along in ground effect just above the Mackenzie's face. Then, as the village of Wrigley appears on the horizon, my chart slips off my lap and disappears between the rudder pedals.

After climbing ten to fifteen feet, I duck my head beneath the panel and reach for the map, taking care not to push forward on the stick. It's quite a stretch, but within a few seconds my fingers close on the map. Just then, I spot a candy wrapper lying against the firewall and, in spite of warning myself to look around before I retrieve it, take a few extra seconds to get it within my grasp.

The Cub is a *light* airplane. Fully loaded, it weighs only thirteen hundred pounds. Shift just fifty pounds a few inches forward and her nose will begin to drop. And though I'm certain that I've cranked in enough trim to keep the nose up as I reach beneath the panel, I'm about to learn that I'm wrong.

As my head comes back above the panel and my hand returns to the stick, the Cub receives two almost simultaneous, staggering jolts as the keels of her floats slice into the Mackenzie at ninety miles per hour. Fortunately, I've just begun to pull back on the stick, and the Cub staggers skyward as I gasp in disbelief.

Fatalists might say that my time just wasn't up, but I credit the nose-up trim for flattening what could otherwise have been a fatal plunge. Without it, the Cub would have descended more steeply and flipped onto its back, like the Cessna of a Minnesota pilot who landed his seaplane with the nose too low. The aircraft flipped, ripping off the front four feet of both floats. The pilot died.

Although I'd known about that accident for many years, its lesson had never hit home. Now, as Wrigley slips past, I curse myself for a fool. Never again will I fly within fifty feet of *anything*, except when landing.

A few decades ago, events at Wrigley and several other northern villages prompted the bush pilot Mike Thomas to write scathingly about the government's entanglement with religion.

In an angry letter, Thomas told Yellowknife's *News of the North* how he'd been hired to fly children away from their homes to church-run schools in the Anglicans' *Norseman* while a friend, Buzz Gresl, flew for the Catholics.

"We'd fly into a settlement, park the plane, and when everybody came down to see the airplane, the Anglican hostel manager would start grabbing kids to take them off to school. Their parents didn't know what was going on.

"I'll never forget Fort Wrigley. . . . The priest and a nun were there grabbing kids and the Anglican guy was grabbing kids. . . . We flew back to Fort Simpson and we went back down the river again, grabbing kids. . . .

"I was back in Fort Wrigley at Christmas. I landed on the ice and this little lady came trudging down on snowshoes. She said 'Where did you take my kids?' She didn't know where her kids were from fall until Christmas. . . .

"Then I started having a better look at this. You see, the church-run schools were getting paid so much a head by the government for each kid they had in a hostel. It was a very competitive business."

Thomas's remarks brought an immediate response. "I got a visitor from Ottawa. He came right to Fort Simpson and he told me to mind my own business. I told him, 'Look, I'm not afraid of you. I don't work for the government. I'm not a Catholic, and I'm not an Anglican.'

"I never got another hour of flying from Northern Health; I never got another hour from Forestry. They completely grounded me. That was the way they worked in those days."

Before the Liard River was dammed, every flood carried a tangle of trees downstream to Fort Simpson, knitting branches and trunks into those contributed by the Nahanni. Reaching the Mackenzie, the aquatic "treeline" divided the big river into parallel halves for hundreds of miles—some say all the way to the ocean.

The first time I followed the waterborne ribbon of trees, a westerly wind had pushed it toward the river's eastern shore. But as Fort Norman approached, the linear snarl suddenly returned to center stream, moving *against* the wind. Puzzled at first, I soon spotted the driving force: the voluminous Great Bear River, the outflow of Great Bear Lake. When I finally left the Mackenzie at Norman Wells, I looked downriver, seeking the end of the backbone of trees. It wasn't in sight.

Expanding north along the Mackenzie River, the Hudson's Bay Company set up posts about every 150 miles, usually at the intersections of major waterways. At the junction of the Great Bear and Mackenzie Rivers, they established Fort Norman, a tiny community guarded by a hulking, spruce-topped headland. For a time, Fort Norman prospered, until the advent of barges and planes and the discovery of oil at Norman Wells, the next settlement downstream.

A few miles up the Great Bear River lies Fort Franklin, a tiny community named for the same captain who eventually led his crews to their deaths near Chantrey Inlet. After barely surviving his first trek to the coast in 1821, Franklin again headed north from Fort Simpson in 1825. (Governor Simpson noted that Franklin was "incompetent" and "ill-prepared.")

Franklin even recorded native warnings in his journal, included the words of Akaitcho: "However, if . . . you are determined to go, some of my young men will join the party, because it shall not be said that we permitted you to die alone." Ignoring Akaitcho, Franklin set off for the Arctic Ocean—and survived only because of native charity. Undaunted, he returned to England, where he re-equipped with a store of delights for his table, then set off to search for the North West Passage and disappeared.

While I clean the flattened mosquitoes and blackflies from my windshield, Pete, the fuel truck driver tells me that he's lived at Norman Wells for close to forty years.

"So when did they find oil?" I ask.

"Just before World War I," he replies. "The Imperial Oil Company built a small refinery for local needs, but they didn't develop the field until the beginning of World War II. By the end of the war, we were pumping close to a million gallons a day through that little three-inch Canol pipeline to the refinery at Whitehorse. But when the war ended they cut production 85 percent and shut the pipeline down."

"Wow, that's a huge drop."

"Yeah," says Pete. "But the pipeline really never worked very well, and it was too expensive to maintain. In the sixties, when demand for fuel increased along the Mackenzie, Imperial added another refinery, and now we pump more oil than during the war. A lot of it heads south through a new pipeline, but nothing goes through the Canol."

An aircraft drones past, followed shortly by two more.

"Are you always this busy?" I ask.

"Most of the time," he says. "Between the airport and the seaplane base, we log about three thousand flights a year. It's the oil, eh? Not bad for a town of a few hundred."

Heavy with extra fuel, the Cub departs for Coppermine. I'll be able to fine-tune my course as soon as I spot massive Great Bear Lake, so I just settle for a northeast heading. But when the lake finally appears, it's directly in front of the cowling, though it should be off to the right.

On checking my chart, I discover that the compass deviation has risen to forty degrees, ten more than at Juneau. Were I to fly above or in the clouds with a ten degree error, I'd miss Coppermine by at least seventy miles.

The Cub angles across Great Bear's northern shore, then crosses the Arctic Circle near a scattering of gasoline drums. Empty fifty-five-gallon barrels, the "Alaskan State Flower," litter much of the North, their red, yellow, blue and white carcasses left to rust whenever the cost of removing them exceeds their value. Canadians call them "arctic poppies," another of our additions to the flora of the North.

Some of the barrels are put to use: docks float on them. They prop up buildings, store water and turn doors or planks into tables. Cut in half, they become basins, barbecues or bathtubs and, when sliced at an angle, the core of a makeshift wheelbarrow. With their ends removed, they find use as well-casings and culverts, and what traveler hasn't seen the empty drum's most frequent application: the barrel stove.

A massive wall of stone appears on the horizon. Rolling over hill and valley like the Great Wall of China, the "wall" is some forty feet across and sixty feet high. Geologists call these formations "dikes" when they're vertical, and "sills" when they're not. Both form when molten rock forces its way through a rift in the earth. As time erodes the softer surrounding rocks, the harder intrusion resists, and the once-buried wall slowly "rises" above the plain.

I decide to follow the wall to its northern end. Ten miles pass, then twenty, with still no end in sight, so I turn east toward a fifty-mile scimitar of water that's known as Dismal Lakes. Surrounded by thousand-foot sunlit hills, the maligned lakes look positively inviting, and I'm tempted to stop and camp despite their depressing name.

Vilhjalmur Stefansson, the Canadian-born American explorer who advanced Arctic exploration by adopting Inuit ways, explored this area in the early 1900s. After living comfortably along the Arctic coastline and on the pack ice for a total of nine years (getting to read his obituary twice) he wrote in *The Friendly Arctic* how Dismal Lakes was named.

A young man by the name of Thomas Simpson had come direct from his home among the woods and hedges of England. . . . here for the first time in his life he was face to face with open country. He came to a lake about thirty miles long surrounded by hills of various form. There were trees at the east end, but he could only see them in the far distance. . . . He named it Dismal Lake. And in his book he goes nearly to the limits of the language in telling us how desolate and dreary, forlorn and forbidding, blasted and barren the country was.

Half a century later there grew up in England a man by the name of David Hanbury [the Hanbury River, with its caribou-devouring Dickson Canyon, bears his name]. . . . For one thing, he had purchased a ranch . . . in Wyoming. He was familiar with the prairie and even the uninhabited prairie. He had read Thomas Simpson's book and the adjectives had made enough impression on him so that when he approached he expected the place to live up to its name. . . . Perhaps partly as a reaction against Simpson, he goes to the other extreme and describes the lake as a wilderness paradise. I have lived a year in the vicinity of Dismal Lake and visited it both summer and winter, and I agree with Hanbury that a man who describes such a place as dismal, desolate and dreary is talking nothing of interest.

Though their beaches beckon, and their rapids promise grayling and char, I decide that Dismal Lakes are just too broad for my taste. I greatly prefer sheltered water, so I leave them behind and land on Elbow Lake, where I climb stiffly from the Cub and tail it onto the beach. Then, attracted by the sparkling ripples at my feet, I fill my hands with diamond-clear water and drink it down. Farther south, I wouldn't do this, but here there are no polluters, and certainly no beavers, which often dispense gut-wrenching giardia.

A sudden wail breaks the silence. Fifty yards away, a loon rides Elbow Lake. Drawing it close with my binoculars, I see it's an arctic loon. Neat and stately as his southern cousins, his body of gentleman's gray has vertical neck stripes of black and white, except for the front of his throat, which is spotlessly black. Unlike the common loon, which needs a long water run to become airborne, the arctic loon can lift off with a shorter, ducklike dash. His call, like his cousins', includes bursts of hysterical laughter and cries of deep despair.

When the ridge top behind my campsite beckons, I gather my binoculars, camera, rifle and a handful of Tootsie Rolls. The westerly breeze suggests I won't need a head net, but I take it anyway.

A narrow band of tussock grass separates the beach from my tent site, which is fleeced with arctic cotton. Spotting a cluster of yellow cinquefoil, I stoop to check their scent, only to find the knee-high brush teeming with wind-bound mosquitoes.

As I climb, my thoughts return to Stefansson, who walked these hills ninety years ago, having acquired an affinity for open country on the North Dakota plains and, as a friend noted, "an unabashed philosophy of eternal youth, complete with revolt and optimism." Combined with his logical mind, those characteristics almost guaranteed his success in the Arctic—a success that heightened his contempt for the British, whom Stefansson regarded as incompetent for having sacrificed so many lives while learning "next to nothing."

Stefansson reasoned that if the Inuit could survive for centuries with ingenuity and patience, those equipped with a rifle and the good sense to adopt their ways should fare at least as well. He also took a dim view of those who headed north in search of "adventure." Thus, when I think of my escapades, it's Stefansson who deflates me: "An adventure is a sign of incompetence."

Stefansson, despite being widely praised, refused to glorify his experiences, remarking that "everything you add to an explorer's heroism you have to subtract from his intelligence." Neither overly proud nor selfish, Stefansson took pains to share his moments of territorial discovery and promoted others' skills. Unlike Arctic explorers who shot their dogs to save weight and dog food on long trips, Stefansson loved his dogs. On the death of Lindy, his favorite, Stefansson wrote, "I lost my best friend in the world, whom I shall never forget."

Stefansson, always the optimist, saw great possibilities for the Canadian north. In 1922, recognizing the coming practicality of transpolar flights, he predicted, "It will be commonplace for Americans and Europeans to travel east by heading north. . . . We shall soon be booking passage from New York to Liverpool, or London to Tokyo . . . by plane in as matter-of-course a way as we now book passage by steamer."

Those who used the term "barren grounds" in Stefansson's presence seldom did so twice. In *The Friendly Arctic*, Stefansson wrote, "Barren Ground is a libelous name . . . better adapted to creating the impression that those who travel in the North are intrepid adventurers than it is for conveying to the reader a true picture of the country. If we want to be near the truth, we should rather follow Ernest Thompson Seton, who is so impressed with the grasslands of the North that he makes the expression, *The Arctic Prairies* the title of his book."

Stefansson scorned the way most hunters use binoculars: "The green man stands erect with his heels together, lifts the glasses jauntily to his eyes and spins slowly around on one heel. Then he announces that there is no game in sight.

"The experienced hunter . . . will lie down flat with his elbows on the ground. . . . There is never any pivoting or swinging motion as he brings the glasses to bear on successive fields of view. He examines one field thoroughly . . . then moves them so the second field overlaps the first. In calm weather . . . it takes about fifteen minutes for one good look around. . . . If, for instance, somewhere near the limit of the power of the glasses is seen a patch that may be a caribou, but which also may be a stone or wolf, it may take an hour of study to make sure."

Fortunately, the bald granite ridge holds no insects to harass me while I emulate Stefansson's methodical search for game. I lie down as instructed. Granite bites my elbows. Cushioning one with a handkerchief and the other with my head net, I stare for three minutes—motionless—then shift to the next field of view. Halfway through, my neck begins to hurt. I cheat by sitting with my elbows on my knees. A blurry butterfly flutters past, all of twenty feet away.

While searching the third field, my eyes begin to water. In the fourth, I find big game—a ground squirrel digging into a distant hillside. In the fifth, caribou antlers catch my eye, but on careful inspection become curved branches, dead and bleached. Discouraged and eye-weary, I rise and swivel like Stefansson's greenhorn and conclude there's "no game in sight."

On a whim, I raise the Marlin to my shoulder, aim at the center of Elbow Lake and squeeze the trigger. The rifle roars, rocketing a nearby well-camouflaged ptarmigan into flight. It's hard to say which of us is more surprised. I lever a new round into the chamber, lower the hammer and pick up the cartridge to savor the sharp but pleasant scent of spent powder. Bringing it to my lips, I blow across its rim, drawing forth a soft and sibilant *C*, then amble back to the Cub, picking poppies along the way.

Fed and soon to bed, I sit elbows on knees on the gently sloping beach with a fire at my side. Overhead, a blanket of cirrostratus clouds slips across the darkening sky to intercept the light of the thousands of stars that our unaided eyes can perceive. To circumvent my censored sight, I envision the Andromeda galaxy, which is said to be our twin, and I wonder whether on the beaches of distant worlds, are other life forms looking up and asking, "Is anybody out there?"

More than two thousand years ago, the Greek philosopher Metrodorus reasoned that "to consider the world the only populated world in infinite space is as absurd as to assert that in an entire field sown with millet, only one grain will grow." Epicurus agreed, as did Lucretius: "Nature is not unique to the visible world; we must have faith that in other regions of space there exist other earths inhabited by other people and animals."

Were Lucretius to return to us, he'd be pleased to find the scientific community firmly on his side, arguing that amino acids, the simple building blocks of life, are easily formed in the billions of galactic kitchens whose starry caldrons brim with primordial soups. In contrast, some fundamentalists embrace a doctrine of "just one earth, just for man." Really? And should pigeons believe that skyscrapers were assembled just for them?

Lucretius and I, being agreed that other life forms almost certainly exist, must respond to the question raised by the American nuclear physicist Enrico Fermi: "If there are others out there, then WHERE IS EVERYBODY?" I don't know, of course, and with Lucretius indisposed, I move on to a more easily answered question: Why don't we know?

In the first place, the distances between stars are so vast that even with fantastic speeds, the timetable for interstellar travel is reckoned in thousands of years.

Second, even if we try to communicate with other solar systems by radio, the time/distance problem is still enormous. Assume that the *nearest* star has planets. Assume that one of those planets shelters a technology equal to ours or better. Assume that their transceiver is aimed at our tiny portion of their sky and is scanning the frequencies we send their way. If *all* of this works, it would require at least ten years to send a message and receive a reply.

Warming to my subject, I conjure up Dr. Fermi and convince him that the odds of nearby celestial civilizations achieving technological parity at the same time as ours are not very good. Most other life-forms will either be primitive compared with our own or more advanced. The primitive society could not receive our signals, let alone reply.

As for the advanced civilization, Dr. Fermi suggests that we might have already been evaluated, using methods beyond our dreams. On observing that we still fight like children, they'd probably not return for several hundred years.

I offer a different approach: when we ask why others haven't contacted us, we assume that life on other worlds will evolve as it has on earth, producing beings with similar technologies. In so doing, we ignore the fact that with millions, perhaps billions of suitable planets to work with, the potential life-forms are limited only by time and the laws of physics. Perhaps there are *nonmaterialistic* intelligent beings out there that communicate among themselves, develop societies, loyalties and show compassion but lack technology.

Consider the whales and dolphins that we believe can communicate over great distances, or the societal patterns of the wolf pack and elephants that not only assist their injured but appear to grieve for their dead companions. Because communicating by radio with these creatures is not possible, does it mean they don't exist? Dr. Fermi, prompted by my mention of whales and elephants, might wryly add that if these great beasts can survive our brutality, they may yet evolve into creatures of brilliance and great sensitivity—and so may we.

Then, like Marley's Ghost of Christmas Past, another voice intrudes, and Lucretius appears. "There is yet another possibility," he says, "And a grim one it is."

"After a few million years of evolution, humans have developed technologies that can bring great comfort or destroy most of life on earth. Fail to use that energy wisely, and power-hungry primitives and fanatics who proclaim holy wars could snuff out our beacons of light when they've just begun to shine.

"Other worlds may well have evolved parallel technologies, broadcast for a few decades, then reaped the whirlwind and vanished into silence, only to begin again the long climb back from the stone age or beyond, if life survived at all."

Lucretius dims and vanishes. Fermi, too, is gone, leaving me to ponder what message I would send were I responsible for SETI, the Search for Extra-Terrestrial Intelligence. Relying on Lewis Thomas, American pediatrics professor and author of *Lives of a Cell*, I'd also use music: "perhaps the safest thing to do at the outset, if technology permits, is to send music." Though Thomas cast his vote for Bach, I'd send the soaring rhythms of Brahms's First Symphony or Tchaikovsky's disquieting "Pathétique" to probe the distant stars.

While tapping my breakfast toothbrush dry on a wing strut, I check the Cub's altimeter. My fair-weather high is moving on, but so will I. If it doesn't slip off too quickly, I just might remain within its embrace for several more sunlit days.

My chart says it's just fifty-six miles to Coppermine, but I call it seventy, for I plan to head east to the Coppermine River and then follow it north to the coast.

A sprinkling of lakes leads the Cub to an extension of the treeline that follows the Coppermine valley north from Great Bear Lake. As the valley steepens, the trees begin to lean tipsily downhill wherever the shallow tundra has slid across the underlying permafrost. Like signposts, they point the way to the Coppermine River, which I join at Sandstone Rapids, then follow its northward flow.

Near Escape Rapids, the river cuts through towering posts of black basalt; a hundred-foot waterfall plunges from the eastern rim, dissolving into mist; the trees disappear. And as the Coppermine expands into a four-mile-wide lake, I begin a long glide that will end at Bloody Fall.

By the time that Samuel Hearne, Matonabbee and his eight hard-working wives and packers finally reached the Coppermine River on their long trek from Churchill in 1771, they'd been joined by a party of Copper Indians. As the larger group passed Great Bear Lake and north along the Coppermine, Hearne began to suspect that the newcomers had come not to be helpful but to murder any Inuit they might encounter. Hearne took his concerns to Matonabbee, who convinced him that a protest or an attempt to leave the war party behind would mean their deaths. As each day carried them closer to the coast, Hearne, in rising turmoil, hoped that the river would end at a vacant beach, but that was not to be.

When they were just ten miles from the ocean, Copper scouts spotted five Inuit tents set beside some cascades. Near midnight, in the waning light of a long mid-July day, the Coppers attacked. Surprised and almost defenseless, the Inuit fought back as best they could.

A young woman ran to Hearne. "She fell down at my feet and twisted around my legs, so that it was with difficulty I could disengage myself from her dying gasps. Two Indian men were pursuing the unfortunate victim, and I solicited very hard for her life. The murderers . . . stuck both spears through her and transfixed her to the ground." More than twenty were slain that night, and the horror-struck Hearne named the site Bloody Fall.

The massacre over, the Indians destroyed the camp, feasted on arctic char and then joined Hearne to walk the last few miles to the ocean, where he claimed the coast for his employer, the Hudson's Bay Company. As for copper, only a single piece was discovered during their eleven-month trek back to Fort Prince of Wales.

I secure the Cub to the rocky shoreline just above the cascades. The air is thick with blackflies, so I slip on a head net, then grab my rod and head upstream over bedrock worn slippery smooth. On either side of the river, the tundra unrolls a blossom-flecked sea of green.

Because the arid Arctic receives about the same amount of precipitation each year as the Mojave Desert, tundra plants have evolved several moisture-conserving tricks. To compensate, saxifrages reduce transpiration with leathery leaves, while dwarf birch have developed evergreen leaves to save the energy required by a yearly renewal of growth.

Constrained by low temperatures and a short growing season, arctic plants fill every crevice that provides sufficient warmth, shelter and moisture. Poppies and Labrador tea increase their range by conserving heat and moisture with hairy stems. Others grow in tight, insulating clusters. Few bushes reach six feet, and then only in the shelter of a riverbank or some other feature that buries them in snow, where they escape winter's desiccating winds.

Animals have also evolved to cope with Arctic climes: the hollow hair of caribou and polar bears, superinsulating coats for musk oxen. Short legs and tiny ears help the arctic fox and musk oxen conserve heat, while willow ptarmigan have feathered their legs and feet to the very tips of their "toes."

A solitary sandpiper patrols the edge of a bay not far above the falls. Less than a hundred feet across, the bay's foam-streaked eddies are a perfect resting place for anadromous fish during their tiring upstream quest. I clip a red-and-white jig to my line, then toss the lure upstream while scanning the tundra for bears. At first, I crank rapidly to counter the river's flow, then slow when my lure meets the swirls.

Something hits the lure—a strike, or perhaps the jig bumping bottom. I cast again. This time, the jig is swallowed by Jaws himself. Line peels from my reel as I hustle along the shore, cranking in line during upstream runs and letting it run when he surges downstream. Suddenly, not twenty feet from shore, he leaps, tail wagging into the sky. It's an arctic char.

A few minutes later, eight pounds of orange-speckled crimson char lie exhausted at my feet. As the hook slides from its crescent jaw, his red belly prompts thoughts of the postmassacre feast held here at Bloody Fall, and I decide to set him free. I wade into the Coppermine and hold him upright until he leaves my supporting hand.

Keeping the windows open to blast away the blackflies, I take off for Coppermine. Within minutes, the rocky cliffs of the river's western shore dwindle, the eastern bank flattens into broad sandbars and the jadeite waters of the Coppermine River blend into the clear, salty water of the Coronation Gulf. A few miles seaward lie the Couper Islands and beyond them a continuous mass of ice.

Coppermine is playing ghost town. Although I look up one gravel street after another past rows of white, boxlike houses, there's not a soul in sight. No clothes flap on laundry lines; not a single four-wheeler whines. When I finally locate the store, it's closed, perhaps because it's lunchtime.

A forty-foot power-sailer has been hauled up onto the beach. Looking it over while I wait for Coppermine to come to life, I picture myself standing at the helm, dodging brash ice and bergy bits along the Arctic coast. As I'm about to wend my imaginary way into Cambridge Bay, someone says, "Hello."

Turning, I discover an Inuk woman with a child at her side. "Oh, hi," I answer. "I'd begun to wonder if the town was deserted. Where is everyone?"

"Oh, they're around," she says, with a casual wave that takes in land and sea.

"How about the store?" I ask.

"It's closed for the day," she replies. "But if you need gas, I can call the truck for you."

"Thanks, but I've plenty of fuel. However, I really should change the oil. If I leave a jug on the beach, will someone dispose of it?"

"Oh sure," she says. "The gas man will pick it up."

As we stroll along the beach, I turn our conversation to her child. "And how old is this little guy?

"He's almost three."

"May I take his picture?"

When she answers, "That's OK," the child beams with delight. With the easy confidence of a professional model, he sets his baby bottle upright in the hub of a large bronze boat propeller lying on the beach, then pulls back his rabbit-fur hood and smiles a benevolent smile. Neither forward nor self-conscious, he stands at ease in rubber boots, plaid pants and a dark green parka. As the shutter captures his serene smile and Oriental ancestry, I think of the next Dali Llama—someone destined to fame.

Two husky pups crawl out from beneath a nearby overturned boat. Cuddly and roly-poly, they're dying for attention. One is pure white, the other a mixture of white, tan and gray. I squat down to rub their bellies and scratch their ears as they try to climb my legs. "My wife would love one of these," I say, then discover that the woman and child have moved on down the beach.

Back at the Cub, I slip a short length of hose onto the oil reservoir's quick drain and snap it open. Four quarts of hot black oil stream into a plastic milk jug that I've brought along for just this purpose. When it slows, I snap the drain shut, remove the hose and add four quarts of oil.

As the Cub climbs away from Coppermine's empty streets, an odd thought strikes me. I'm really not serious, but I can't help thinking that if my ancestors had been massacred so close to home, I might be reclusive, too.

15

Coppermine to Yellowknife, Northwest Territories

*Is civilization progress?... the final answer will be given
not by our amassment of knowledge, or by the discoveries
of our science, or by the speed of our aircraft, but by
the effect our civilized activities have as a whole
upon the quality of our planet's life—the life of
plants and animals as well as that of men.*

— CHARLES LINDBERGH

I T'S BUMPY DOWN LOW, so I climb to smooth air
for the 150-mile flight to Port Radium. An hour
later, as the Coppermine River skirts the September Mountains, the massive blue gemstone called Great Bear Lake
peers over the horizon.

Great Bear is the world's seventh-largest lake, a ranking that includes the much larger Caspian Sea, which is really a lake, and the

once-great Aral Sea, which, because of Russia's diversion of its headwaters for irrigation, is rapidly disappearing. Despite being larger than Lake Erie, Lake Ontario and eight of our fifty states, Great Bear and Great Slave Lakes are almost unknown within the United States.

Two hours out of Coppermine, the Cub crosses Great Bear's stony shoulders, lands on Echo Bay and drifts to a stop beside a rocky point that might well have written the end to World War II.

In 1900, two years before Marie Curie finally succeeded in extracting radium from pitchblende, MacKenzie Bell and Charles Campbell were cruising the Great Bear shores, taking samples of the region's copper and silver ores and of some odd-looking ocher deposits that they'd never seen before. Bell returned to Ottawa, where he reported the find to his government employers, and there the matter lay until a prospector named Gilbert Labine chanced upon Bell's report.

In 1930, Labine headed for Great Bear Lake, where he confirmed the presence of silver. But more important, Labine realized that the yellow ore was pitchblende, the source of two radioactive elements—uranium and its close relative radium—which, once refined, would bring a spectacular $400,000 an ounce. Ignoring the silver, Labine attacked the pitchblende, and Port Radium found its name. Although Labine didn't know it, he'd broken a monopoly, for until the Great Bear discovery, the Belgian Congo had been the world's only source of pitchblende.

Lacking a refinery, Labine had one built on Lake Ontario. For every *gram* of radium produced by the refinery, more than a thousand tons of pitchblende were removed from galleries reaching far beneath Great Bear Lake. And then came World War II.

The Canadian government took over the mines and began to ship refined uranium to the Manhattan Project, which produced the atomic bomb. Today, rumors persist that it was Great Bear Lake uranium that fueled Little Boy, the bomb that leveled Hiroshima and brought an end to World War II.

When the pitchblende ran out in 1960, the owners shut the Port Radium down, believing that the less valuable silver could not be profitably mined. They could hardly have been more wrong.

In 1962, Echo Bay Mines leased the property. Sinking shafts more than a thousand feet deep, they found ore that assayed a whopping 70 percent silver, and Echo Bay Mines quickly became the world's largest silver producer. (In many silver-bearing ores, the value lies in the copper and tin, and the silver is just a by-product.)

A decade later, when Wes asked mine manager John Zigarlich what the drums being rolled into a waiting Otter contained, Zigarlich casually replied, "Just silver."

"Ohhhh . . . and what about security?" asked Wes.

"First of all," said Zigarlich, "you might call us a company town, although, as you've noticed, there isn't any town. In addition, we're pretty isolated, so security isn't a big concern. Except for rare tourists like you, those barrels get no more attention than a stack of bricks in Edmonton."

"What about winter?" I asked. "What the heck do you do for entertainment?"

"Well," said John, "we play cards and billiards, and there's the radio." Then, pointing to Echo Bay, he added, "But when this turns to ice, we curl."

Not knowing if we understood what curling was, John played it safe. "It's like shuffleboard, only we slide forty-pound stones along the ice and sweep like mad in front of them with brooms to alter their speed and trajectory. Up here, curling's our winter sport. Given half a chance, we fly to Yellowknife whenever there's a bonspiel."

"A bonspiel?"

"That's right," he said, "a curling tournament."

As I transfer fuel from floats to wings, a raven flaps to a landing atop the fuselage, then hops toward me. Eye-to-eye, I talk to a bird that many natives revere.

"What a handsome fellow you are. Would you like some bread for that strong beak of yours?"

He nods, and I duck into the Cub to retrieve my food supply. Within minutes, the raven consumes a slice of bread, an Oreo and a chunk of cheese, the last lifted carefully from my fingers, then watches me, tilting his head from side to side as I resume transferring fuel from bags to wings.

A truck pulls up, "Quite a bird you have here," I say to the driver.

"Sure is," he answers, "and he's not the only one. Place is full of them, and they're first-rate panhandlers. But watch it if he takes a dump on your wing, eh. That stuff will bleach your paint, so be sure you rinse it off."

Eyeballing the raven, I say, "Watch it, buster." He behaves. As the Cub leaves Port Radium behind and races south across the open, parklike forest below, I imagine exploring the country by snowmobile. Weaving gracefully between the widely spaced jack pine and spruce, I'd hardly have to slow down.

Near Indin Lake, a grayling haven about halfway to Yellowknife, I descend to within a few hundred feet of the maze of rivers and lakes. Perched on a midstream boulder in the Snare River, a bald eagle tears at a fish in its talons—an innocuous, natural act. Yet years ago, when I read that Tibetan eagles were served human dead, their skulls smashed by priests to grant the eagles easy access, and that Indian Parsees similarly supplied corpses to the vultures of the Towers of Silence, I initially took offense. How could they do such a thing, I thought. I no longer share that bias.

Have we not, with great ceremony, fed bodies to the worms and delivered our dead to the creatures of the sea? In what way is confinement to casket and vault superior to dissolution by eagles, insects or fire?

The aviator-author Antoine de Saint-Exupéry accepted the rightness of a natural, unembellished death. Having sustained life-threatening injuries many times, once nearly drowning and, on another occasion, almost perishing from thirst, he made peace with death and gave up on conventional religion, which he saw as a construct built to ease human fears. "There is no more death when one meets it," wrote Saint-Exupéry. "When the body breaks apart, the essential is revealed. Man is only a knot of relationships."

The Snare River eventually leads to an Indin Lake esker that ends at a west-facing beach, then climbs from the depths on the opposite shore to continue its sinuous trek. My campsite will be a raised strip of level ground at the edge of the esker, where two hardy dandelions quiver in the breeze. Glowing brightly, they confirm my southward progress.

I'm eager to cast for grayling, but I force myself to clean and organize the Cub's interior, which has again degraded since leaving Little Doctor Lake. That done, I clip a silvery spoon to the end of my line and stroll down the beach while enjoying my favorite hyperbole—that *up here* you can hang a hook on a bowling ball and still catch plenty of fish.

As the lure arcs out over Indin Lake, I consider how spoiled I've become, accustomed to fishing that is often little more than cast, retrieve, remove fish; cast, retrieve, remove fish. Thus, I'm not surprised when my spoon is taken by a lunch-size grayling as I begin my first retrieve.

While the grayling simmers on the Coleman, I load two rumpled slices of Whitehorse bread with marmalade and decide how to end my day. Do dishes. Read. Build a fire. Take a hike. But with the dishes done, I'm too antsy to read, so I begin to assemble a fire.

Although making a fire should be one of our most satisfying acts, it's become unremarkable for most of us—like breathing. For me, fire building's a heart- and hand-warming art. Without fail, a budding fire's first wisps of nostril-biting smoke liberate visions of our prehistoric ancestors worshipfully urging flames from flint-struck sparks. In the first tiny flames, I see images from Jack London's masterful story "To Build a Fire," in which a freezing trapper struggles to fend off death.

After scraping aside the earth's mossy coverlet, I begin with a few candy wrappers and paper scraps, then add a mesh of tinder-dry twigs and move on to thicker branches before gently capping the assembly with bone white driftwood. Were I farther south, I'd begin with nature's pungent-burning, waterproof paper—birch-bark.

In my pocket, I carry wax-coated wooden matches that can survive a dunking. Packed elsewhere are a flint, a propane cigarette lighter and a candle that can, with patience, ignite wet kindling. Triple O steel wool burns fast and hot. Given none of these, one might ignite gasoline with sparks struck from rocks or with almost any battery, its terminals bridged by a fine wire, which heats to incandescence, or with a camera lens to concentrate the heat of the sun.

I decide to try my widest diameter lens—a Tokina F2 80–200 mm telephoto. Opening it wide, I align the lens with the sun while adjusting its distance from a candy wrapper to concentrate the sunlight on a tiny, brilliant point.

A wisp of smoke appears, followed by a widening hole in the wrapper. Thin, glowing margins spread outward as the paper "burns," but not with an open flame. Laying a crumpled tissue on the smoldering wrapper, I gently blow across it. With a sudden puff, my fire bursts to life.

When the flames are well established, I wet the surrounding ground and stand a wide slab of rock at the fire's windward edge to foil the spark-carrying breeze. Then, with my camera and a little bug dope, I head for the crest of the esker that has formed my beautiful beach.

The esker's fifty-foot slopes are dappled with ground-hugging bearberry bushes and patches of caribou moss, but its well-worn crest has been denuded by thousands of migrating caribou. As I stroll above a sea of scattered treetops, a few blackflies dance in my wind shadow while the bug dope keeps them at bay.

How good it feels to be free from the confining Cub. I jog briefly, then settle into wide strides. Thirty minutes pass, and the esker finally ends as it began—at another beach, another lake.

Dropping onto the sun-warmed sand, I let my thoughts skip back through the years. I see an eight-year-old eagerly peddling sled-loads of homemade balsam Christmas wreaths. I recall a family friend who offered his mind-opening science fiction books to a bedridden fifteen-year-old to help him pass the time. I remember a college student who needed ten minutes to walk a single city block, impeded by a chronically collapsing lung that would require surgery just weeks before the blur of his final exams, his state and national board exams, his graduation, his wedding. I think of my wife and our marriage, once green, now mature. Finally, I remember my two sons, who mean so much to me, and things unsaid, undone. Suddenly lonely, I select a pristine stretch of sand and, with a slender wand of driftwood, inscribe my wife's name in sweeping script.

I stroll back to camp beneath a sky aglow with primrose light. Not far from the tent, I spot a skull-like dome protruding from the sandy soil. A touch confirms its bony nature, and a few finger scoops later, a human skull emerges. Probing further, I find no vertebrae, no ribs, no other bones.

If I'm to have company, my guest must have a name, and Yorick springs tritely to mind. Kneeling before the skull, I try to imagine its owner's past as Yorick evolves into Urok, then becomes Unok. A beretlike lichen decorates Unok's brow. Inches across, its maroon expanse testifies that Unok's skull has lain here for at least one hundred years.

"Unok," I softly inquire, "would you like to join me at one more campfire?" Hearing no response, I reverse our roles. Now Unok's the host and I'm the vacant skull. How would I respond to such an invitation? Yes, YES. Of course, YES!

With Unok's skull cradled in my hands, I return to the dwindling fire, add a few sticks of driftwood and blow its embers to life. Forcing a solid stick into the fireside tundra, I brace it with rock, then guide Unok's foramen magnum over the shaft so that his skull stands upright, supported on a spine of spruce. Beneath a purpling sky, Unok and I commune.

How many generations, how many millennia, have passed since our ancestral kinfolk shared a common fire, not knowing that some of their descendants would migrate north toward Scandinavia to become my ancestors, while others might eventually cross the Bering Strait to become native Americans, each to invent and refine stories of how the earth and the universe were born?

Some North American tribes tell of a muskrat that dove to the bottom of an eternal ocean and returned with a trace of mud; for others, a deep-diving loon retrieved the first lump of clay. Tahitians also created an aquatic myth, believing that their islands had been pulled from the ocean floor by gods. A hemisphere away, Sumerians claimed that the earth was formed from a clod of mud thrown by wrestling giants.

Letting my mind flow into the recesses of Unok's omniscient skull, I find an African tale to brighten the darkening sky: Bushmen tell of a lovely girl who dipped her hands into a fire and threw hot ashes into the sky to form the Milky Way. The sparks flew even farther, and now live on as stars.

As firelight flickers across Unok's brow and cheekbones, I have a brief qualm about moving his skull. As if in response, he fills my mind with a scene from ancient Egypt, where skeletons have been reverently seated beside feast tables as a reminder that the reward for life is death. "Live life while you can," whispers Unok. "Let judgment, not fear, be your guide."

With our fire reduced to embers, Unok and I search the darkening sky for a few of the thousands of meteors that plunge into our atmosphere every minute, escaping notice by day, and lighting tiny flares at night. As we watch, one spark after another streaks across the sky, adding tiny bits of mass to the earth in an accretion process that began billions of years ago.

When my neck cramps from looking upward, I lie back, cradle my head in my hands and smile. The northern sky has donned its luminous negligee of the night, the aurora borealis. Turning to Unok, I tilt him backward against a stabilizing mound of sand so he can enjoy the view.

Some of Unok's ancestors believed the aurora to be the spirits of dead elders playing with a walrus skull; others reversed the tale, allowing walrus spirits to toy with human heads. One Inuit group described an enormous wedding, with the guests arriving on glowing *komatiks* (sledges), and though some whistled to bring the aurora close, others whistled to hold it at bay. Point Barrow Inuit, believing that the numinous lights could attack with evil arms, kept their knives close at hand and threw dog excrement skyward to repel the ominous glow.

Finland's Sami warned their children that they'd be burned or turned to stone if they mocked the shifting lights, while in Norse mythology, the Vikings beheld a sky that mirrored Vulcan's forge. In their search for profits, Alaskan miners envisioned the glow of radium mines, while sixteenth-century explorers saw the reflections of polar ice.

In 1570, when an exceptional aurora illuminated central Europe, Bohemian scribes wrote that people were horrified: "No such gruesome spectacle had been seen or heard of within living memory." Fifteen hundred years earlier, when the lights lit Italian skies, the Roman senator Seneca reported that citizens rushed off to Ostia, expecting to find it in flames. (Seneca emphasized honor in ethics, science and philosophy, and rejected religion, saying, "Religion is regarded by the common people as true, by the wise as false and by the rulers as useful.")

Unok and I, however, see wavering curtains set aglow by the sun's charged-particle breath—the solar wind. Bestirred by the sun's exhalations, the earth's ionosphere blushes a palette-spanning array of nitrogen blues, hydrogen greens and oxygen yellows and reds. We also know that tonight's evanescent skies are only standard fare. Let the sun sneeze and its gusts can destroy communications, disrupt power transmission, induce electrical currents in the Alaskan pipeline, and, with ghostly humor, raise your garage's remote control door.

As the aurora flares above our evergreen-fringed amphitheater, I listen for the crackling sounds that so many claim to hear. But the skies have an antidote for eavesdroppers like me, and I soon succumb to sleep.

Later, awakened by the cooling night, I lift Unok from his wooden spine and, with the aid of my pocket flashlight, return him to his bed of flowers. When he's properly ensconced with his brow protruding from the sand and his lichen beret tilting jauntily to the south, I bid my friend good-night as the aurora borealis prances on through coal black skies.

Settling into my sleeping bag, I drift off to sleep. Far above, the aurora drapes the sky with curtains of shimmering light as the eyes of night follow skeins of migrating caribou, search the tundra for howling wolves and squint in puzzlement at a wilderness beach inscribed with the name Sally.

The western horizon bears popcorn clouds, but the sky overhead is clear. At my feet, scarlet-rimmed bearberry leaves proclaim that fall is on the way, and a glance at the Cub confirms what my hands already know: it's cold. The bushes sparkle with dew, but the Cub's easily cooled wings are white with dangerous frost. I'm unwilling to wait for the sun to melt it away, but I'm even more reluctant to take off with the innocent-looking frost, so I toss a few pails of Indin Lake onto the wings. Then, realizing that my wet hand might slip on the propeller, I dry my hands and the prop, for I don't want to repeat the mishap that crippled pilot J.

J. had run a bush operation for years, routinely hand-propping Cub-like planes to life and even larger aircraft whenever their batteries failed. After landing at a remote lake to cache a load of supplies, J. climbed into his Cessna and found his battery dead. Behind schedule and irritated at the delay, he scrambled onto the float and began to swing the prop.

My Cub, which produces 22.5 horsepower for each of its four cylinders, props fairly easily. But J.'s Cessna, which generates almost twice as much power per cylinder, required a muscular thrust. After propping the reluctant engine for a few minutes without success, J. began to tire. Frustrated, he gave the prop a mighty heave—and slipped—as the engine sprang to life.

The spinning prop severed his arm, sending blood spurting into the slipstream as he desperately clung to the plane. Climbing inside, he removed his belt and looped it around the bleeding stump, then pulled it tight with his teeth.

Knowing that he would die without help, J. poured on the power and flew back to his base, his teeth tugging on his life-saving belt while he fought the urge to faint. After making a passable landing, he ran the Cessna ashore, bringing help at a run. J. almost lost his life to impatience, but saved it with good sense and guts. And in so doing, he taught twitchy pilots like me a lesson: slow down.

Hindered by a southerly wind, the Cub drones toward a town that takes its name from the knives of the Copper Indians—Yellowknife. To the east of the capital of the Northwest Territories, lie millions of acres of tundra that are being "opened up" by prospectors seeking a new aurora: the reflections of garnets and diamonds, the mother lode of gems.

Unlike the prospectors of the Yellowknife Gold Rush of the thirties, today's geologists search not so much for gold as they do for kimberlite pipes—the remains of diamond-bearing volcanoes. Because kimberlite is softer than the surrounding rock, most of the surface ore has been scraped away by glaciers, leaving depressions that have turned into lakes. Thus, mining companies must either pump the lake dry when they find a pipe, a daunting project, or mine beneath them, which has hazards of its own.

After years of searching, a prospector named Charles Fipke realized that he'd have to head "upstream" toward the source of the glacial flows to find the origin of the diamond indicators that lay scattered across the Territories. Year by year, Fipke ranged farther east from the Mackenzie Mountains, discovering increasing numbers of "indicator stones" every few hundred miles.

By 1985, Fipke ran out of funds, and founded Dia-Met, selling stock for as little as 17 cents a share. That summer, while prospecting near Little Exeter Lake, Fipke took samples that fairly screamed of diamonds. Still, because he couldn't be sure of the pipe's location, he delayed staking (which would ensure a rush of competitors) until 1989, telling those who asked that he was searching for gold.

The following spring, Fipke hired a helicopter to speed up staking his claims. On the day that his money ran out, he landed beside a small oval lake. There, he found a tiny piece of chrome diopside, a kimberlitic mineral that usually disintegrates before it gets far from the pipe. Fipke promptly sold 51 percent of Dia-Met to Australia's Broken Hill Proprietary.

BHP began drilling immediately. One core yielded nearly a hundred small diamonds, many of gem quality, while later cores produced gems of even higher value. Within weeks, Fipke's find had attracted two hundred competitors, including De Beers Consolidated, which controls three-fourths of the world's diamonds.

Although the boom might be short-lived, its effects are bound to be huge. BHP alone proposes to spend $0.5 billion just to get into production. A single mineral analysis can cost $1,000, and the all-essential chopper goes for $700 an hour. In the long run, BHP expects to extract $25 billion of diamonds in twenty-five years while paying $2.5 billion in taxes. It's a gamble, too, for although kimberlite pipes exist in Africa, Australia and Siberia, until Fipke came along, not one major pipe had been found in North America.

Even so, Fipke's find is just one of a hundred pipes discovered to date. BHP owns twenty-five, including Misery, a misnamed pipe that's yielding a remarkable three carats a ton. As for Chuck Fipke, whose net worth has topped $400 million, he retained his well-worn pickup and shuns the trappings of wealth.

Development of the diamond fields is proceeding under tight scrutiny, as it should. In just one year, 8 percent of the area's grizzlies had already been shot by the expanding human population. As a result, many organizations, including the World Wildlife Fund, have asked the Canadian government to put BHP's permits on hold while the effects of development are evaluated. Once again, it's ecology versus economy. In the meantime, Yellowknife continues to live up to its Dogrib Indian name—"the money place."

Tuning my radio to 128.4 mhz, I listen to a recording of Yellow-knife's landing conditions, then switch to the tower frequency. While I wait for a break in the pilot-tower transmissions, I offer thanks to Hertz and Marconi, two scientists whose work led to radio, television, cellphones and my small but potent transceiver. Because of them, our words can travel thousands of miles, and we're no longer limited to sending notes, waving flags, flashing lights and yelling into tubes.

After receiving clearance to land at Back Bay, I scan the land below for the hull of a DC-3 that undershot the airport in the forties, and crashed onto the first tee of Yellowknife's primitive golf course. Yellowknife golfers, being resourceful and disinclined to waste, promptly converted the twin-engined airliner into their first club-house.

At the Spur fueling dock, I find a locked office and a sign saying, "Back at 2:00." At 3:15 a pickup rattles up. The driver is all smiles and no apologies. I top off the Cub with thirty-one gallons of fuel.

By the time I eat lunch and hike to a two-story wooden box called the Igloo Hotel, then shower and wash a few clothes, it's almost five. Having agreed to pay $118.15 Canadian to stay in the Igloo's plywood cubicle splendor, I decide to economize by walking uptown. Besides, if the cabs follow the Igloo's example, they'll be called Comfort Econo-Cabs, run on square wheels and charge $40 a mile.

That said, it's easy to like Yellowknife, especially old Yellow-knife, where a few Old Town shanties still bear tin cans nailed to their walls in which nasturtiums and marigolds bloom.

Spotting a granite dome topped by a stone obelisk, I briskly climb the stairs, then lean against the Bush Pilot's Memorial while drinking in the view. Here, from dawn to dusk, the skies reverberate the throaty roar of bush planes while the obelisk points a finger to the sky.

Located some six hundred miles north of Edmonton, Yellow-knife sprang to life in 1933 when C. J. Baker and Herb Dixon discovered veins of gold-bearing quartz, the Slavey Indians' "rock fat."

Baker, using innovative spelling to capture Dixon's exclamation over their find, named the site Quyta Lake. Then another strike followed on Yellowknife Bay, and the rush was on, taking the price of a room at the Corona Hotel to all of $1 a night. By 1938, the year that Yellowknife poured her first gold bar, the town had fifty-two bootleggers and seven houses of prostitution. One saloon, the House of Horrors, found its name when a miner noticed the legs of a patron who'd drunk his last protruding from a water barrel beside the front door.

Like any frontier city, Yellowknife has had its heroes, and among them, a former Minnesotan named Vic Ingraham personified grit. It was late in October 1933 when Vic's tugboat caught fire while heading for Port Radium. Vic dove into the engine room to rescue two men. Driven back by burning gasoline that cost him his boots, his socks and his mittens, Vic and his companion, Stewart Curry, abandoned the flaming tug in a tiny life raft intended just for one. Adrift for hours in subfreezing temperatures on a lake that never warms above thirty-five degrees, Vic suffered severe frostbite on his hands and feet. For eighteen days, the pair awaited rescue on Great Bear's frigid shores. When rescue finally came, Vic was flown first to the Aklavik hospital at the mouth of the Mackenzie River, where the first of many operations began, and then to Minneapolis, where doctors finished the surgeries that left Vic with stubs for six of his fingers and no legs below the knees. His Yellowknife friends provided him with a new set of legs, and he headed north again, working as an agent for a barge operator on Great Slave Lake. When gold was discovered at Yellowknife, Vic turned his back on barging to build its first hotel. A larger replacement followed, and then a third, the Yellowknife Hotel, which he managed for the rest of his life. As word of Vic's ordeal and his resilience spread at the end of World War II, his story found print in *The Reader's Digest*, giving hope to the many disabled returning home from the war.

By the end of the war, Yellowknife had a few miles of road. Fifteen years later, the "highway" from the south finally reached town, thanks to a long Mackenzie River ferry ride that's still required today.

During the sixties, the smaller mines shut down, leaving only the Con (Consolidated Mining and Smelting) and the Giant. When labor troubles culminated in a fatal explosion at the Giant, the desk clerk advised against an evening on the town. Heeding his advice, I confined myself to the Bush Pilot's Pub, where drinks are served on an aircraft-wing bar.

Designated the capital of the Northwest Territories in 1987, Yellowknife, then a town of only eight thousand, became the headquarters for a third of Canada. Now twice that population and growing, the capital boasts modern hotels, art galleries, fine restaurants, a Northern Heritage Centre to showcase the North's people, land and animals, and a $25 million legislature building with a round assembly chamber to inspire the consensus philosophy of government.

When I return to the Igloo Hotel, I tell the clerk that I'm surprised to see so few mosquitoes. "Is that normal?" I ask.

"Jeez, no," he replies. "It's been a dry year, eh? Most summers, it's almost as bad as camping in the bush."

"Oh . . . I thought you might have been spraying."

"Yeah, we tried that back in the eighties. The city funded a big drainage and pesticide program that was supposed to get rid of every mosquito within five miles of City Hall, but it flopped. When a wet summer came along, the bugs were as bad as ever."

He stops for a moment, smiling at a thought that he decides to share. "One old-timer who'd been living in a drafty log cabin even had to put up a tent in his living room so he could get some sleep. Then somebody introduced a referendum asking for more spraying. It won by a landslide, but the cost came close to a dollar a bug, so we gave it up. Better enjoy it, 'cause they'll be back next year."

Changing the subject, I ask a final question. "I understand why you have streets named for Hearne, Matonabbee and Franklin, but what about Ragged Ass Road?"

With the look of someone compelled to answer an oft-asked question, he replies, "It's named for a mining consortium, but beyond that, your guess is as good as mine."

Back in my room, I scan *The Yellowknifer* and *News North* to take the community's pulse. Unfortunately, it's a slow news day, and Yellowknife's pulse, when I find it, is weak and thready. Even the letters section, always one of my favorites, is surprisingly mild, containing only a complaint about barking dogs and off-road vehicles, but there's nothing about national policy, as if such matters were a planet away.

In the classified ads, however, I strike it rich:

Dog team for sale—malamute/husky cross with harness. Healthy. Moving—best offer. (My wife loves dogs. Wouldn't she be surprised!)

Proven silver claim. Write Pete at xxxxxxx. Bargain for quick cash or might take partner.

Wrecked Cessna 185, 60 mile from YLKF. $9,000 as is, where is. Call room xxx at the hospital.

Hoping to catch the news, I turn on the television just in time to see a presentation about Canada's immigration policy, which has been revised to slow the country's growth on a planet that already houses some six billion people, the last billion having been added in just twelve years! Smiling now, I recall my irritation at once seeing a CBC television clip of then Prime Minister Brian Mulroney distributing awards to mothers of twelve or more children in his home province of Quebec. On returning home, I learned that our diocese had once again given its "Mother of the Year" award to one of its more prolific women.

Though I'm years removed from the events, I still fume. Why not give awards to rabbits, to hamsters or termites? Are they not infinitely more prolific? Grumbling, I wonder what our planet will be like by the time we begin to present awards to parents of one or two children. What might it be like if we'd heeded Thomas Malthus instead of plunging on, using unforeseen advances in agriculture to paint his predictions wrong?

Both Darwin and Wallace gave Malthus credit for the idea that led to their theories of natural selection. According to Darwin, "In October 1838 I happened to read for amusement, Malthus on population, and being well prepared to appreciate the struggle for existence which everywhere goes on . . . it at once struck me that under these circumstances, favorable variations would tend to be preserved and un-favorable ones destroyed. The result of this would be the formation of a new species. Here then I had a theory by which to work." Malthus, in turn, credited the philosopher/scientist/statesman Benjamin Franklin with remarks about population and the food supply that Malthus would later mature.

Turning to U.S. news, I see a commentator reporting that the Christian Coalition has mounted a new push for government funding of religious schools and has expanded its crusade against gays. Smoldering now, I wish I'd never turned the TV on.

Stephen Coonts, former Vietnam pilot, and author of *Flight of the Intruder*, summarized my opinion of these zealots in a comment in *Cannibal Queen*: "Little people in little rooms in little places purport to tell us the eternal truths. People who don't understand the most basic laws of physics tell us with straight faces that they have mastered the incomprehensible. How could they know?"

16

Yellowknife to Stony Rapids, Saskatchewan

Wilderness is the one thing we can not build to order.
When our ciphers have choked out the last vestige of
the Unknown places, we cannot build new ones.

– ALDO LEOPOLD

I N THE LOG-WALLED Wildcat restaurant at the edge of the seaplane base, conversations focus on three related issues: forest fires, flying and the weather.

"Dry enough for you?"

"Hell, yes. Country hasn't been this thirsty since '88—or was it '89? Fires all over the place."

"Great year for business, eh?"

"You can say that again." (Charter operators do well during dry years by flying men and equipment to remote blazes.)

"Sid get back?"

"Yup—last night about ten. Says the Duncan Lake burn is still hot and there's a new one near Desperation Lake. Oh, yeah, there's a big one south of McDonald. He's flying two crews from Snowdrift to the McDonald burn today."

"That Sid—if we didn't have enough to keep us busy, he'd probably be tossing flares out the window right now." Laughter circles the table.

"Naw, Sid wouldn't do that," someone says, then adds, "not this year." More laughter.

Back Bay is mirror-perfect calm as the Cub rips across the smooth water and leaves its inverted image behind. I glance back over my shoulder at a taxiing Norseman, wishing now that I'd waited, for I love the throaty roar of radial engines. Unlike my diminutive Cub, the Norseman will shatter Back Bay's serenity, setting the pattern for yet another busy day.

Forty minutes pass. Far off to the north, a nuclear-bomb-like cloud billows up from the Duncan Lake burn, lifted high by an inferno hot enough to incinerate the tundra soil.

My destination is Utsingi Point, a long sliver of land at the tip of the Pethei Peninsula where I hope to find the stony remains of the organisms that brought to life all fish and fowl, all insects, reptiles and mammals. Called stromatolites, they're petrified colonies of blue-green algae, an early life-form that some two to three billion years ago began to produce oxygen in the shallows of our ancient seas.

An hour east of Yellowknife, I descend over Hearne Channel, turn north and follow Utsingi Point while searching its weathered limestone shore for stromatolite remains. Seeing nothing but elephant-skin-like rock, I descend even lower and skim the barren shore.

Finally, discouraged and unwilling to fly farther north, I land and taxi ashore. As I scan Utsingi's rippled surface for something to tie to, the scene suddenly snaps into focus. The entire shoreline is an exposed stromatolite reef! Expecting to see only isolated examples of the washtub-size colonies, I hadn't recognized the mottled mass of thousands as they passed beneath my wings. I'm surrounded by the petrified remains of the cells that breathed us into life, and filled with a sense of awe.

For aeons, the earth was a carbon-dioxide-rich oxygen-starved planet. But when early life-forms finally appeared, one of them, an algaelike organism called cyanobacteria, began to split water into hydrogen and oxygen by photosynthesis, then combined the hydrogen with carbon dioxide to make the forerunners of the carbohydrates that we enjoy today. In so doing, cyanobacteria changed the parameters of life on earth. Time passed, and as their numbers mushroomed, the cyanobacteria accumulated in colonial structures called stromatolites, which eventually formed the oceans' first biological reefs.

With an abundant supply of carbon dioxide and no competition, the thriving cyanobacteria soon became the ascendant life-form. Oxygen, the algae's "waste product," accumulated for ages, fueling an explosive evolution of oxyphilic organisms while simultaneously protecting them from ultraviolet radiation with a by-product called ozone, which we are now, to our peril, depleting.

Scientists now propose that many of the earth's iron deposits are the result of stromatolite activity: the cyanobacteria released oxygen into the ocean, which combined with dissolved iron, forming iron oxides that accumulated in the shallows. Thus, when prospectors discovered Minnesota's Mesabi Iron Range, they often found the ore beneath masses of unyielding, quartz-like rock, which they roundly cursed, unaware that it housed the remains of the algae that had laid down the ore that they prized. When the same Luis Alvarez who investigated the clay layer that marks the end of the dinosaur era thought to examine stromatolite sections with a microscope, we learned that these odd-looking rocks were formed from our humble precursors.

In the United States, fossilized reefs can be found on Lake Superior's northern shore, or in Wyoming's Medicine Bow Mountains. Fortunately, a few viable stromatolite colonies have survived. Some are actually thriving, the largest being located in Australia's Shark

Bay. Minnesota even hosts a few *living* colonies in the depths of its freshwater lakes, all of them spring fed, their locations kept secret to protect them from careless humans.

As I taxi away from Utsingi's rumpled shore, I recall reading that 99 percent of the earth's life-forms have already become extinct, and I'm immensely pleased that among the survivors are the simple algae colonies that brought us the breath of life.

Beneath an immaculate sky, the Tundra Cub slips past Redcliff Island's russet crags. And although the sky overhead is a great blue dome, far ahead, beyond the McDonald fault, the horizon is hidden in smoke.

Rutledge Lake looms through the smoky veil, but there are still no fires in sight. Rejuvenating myself with a candy bar, I push on as the visibility falls to eight miles, then six, then four while the smoke invades the cockpit. Though I'm miles from any fire, the scent bothers me, for no pilot relaxes when the cockpit smells of smoke.

I climb to four thousand feet, hoping to escape the acrid odor without losing sight of the earth, only to have it almost disappear behind a blanket of mahogany-tinted smoke. Dancing on the edge of instrument flight, which neither the Cub nor I are equipped to handle, I return to a thousand feet. With my nerves set a-jangle by the nostril-biting fumes, I cross the Talston River in two-mile visibility.

The earth's green face suddenly darkens. Burned just yesterday, or perhaps the day before, the forest lies in smoldering ashes. Blackened hills still flicker with orange fire where pitch-rich stumps burn on. Bouncing through a potholed sky, the Cub spans miles of blackened trees interspersed with water-lily-greened lakes. Like oases of color, they ride a pitch-black sea. Though they're widely scattered, clusters of still-verdant trees reveal a capricious fire that torched here, skipped there. I press on as, chart in my lap, I map a careful record of my progress. As I pencil in my track, sunlight gilds my skeleton key with brassy, smoke-obscured rays.

The Cub crosses a struggling, amoeba-shaped burn. Thwarted by nearby marshes, the fire has sent pseudopods flickering up the ridges in an attempt to pass them by. As the flames devour the wooded slopes, I see a cancer gnawing the forest's flesh—a very misleading vision, for when fire releases minerals from torched vegetation, it renews a forest. Flooded with a sudden wealth of calcium, phosphorus and magnesium, seemingly lifeless burns soon erupt with shoots of fireweed, jack pine and aspen.

The air suddenly calms, as if I've flown into the eye of a hurricane, but within minutes I'm once again dancing in the hot breath of nearby smoke-hidden fires.

Visibility abruptly lifts to five miles. Dead ahead, a twenty-mile fire front dances in flames where a sinuous blaze is torching its way upwind. In the swirling air downwind from the ridges, flames rush upward, exploding evergreens in an incandescent storm. On the windward slope, the blaze gnaws its way downhill, opposed by both gradient and wind.

The Cub punches through bubbles of fire-heated air, leaves the flames behind and returns to a forest pockmarked with the scars of older burns. When a long, slender lake beckons, I angle into the wind, land and taxi toward acres of charcoal gray turf and ebony stumps that look like a black-and-white photo of a World War I battle zone.

This isn't a recent burn. On fresh burns, each step lifts clouds of ash. But here, though the acrid odor of charred wood still tweaks my nose, wind and rain have tidied up, and the ashes are all but gone.

At my feet, aspen shoots proclaim a burn that's a month or more old. I walk inland through a scattering of inch-high ferns. At the base of a charred pine ahead, I spot a cluster of emerald greenery. Moving closer, I discover a wild rose with a gloriously healthy blossom that somehow escaped the flames and return to the Cub for my camera.

As the Nikon's shutter clicks, I'm struck by the absence of sound. No insect hums. No jays cry out, no ravens call. Here, with neither seeds nor berries, and very few insects, no bird will waste its time. In mid-August, a winterlike silence reigns. Still, like the ocean from which we arose, the lake remains a reservoir of life. Near its center, a common loon surfaces, fish in mouth, and with a toss of its head, gulps it down. Given time and moisture, the forest, too, will spring to life and rise like a phoenix from the ashes.

Heading south again, I follow the Tazin River toward a lake that bears the crème de la crème of northern campsites, which is a very high honor, given its many competitors. As the well-shaded moss-cushioned campsite passes below, I think of the first time that I saw this lovely spot.

The day was a hot one. By the time the Brugemmans' Super Cruiser and my Cub finally reached the Tazin River, I was flying with the windows open, with one arm resting on each sill like a kid in a narrow convertible. I'd been shedding my clothing for miles, carefully tucking each garment under my seat so they couldn't fly out a window. By the time we spotted the sandy point on the Tazin's eastern shore, I was down to nothing but shorts.

Baked by the full-bore incandescence of a midsummer sun that had lifted the temperature into the nineties, the Bruggemans soon followed my example as the three of us cast from the beach into deep Tazin water. Only northerns took our lures that day, and when I hooked a forty-incher, Homer and I stopped for photographs while Paul stripped down for a swim. When Paul emerged from the Tazin, I yelled, "Hey, Paul, hold this pike in front of yourself and I'll take your picture!" A shutter click later, my camera captured a dripping naked Paul behind a discreetly positioned pike.

With Paul's permission, when I present programs about my travels, I include slides of our picturesque campsite. Next comes under-wear-clad Homer, struggling to beach a thrashing pike, and laughter ripples through the crowd. When naked Paul appears, grinning above the fish, the audience roars.

I wait for the laughter to subside, then add, "According to my feeble and often inventive memory, I once asked Paul's wife what she thought of that photo. And though I'm no longer certain of her response, I like to think she replied, 'It's OK, but he could have used a smaller fish.'" And the audience roars again.

As the rolling Saskatchewan hills cup blue sapphire lakes in chaliced evergreen hands, the Cub nears Uranium City, a modern ghost town where, in the fifties, an entrepreneur named Gus Hawker greeted newcomers with cries of "stake your claim and make your fortune." Gus heeded his own advice, first becoming a store owner and then the president of his own mining company.

Uranium City boomed in response to the postwar demand for nuclear bombs and power plants, growing quickly into a town of ten thousand with a modern airport and first-class schools. But then priorities changed, and the mine shut down in '82. The town collapsed, leaving behind an empty city—no maple leaf flags, no laundry lines, no children, cars or dogs. Attracted to the barely used homes, entrepreneurs trucked a few to Lake Athabasca, then carted them over the frozen lake to begin life anew at Black Lake or Stony Rapids.

The Cub descends to a hundred feet and crosses Lake Athabasca. Along the lake's southern shore, submerged swirls of butterscotch sand break through the lake's frolicking surface, becoming sandbars fringed with foam. On the horizon, trees strangled by the Athabasca dunes reach for the sky like the masts of foundering ships.

A mile-wide lake at the edge of the dunes beckons, and I'm soon tying the Cub to a bone white spruce that's protruding from the lake's craterlike shoreline. But when I hoist a bag of fuel to the top of the wing and reach for the gas cap, it isn't there! I must have left it lying on top of the wing when I fueled in Yellowknife, an error I've made before. Fortunately, I used that tank first, so most of the fuel has been burned and not sucked overboard. Grumbling at my negligence, I empty the bag, dig out the duct tape and lay several overlapping strips across the opening, then poke a slit in the silvery patch with my pocket knife. (Fuel can't flow to the engine if air can't get into the tank.)

Although I leave the stove behind, getting my gear to the top of the shoreline dune takes three frustrating, back-sliding climbs. Then, with my camera and my ever-present compass clipped to my belt, I set out across the sand.

A hundred yards from camp, I stop to memorize the features surrounding my tent: the blank space with neither dunes nor trees that hints of the lake where the Cub awaits and a tall clump of spruce to the east. Another hundred yards later, I turn again. The tent has disappeared behind the dunes, but the landmarks remain.

The Athabasca dunes are interspersed with humps of low vegetation, little islands of struggling trees and patches of hard-packed clay. Around these islands weave ribbon-like dunes, breaking-wave dunes and dome-shaped dunes, not a one of them fifty feet high.

I've always liked sand dunes. Like ocean waves trapped in midcurl, they wait for the wind to shift their shapes. Beguiled by their herringbone patterns and graceful contours, I've spent hours photographing their endless array of curvaceous crests under deep blue contrasting skies.

Because deserts are not necessarily deserted, I scan each slope and probe every island of struggling vegetation but find only insects, and even they are scarce. The plants, however, intrigue me. Stunted pine and birch rise from patches of yellow-green tansy and feathery sand heather. I've read that the Athabasca dunes contain fifty rare plants, plus ten that grow nowhere else, so I'm not surprised to come upon plants that I've never seen before. In part because of this rarity, the dunes became a Provincial Wilderness Park in 1993.

I climb to the top of the nearest dune and stretch out along its crest. As I bake in my sandy surroundings, I can easily believe that just 1 percent of the earth's water is fresh, with 2 percent locked up as ice and the remainder salted away in the seas. Like Coleridge's Ancient Mariner, who found "water, water everywhere, nor any drop to drink," I, too, ride an undrinkable sea, but here no wave breaks, no albatross hangs from my neck and no gulls or cormorants cry.

When the silence grows heavy, I begin to retrace my steps, then veer west to cover new terrain. I pause at a cluster of sand-blasted spruce, where I discover an empty bird nest. Poking around, I find a tiny anthill and, a few yards away, some small animal tracks heading north toward ninety miles of barren shoreline. They look like house-cat tracks, too small for a young fox or a bobcat. But a house cat? Here?

Because I've left the Coleman in the Cub, supper becomes an eclectic mix from package and can: a sardine sandwich, a handful of raw carrots, dried apricots, a half-dozen cookies and a can of soda. That done, I retrieve *A Natural History of the Senses*, and, as the sun descends, build a fire from the forest's bones. Maturing, it crackles, emitting explosions of sparks as if to confirm her opinion that "a campfire wouldn't be as exciting if it were silent."

I try to imagine a silent campfire. Seeking the real thing, I stuff my fingers in my ears. She's right, of course. Though the resinous scents, the radiant warmth and the leaping sparks remain, it really isn't the same.

As I set up the tent, a faint rumble turns my head to the west. An advancing line of thunderstorms is about to obscure the setting sun behind burgeoning castles of white. The storms probably won't be severe, but I quickly double the lines to the Cub and seal the gas-tank cap slit with another strip of tape. Thinking ahead, I slap a second piece onto the windshield as a reminder to unseal the tank tomorrow.

Back at the tent, I lay several logs across the tent stakes and heap sand against the lower six inches to keep the wind from getting underneath, then I lean against a jack pine and survey the approaching storm.

Advancing along a two-hundred-mile front, mature male cumulonimbus storms containing a half-million tons of water are muscling their way into the stratosphere, where the subarctic jet drags cirruslike streamers downwind. Because of their flat-topped profile, and perhaps in memory of Thor, we call these lofty tops "anvils." I imagine Thor hammering out a lightning overture while his hair streams off to the east as the sky darkens and drumrolls of thunder rumble over the dunes.

The female thunderheads, not quite tall enough to reach the jet stream, wear beautifully rounded but treacherous curves. Hidden within those soft whipped cream contours lie tumultuous cores of power that can rival nuclear bombs. Fly into one of these mobile explosions, and like a hungry spider, it can pluck your wings and eat you for lunch. As for her five-mile-high teenagers, they'd probably maul you and then let you pass. No sensible pilot will test them, for the cumulonimbus crowd is a violent, dangerous clan.

The thunderheads draw close, preceded by a low, ominous-looking roll cloud—the leading edge of a cold front, the tsunami of the sky. Wedging low, the roll cloud shovels lighter dune-warmed air into the growing storms. Rammed aloft on 150 mph updrafts, its moisture condenses, releasing heat, which further expands the air. The storms rocket higher as shards of lightning arc from cloud to cloud, and the families begin to commune.

As the sooty roll cloud advances, not a single raindrop falls, and the air is eerily calm. A mile to the west, stump-legged torrents of rain march forward. Black as basalt and as solid-looking as posts, they press on, their paths illuminated by pulses of lightning hotter than the surface of the sun. Like fleeing animals, dust devils waver ahead of the storm, racing a wall of wind.

Bracing myself against the quivering jack pine, I capture the storms' explosive drama with my wide-angle lens. Self-lit by their own internal strobes, the towering clouds glow white, gray, gold and purple while the wind pelts my face with sand. As the Nikon seizes the flashing scene, goose bumps flare across my flesh and fire up my brain. Blinded by lightning, deafened by thunder and peppered by wind-driven sand, I revel in Ms. Ackerman's "sense-luscious" world.

As huge drops of water begin to punch craters in the sand, a flurry of lightning reveals a sky streaked with green, and green means hail. Like a rabbit fleeing to safety, I scramble into my tent between great gobs of rain. Within minutes, the sky's green promise is fulfilled when hail the size of pearls begins to fall. Fortunately, my springy tent can tolerate marble-size hail, as can the drumlike skin of the Cub, but golf-ball-size hail or larger could reduce the tent and the Cub to rags, and larger hail can kill. Were the Cub to be trashed and I survive, having hidden beneath my foam mattress and sleeping bag, I'd be forced to wait for Search and Rescue planes to find me when I failed to reach Stony Rapids.

As hail, the farmers' "white plague," bruises parched spruce and birch, I sit in my shuddering tent. The pounding increases, leading me to the edge of worry, and then abruptly stops.

Outside, the crunch of inch-deep hail accentuates my steps. The deluge has bleached the yellow dunes, leaving snow-white drifts behind. Bedraggled foliage dangles from tree and shrub. But the stones are small; the tent is fine, and the Cub's unscathed.

I scan the storm's receding bulk. White-topped, with salmon pink backs rising from bulging purple bases, they rumble off to the east like a colorful crowd of Michelin men set aglow by the setting sun.

17

Stony Rapids to Minnesota

There's no place like home.
– FRANK BAUM, *The Wizard of Oz.*

HE CUB SLIPS ACROSS the freshly scrubbed forest in smoky orange light while I wonder if more fires await to the east, spawned by yesterday's storms. An hour later, with neither storms nor fires in sight, I arrive at Stony Rapids, where two Beavers are tied to a pier on the south side of the Fond du Lac River.

As I approach the only opening at the pier, a forty-foot space between the aircraft, I throttle back just enough to keep the Cub dead in the water, its forward speed canceled by the river's steady flow. With a touch of right rudder I angle the Cub toward the dock. When the side of the float bumps the pier, I kill the engine, leap out and secure the Cub.

An hour later, brimfull of Athabasca Airways fuel and stuffed with eggs and pancakes, the Cub and I leave Stony Rapids behind. On one wing, the Cub wears a rusty gas cap retrieved from a derelict truck, its $15 price the penalty for being careless in a sellers' market.

Turning south, I meet the northward flowing Cree where it winds through the Black Lake flats as if worn out from stringing sapphire ponds between rapids of pearly foam. An hour later, when Cree Lake finally becomes a slit on the horizon, I reach for my camera to capture its sunlit islands, its azure shallows and beaches of golden straw. Like a miniature Athabasca, Cree Lake's curvaceous shoals convert the lake's blue-green depths to a multi-hued topographical map.

Lazing along at seventy mph, I evaluate each beach: is the water too shallow, likely to leave a seaplane grounded ten feet from shore? Is it too exposed, or tucked into a sheltering bay? Are there open spaces beyond the sand on which to pitch a tent? Then, with my map bearing fourteen new *S*'s, I turn southeast toward an aptly named Reindeer Lake village called Southend.

From Cree Lake to Southend, a thriving forest rides a washboard of north/south ridges and valleys. Between the crests, linear lakes and streams flow through glacier-plowed troughs. One after another, the grayling-rich waters of the Wheeler, Geikie, Thompson, Wathaman, Foster and Pink Rivers pass below, their parallel flows herded northward by the lush corrugations of a deeply grooved earth.

When the Cub is refreshed with Southend fuel, I lay out a course to Fort Paskoyak, which everyone calls the Pas—pronounced "paw." Later, as Sandy Bay falls behind, I pass the time by recalling films with great flying scenes—films like *Mother Lode, Always* and *The Empire of the Sun*—then move on to my flying dreams.

For as long as I can remember, I've dreamed that I could fly. As a child, my dreams began with floating just above the ground with effortless block-long strides. While others plugged away, I'd float gracefully from step to step, immune to all but a tiny part of the earth's pervasive pull. Half realizing that I was dreaming as I glided from jeté to jeté, I'd tell myself, This is so easy; I *must* remember how to do this when I return to the light of day.

As the years progressed, I soared higher, flying prone like Superman while holding a small board in my hands, which I'd angle to direct my flight to lands that no others have seen. There was always a slight sense of danger, should I lose my grip on the board, but I soared through the nights for year after year and never fell out of the sky.

The nickel mines of Flin Flon lie far behind; to my right is Cumberland House, the Hudson's Bay Company post established by Samuel Hearne in 1774. Hearne knew that the Bay's competitors (whom they mockingly called "pedlars") had a post on the Saskatchewan River at the Pas, so he sited Cumberland House forty miles upstream to intercept the fur-laden eastbound trappers and promised his men a two-pound bonus for every trapper they induced to switch to the Bay. Recruiting a "pedlar" brought a munificent hundred-pound sterling reward.

When the Pas finally slips into sight, I open a window and thrash around in my seat. I'm stiff and weary from hours of sitting, so I grasp the overhead tubing and slide up and down to awaken my body and brain.

At Beaver Air Service, I ask Raymond, a Métis, for a ride into town, where I buy him lunch. Over burgers and chips, Raymond reports that the Pas is about half white and half Cree and Métis. Employment, according to Raymond, depends on the pulp mill and on the railroad (now owned by a U.S. firm) which divides at the Pas, sending one branch north to Lynn Lake and the other northeast to the nickel mines at Thompson and then on to Churchill.

As I down the last of my milkshake, I ask Raymond if he knew a local pilot whom I'd met in '92.

I'd just finished fueling the Cub when a dozer operator throttled down his Cat and walked over to ask where I'd been. Half expecting the usual display of envy, I said that I'd just arrived from Baker Lake by way of Reliance, Fort Smith and Lac La Ronge. That day, however, I was in for a surprise. In response, my questioner mentioned that he'd also made a rather nice trip—just that spring, in fact.

"Really," I said. "Where'd you go?"

"To the north pole."

In a classic role reversal, I became the slack-jawed amateur and he the veteran.

Knowing that flying to the north *magnetic* pole would not be a difficult task, I asked, "Do you mean the north magnetic pole?"

"No," he replied, "I mean the *geographic* pole. During the winter, I installed extra tanks in my Super Cub, put on a pair of wheel-skis so I could land on runways, ice or snow, and set off for the pole in April." Telling of places like Resolute, Eureka and Alert, he reduced my wanderings to minor suburban tours.

When I ask Raymond if he'd heard about the flight, he draws a blank.

"Surely it made the papers?"

When he replies, "Not that I know of—it's news to me," I begin to wonder if the cat driver was only pulling my leg.

The Tundra Cub rises from Grace Lake's weedy face and heads toward Norway House, a sprawling settlement of about three thousand at the north end of Lake Winnipeg. For close to two centuries, yearly brigades of voyageurs fanned out from Norway House, laden with goods for fur trade posts lying far to the north and west. The York boats carried homesteaders to farmlands along the Red River, while the big canoes headed west toward a tiny settlement called Edmonton, now reaching for 700,000.

Those who remained at Norway House planted potatoes and set nets for fish, twenty thousand being taken at Norway House alone in 1861. With the first crisp days of fall, the tide would turn, bringing a flood of fur from the north and west to Norway House, then down the Nelson and the Hayes to York Factory. But as roads and rail marched westward from the East Coast, the need for Norway House waned. By the twentieth century, it was just another HBC outpost, its administrative role having been usurped by Winnipeg.

But Norway House hangs on. Its schools, hospital and homes somehow survived a plague of forest fires that hopscotched through town in 1989. In that year alone, eleven hundred fires incinerated more than nineteen hundred square miles of forest, a comeuppance, perhaps, for years of extinguishing every little blaze, which stockpiled wood for '89, the year of the megaburn.

Descending to one hundred feet to follow Lake Winnipeg's scalloped shoreline, I pass one lovely crescent-shaped beach after another, their arcs separated by linear lichen-dappled outcroppings that rise like humpbacked whales from the lake's algae-laden depths. These long, fingerlike reefs reach far out into the shallow lake, making small boat travel treacherous when the wind comes up.

At Poplar River, I turn inland toward a hidden treasure at the east end of Black Birch Lake where, sheltered by aspen and birch-shaded slopes, I've often pitched my tent at the side of a reed-rimmed beach. An hour later, ripples chatter beneath my floats, the Cub slows and I toss a lure out the door.

Just as I enter the reeds, I feel a twitch, a tug and a flurry of jerks. I let the Cub ground itself while I crank in line. A few minutes later, I'm knee-deep in Black Birch Lake, filleting a gold-flecked walleyed pike on one of the Cub's flat-topped floats.

While I dine, my eyes wander past the Tundra Cub to the forest. Warm and inviting, every bush, needle, leaf and branch glows with the marmalade shades of evening.

A Canada jay floats down to a nearby branch, announcing its presence with a soft coo. When I toss a bit of bread across the fire, the jay cocks its head, then glides down to accept my gift. Playing its traditional role as a traveler's companion, my "Whiskey Jack" listens to whatever tales I offer while he eyes me from beyond the flames.

The more lyrical Cree called my guest wiska-zhon-shish, which is variously translated as "the little one that works at the fire" or "he who comes to the fire." Trappers dropped the ending "shish" to arrive at Whiskey John, then Whiskey Jack.

As dusk descends, I hike down the beach to stretch my legs. Shifting a few yards inland for my return, I discover a long-dead campfire. At its side, the fading light illuminates a small mound of metal. Moving closer, I discover a heap of rusting leghold traps and a crumbling snarl of snares. Someone, perhaps a native, once padded his income and warmed his body with these now-useless tools. The animals paid with their lives, of course, but their loss never stilled the trapper's lament: when prices are low, who gets skinned worse, the fox or the trapper?

When I was young and eager to own all the things that fur could buy, I sided with the trapper. Since then I've seen enough needless killing to make me change my mind: an otherwise principled friend who liked to shoot prairie dogs just for fun; a teenager threatened by cancer whose last wish is to kill a grizzly bear and films of whalers spearing mother whales while their calves continue to suckle.

As I draw my sleeping bag around my shoulders, my mind, still entangled with traps and snares, scrolls back through the decades to a forest scene and a boy just barely ten. It's the night of the winter solstice, a time of deep cold and long northern Minnesota nights. Under a black sky glittering with the sparks of distant stars, the border country sleeps.

Inside a small cabin, a pale hand slips from beneath a stack of gray woolen blankets, then moves from side to side to sense the cold. The hand gropes for a pair of wire-rimmed glasses and, having found them, disappears beneath the covers. A moment later, the hand returns to retrieve wool socks, long underwear, melton pants and a wool-flannel shirt. Beneath the blankets, the occupant curls himself around the clothing, preheating the layers that will have to keep him warm.

A clock strikes seven times. Poking his head from beneath the covers, the boy turns toward a window. Seven o'clock and still dark. He considers staying in bed a little longer. I'll wait for the sun, he thinks, but thoughts of his trapline widen his eyes.

He quickly pulls on his clothes, hurrying not so much because of the waiting riches, but to pile on the layers before they cool. As he turns to leave the room, he runs a finger down the frost-feathered window, carving a furrow a quarter-inch deep.

In the darkened living room, a wood burner smiles toothily through rectangular inlets beneath its cast-iron door. Feed me, it pleads. Quietly (his parents are still sleeping) he lays a few pieces of well split cedar on the coals, then blows across the radiant bed. The oily cedar bursts into flames. Birch follows, and the woodburner springs to life.

His boots, still warm from a night near the fire, exude the tarry aroma of Nor-V-gen boot grease. Bending over, the boy laces rawhide thongs through their tall ladders of hooks, then touches the pouch on the side of his boot to be sure that his pocket knife's there. He struggles into a jacket that was loose two years ago, fit last year but now grows tight. Pulling on a woolen cap, he lowers the earflaps, tugs a pair of leather choppers over wool mittens and quietly slips out the door.

Cold, dry air pinches his nostrils; the metal frames of his glasses bite into his nose and temples. Far out on the lake, a snow-muffled rumble ruptures the silence as the lake's lens of shore-fast ice contracts, shrinking from the cold until it cracks with the sound of distant thunder.

Guided by the feeble light of a dying aurora, the boy picks his way along a cement-hard trail. Squeaaach, squeaaach, squeaaach—his boots wrench protests from the bone-dry snow as he envisions the bicycle that a few more rabbits will buy—a red-and-white Schwinn with a battery-powered horn and headlight, two rearview mirrors and tasseled handle grips. The boy pauses beside a rock-hard brook to marvel at the change a few months can bring, then heads for a cluster of towering cedars that mark his first trap.

The leghold trap is empty. He carefully walks around it to admit the meager light of the purpling predawn sky. The trap is set correctly, but nothing has come this way.

The boy has but one leghold trap. All the rest are snares—supple braided-wire nooses that hang suspended just a few inches over the trail. A passing rabbit, accustomed to pushing its way through twigs and brush, feels nothing unusual until the noose draws tight around its neck. In the boy's mind, the rabbit dies quickly, aided by the numbing, merciful cold.

His first snare hangs as he'd set it—a perfect circle, a zero, a delicately frosted cipher hovering over the trail. Dropping to his knees to examine the pathway, he finds no tracks on its crystalline face.

The second sparkling loop reminds him of his mother's rhinestone choker. "Choker," he thinks, then retreats from the word with a twinge of regret.

When he finds his third snare empty, his dreams of a bicycle slowly begin to fade. He moves on, repeatedly wiping his dripping nose on the back of his choppers. Paralyzed by the subzero cold, the fine hairs that line his nostrils can no longer sweep back the flow, and the leather slowly hardens beneath a film of mucus ice.

The boy pushes his way through an alder thicket and carefully approaches his fourth snare. There, centered in the trail lies the largest rabbit he's ever seen, curled up as if sleeping—frozen solid. Slipping his knife from his boot, the boy slides the blade beneath the noose and pries it open. After ascertaining that the snare is still securely tied to it's heavy, club-like stick, he resets the snare, drops the rabbit into a burlap bag and heads for a pine-fringed bog. The sky, now indigo, dyes the snow the deepest blue.

As he nears the edge of the cranberry bog, something moves. He stops, motionless, scanning the trail. A rabbit materializes. Blue-white on blue-white, the rabbit is almost invisible in the slowly maturing light. The boy waits, hardly daring to breath, not knowing what to do. A minute passes. His unmoving feet protest the cold. Still he waits. A shiver runs down his body, and the rabbit races off down the trail—into a waiting snare.

Yanked off its feet, the rabbit tumbles, then dashes blindly back and forth, jerking against the drag as the noose tightens round its neck. The boy stands transfixed. It won't take long, he reassures himself as his eyes widen in disbelief at the animal's extraordinary gyrations.

The rabbit plunges on, thrashing violently through one long minute, then two, making frantic but futile attempts to escape. Anguished and hoping to put an end to its misery, the boy drops to his knees, reels in the convulsing animal and jerks the noose tight.

Caught in a ghastly scene of his own making, the horror-stricken boy pulls on the noose as tears yield to sobs of remorse. The rabbit, drawing on unimaginable reserves, twists and turns, striking out with its legs. Appalled at its frantic exertions, the boy whips off his mittens and tries to open the noose, but the wire, the strong, braided wire, has become so ensnarled in the animal's fur that release is impossible. Desperate to end the animal's pain and his horror, the boy pins the thrashing rabbit down with one hand and, with the other, raises high the club to which the snare is tied. Surely one blow will end its pain.

The first impact drives the rabbit's head into a cushioning pillow of snow. The second, though aimed through tear-flooded lenses, lands more solidly, squirting an eye from its socket in a gush of blood. Still the rabbit thrashes on, fighting for its life. The boy, totally undone and awash with pity, anguish, and a pain he's never known, strikes again and again. Frustrated by the pillowy snow and repelled by the crimson carnage, he pleads for an end to the horror, crying, "die, DIE, oh please, please Diiiieeee."

The rabbit finally quivers, then softens beneath his hand, taking with it his fantasy of quick and quiet, painless deaths. On his knees beside the limp body, the blood-spattered boy sobs while the silent forest watches. Far above, the first breath of dawn brushes crystals of frost from the towering Norway pines. Descending, they glitter the air.

With shaking hands steaming in melted snow, the sweating boy wipes his blood-smeared glasses while he tries to regain control. Opening his pocket knife, he saws away at the noose, then lays the limp body beside the trail. Still weeping, he carefully places the frozen rabbit alongside its companion and covers the bodies with snow.

The boy rises, shaking his lowered head, as he mourns an innocence lost. Racked with lingering sobs, he walks to the end of his trap line, pulling shut noose after noose after noose. He springs the leg-hold trap and leaves it behind to rust. As the boy trudges back to the cabin, his brow furrows at the thought of his mother, frightened by his empty-handed, blood-spattered return. When she asks, "Son! What happened? Are you alright?" What will I say? How will I hold back the tears?

I awaken at six o'clock. It's light enough to fly, but what's the rush. Scrunching down in my sleeping bag, I try to emulate the starlet who preferred to rise at the crack of noon, but hunger prods me awake.

When I taxi up to the Red Lake pier, there sits Large, his tail flopping from side to side. I slide a hand along his body, searching for ticks. But the season's waning, and his count is down to two. I pay my bill, then ask about Laura. "She's off today," they say.

At a nearby Waterfront restaurant, I hungrily toss down fried eggs, hash browns, bacon and cakes while two charter pilots try to one-up each other.

"Shit, Charlie," says one, "you've never seen such a head wind. It blew so hard that my shadow got left behind. Must have snuck in after dark though, 'cause it was right there in the morning."

Not to be outdone, Charlie begins a long-winded story about paddling his seaplane the length of Lake Winnipeg. I'd like to hear the ending, but I have to get back in the air.

Two hundred miles farther south, where Kanata ends and the Boundary Waters begin, I punch up 122.8 mhz on my radio and send out a call to Crane Lake.

"Crane Lake radio, this is Piper 4745 Mike, thirty minutes north for customs. Please confirm."

"Piper 4745 Mike. Crane Lake customs in thirty minutes."

The Cub descends through a gusting southwesterly wind, then taxis up to the pier. After greeting the sweating officer, I check the thermometer, which is pegged at ninety-four. Two minutes later, I'm free to go.

Just then, a slender, middle-aged man in an "I'd Rather Be Flying" T-shirt walks up.

"Excuse me," he begins, "aren't you the fellow who's done programs for the Seaplane Pilots Association?"

"I have," I respond.

"Oshkosh, too?"

"Yes."

"Loved 'em," he says, "Just loved 'em. You heading north?"

"I'm just getting back," I reply.

"Gosh," he says, "I'd love to take one of those trips, but I really don't think I should."

"Why is that?" I ask.

"Well, what if I got lost or something happened?"

"Look," I respond. "Would you fly from here to Red Lake?"

"Sure," he says.

"How about to Winnipeg?"

"I'd do that."

"Well, in the unlikely event of an engine failure, those heavily forested routes aren't as safe as flights in the open country farther north where a plane is easy to spot, and there are even more lakes to land on."

"Yeah, well," he says. "You're probably right. Still . . ."

As he searches for words, I consider telling him about Marion Hart, the grandmother who soloed a single-engine Beechcraft across the Atlantic Ocean at the age of seventy-four, but decide to let it go. Why should I pressure him or make him feel less a man?

When I taxi away, he stands on the pier, dreaming dreams that might never mature. He's owned a seaplane for fifteen years, but something's held him back. Do his maps bear the mythical beasts that rimmed the charts of old, or does he still hear the ancient cartographers' warning: beyond here lurk dragons!

Hot, gusting winds punish the Tundra Cub all the way to Lake Vermilion, where I fly the roughest approach of my life. When I'm four feet above the wind-whipped lake, the Cub enters rolling air, loses lift and slams into the water. Unbelievably, nothing breaks.

As the Tundra Cub drifts to a stop, a common loon trailed by two fluffy chicks cruises leisurely past my pier. I slump in my seat, glad to be home, then begin to unload the Cub. Before I call my wife, I drop into a chair and reach for the TV remote, only to discover that I've forgotten which of its faded buttons to press. Fortunately, it's news time. On the up side, the Israelis and Palestinians are still talking peace, and scientists have found even more fragments on earth that might have come from Mars, where a little robot called Sojourner once sampled the surface and sent home intriguing notes.

On the down side, graft and corruption are undermining Russia's struggling economy; inter-religious strife still troubles Ireland, the Middle East, India, Pakistan and the area that once was Yugoslavia while the wealthy still complain about taxes that force them to survive on a mere quarter million per year. Still, across much of the world, people are learning, caring and sharing, giving reason to hope that we'll someday outgrow our divisive superstitions, our greed and vicious squabbles and fall in love with life.

Though our lives begin with a cry of surprise,
and a question awaits at their close,
in between lie days filled with wonder
for all to slowly unfold.

In forest and canyon cathedrals,
in treasured libraries and halls,
welcome them, open them, savor them,
for after the question, who *knows*.

A Brief Chronology of Powered Flight

1903   The Wright brothers make the first piloted, powered, heavier-than-air flight, flying 120 feet in twelve seconds.

1911   Glenn Curtiss flies the first seaplane.

1922   Jimmy Doolittle makes the first one-day flight across the United States.

1926   Robert Goddard demonstrates a liquid-powered rocket.

1927   Charles Lindbergh completes the first solo nonstop transatlantic flight.

1933   Wiley Post completes the first solo round-the-world flight.

1935   Howard Hughes sets a world speed record of 352 mph.

1942   The first commercial round-the-world flight is completed in a Pan American Pacific Clipper.

1947   Chuck Yaeger exceeds the speed of sound.

1954   The Boeing 707 becomes America's first jet transport.

1961   Yuri Gagarin orbits the earth.

1969   Apollo 11 astronauts Aldrin and Armstrong land on the moon.

1977   The Concorde completes the first commercial supersonic London to New York flight.

1977   The Gossamer Condor becomes the first human-powered heavier-than-air craft to sustain controllable flight.

1981   The first United States space shuttle is launched.

1986   Jeana Yeager and Dick Rutan complete the first nonstop round-the-world flight without refueling.

Bibliography

Ackerman, Diane. *A Natural History of the Senses*. New York: Random House, 1991.

Alexander, Bryan and Cherry. *The Eskimos*. New York: Crescent Books, 1988.

Anderson, Barry. *Lifeline to the Yukon*. Washington State: Superior Publishing, 1983.

Atwood, Margaret. *Strange Things: The Malevolent North in Canadian Literature*. New York: Oxford University Press, 1995.

Ballantyne, Robert. *Hudson's Bay*. New York: T. Nelson, 1848.

Bronowski, Jacob. *The Ascent of Man*. New York: Little, Brown & Company, 1973.

Bruemmer, Fred. *The Arctic*, New York: Quadrangle, 1974.

Bruemmer, Fred. *Encounters with Arctic Animals*. New York: American Heritage, 1972.

Brueton, Diana. *Many Moons*. New York: Prentice Hall, 1991.

Brody, Hugh. *Maps and Dreams*. New York: Pantheon, 1982.

Burke, James. *Connections*. Boston: Little, Brown & Company, 1978.

Berton, Pierre. *The Arctic Grail*. Toronto: McClelland & Stewart, 1988.

Berton, Pierre. *The Klondike Fever*. New York: Alfred A. Knopf, 1972.

Calef, George. *Caribou and the barren-lands*. Toronto: Firefly Books, 1995.

Coonts, Stephen. *The Cannibal Queen*. New York: Pocket Books, 1992.

Davis, Richard and Guravich, Dan. *Lords of the Arctic.* New York: Macmillan, 1982.

Dawkins, Richard. *The Blind Watchmaker.* New York: W.W. Norton, 1996.

De Poncins, Gontran. *Kabloona.* New York: Reynall and Hitchcock, 1941.

De Remer, Dale. *Water Flying Concepts.* Self - published in Grand Forks, N.D., 1989.

Dyson, John. *The Hot Arctic.* Boston: Little, Brown & Company, 1979.

Ferris, Timothy. *Coming of Age in the Milky Way.* New York: Morrow, 1988.

Freuchen, Peter. *Book of the Eskimos.* New York: World Publishing, 1961.

Frey, Jay. *How to Fly Floats,* Melville, New York: Edo Corporation, 1972.

Gingerich, Owen. *The Great Copernicus Chase.* Cambridge: Sky Publishing, 1992.

Hall, Sam. *The Fourth World.* New York: Random House, 1988.

Harrison, Edward. *Darkness at Night.* Cambridge: Harvard University Press, 1987.

Hearne, Samuel. *Journey From Prince of Wales Fort in Hudson's Bay to the Northern Ocean in the Years 1769-1772.* Philadelphia: Joseph and Jane Crukshank, 1802.

Helmericks, Harmon. *The Last of the Bush Pilots.* New York: Alfred A. Knopf, 1972.

Hildebrand, John. *Reading the River.* Boston: Houghton Mifflin, 1988.

Hing, Robert. *Tracking Mackenzie to the Sea.* Manassas: Anchor Watch Press, 1992.

Hummel, Monte. *Arctic Wildlife.* Toronto: Key Porter, 1984.

Innis, Harold. *The Fur Trade in Canada.* New Haven: Yale University Press, 1962.

Kurelek, William. *The Last of the Arctic.* Toronto: Pagurian Press, 1978.

Leopold, Aldo. *Sand Country Almanac.* New York: Random House, 1970.

Leslie, Edward. *Desperate Journeys, Desperate Shores.* Boston: Houghton Mifflin, 1988.

Lindbergh, Anne M. *North to the Orient.* New York: Harcourt Brace, 1963.

Lokke, Carl. *Klondike Saga.* Minneapolis: University of Minnesota Press, 1965.

Lopez, Barry. *Arctic Dreams.* New York: Bantam, 1987.

Lyall, Ernie. *An Arctic Man.* Edmonton: Hurtig Publishers, 1979.

MacDonald, Malcolm. *Down North.* New York: Oxford University Press, 1943.

Matheson, Shirlee Smith. *Flying the Frontiers*. Saskatoon: Fifth House Publishers, 1994.

McPhee, John. *Coming into the Country*. New York: Farrar, Straus & Giroux, 1976.

Mirsky, Jeannette. *To the North*. New York: Viking, 1934.

Morrison, Philip and Phylis. *The Ring of Truth*. New York: Random House, 1987.

Mowat, Farley. *Never Cry Wolf*. Boston: Little, Brown & Company: 1963.

Mowat, Farley. *Canada North*. Boston: Little, Brown & Company, 1962.

Mowat, Farley. *The Desperate People*. Boston: Little, Brown, 1959.

Mowat, Farley. *People of the Deer*. Boston: Little, Brown & Company, 1952.

Murie, Olaus. *Journeys to the Far North*. Palo Alto: America West Publishing Co., 1973.

Newman, Peter. *Company of Adventurers*. New York: Penguin, 1988.

Newman, Peter. *Empire of the Bay*. Toronto: Viking Canada, 1995.

Norment, Christopher. *In the North of Our Lives*. Camden: Down East Books, 1989.

Olesen, Dave. *North of Reliance*. Minocqua:NorthWord Press, 1994.

Patterson, R. M. *Dangerous River*. Toronto: Stoddart Publishing, 1989.

Perkins, Robert. *Into the Great Solitude*. New York: Bantam, 1991.

Place, Marian. *The Yukon*. New York: I. Washburn, 1967.

Raffan, James, ed. *Wild Waters*. Toronto: Key Porter Books, 1986.

Raymo, Chet. *The Crust of Our Earth*. New York: Prentice Hall, 1983.

Redfern, Ron. *The Making of a Continent*. New York: Random House, 1983.

Rytchetnik, Joe. *Alaska's Sky Follies*. Anchorage: Epicenter Press, 1995.

Sagan, Carl. *The Demon-Haunted World*. New York: Random House, 1995.

Seldes, George. *The Great Quotations*. Secaucus: Lyle Stuart Inc., 1960.

Shomon, Joseph. *Beyond the North Wind*. Cranbury: Barnes &Co, 1974.

Sobel, Dava. *Longitude*. New York: Penguin, 1996.

Stefansson, Vilhjalmur. *My Life with the Eskimo*. New York: Macmillan, 1922.

Stefansson, Vilhjalmur. *The Friendly Arctic*. New York: Macmillan, 1921.

Tryck, Keith. *Yukon Passage*. New York: Quadrangle, 1980.

Turner, Dick. *Wings of the North*. Surrey: Hancock House, 1980.

Turner, Dick. *Nahanni*. Surrey: Hancock House, 1975.

Weiner, Jonathan. *Planet Earth*. New York: Bantam, 1986.

White, Andrew. *A History of the Warfare of Science with Theology*. Gloucester: Peter Smith Publishers, 1896.

Walker, Barbara G. *The Woman's Encyclopedia of Myths and Secrets*. New York: Harper & Row, 1983.

Young, Steven. *To the Arctic*. New York: John Wiley & Sons, 1989.